PARALEGAL PRACTICE

Complete College-Level Course

Volume 1

Jari Davis

Course Shift

Table of Contents

CHAPTER 3

CHAPTER 4

CHAPTER 5

CHAPTER 8

CHAPTER 1
The Profession

In this Chapter, we will discuss:

A. The Course

B. What You Will Need

C. What is a Paralegal?

D. Paralegal Functions

E. Paralegal Employment

F. Career Opportunities

G. Personal Assets and Skills

H. Education

G. Regulation, Ethics & Professional Responsibility

H. Licensing

A. THE COURSE

The Paralegal Training home-study course focuses on the legal concepts, procedures, and skills that are used in a wide variety of legal environments. It is designed to teach the functions and processes of institutions in the U.S. legal system, roles and issues in the paralegal field, legal ethics, and selected specialties of law. It includes a listing of important skills, including legal analysis, communication, legal research, computer knowledge, legal drafting, investigation, interviewing witnesses, client relationships, and office organization. If you complete it, you should be prepared for a challenging and responsible career in the legal environment.

We will cover:

- Issues relevant to the paralegal profession.

- American law

- Court systems

- Analysis of facts, law and legal issues

- Legal writing

- Research and citation

- Interview and investigation

- Civil litigation

- Criminal law

- Law specialties

- Optional dictation and transcription module

B. OPTIONS FOR COURSE REFERENCES

Substitutions are acceptable. You may find enough Internet resources to avoid purchasing any other references at all.

a. Merriam Webster's Collegiate Dictionary (latest edition) or comparable

b. The Blue Book: Buy the hard copy or subscribe to the online version

c. https://www.legalbluebook.com/

d. A Handbook of Basic Law Terms by Bryan A. Garner (or comparable)

Throughout the course, you will be provided websites for research purposes; this activity will facilitate your ability to use such sites in your training and your career. Some of the exercises may be based on the research you do, so take the time to familiarize yourself by reading what they offer, moving around to find other topics which may be of interest and looking at the *links* various sites will provide. Bookmark those you frequent most for a ready resource.

The questions related purely to web research may or may not have answers in the answer sections. Also be aware that those listed were available at this printing. Since websites come and go, the ones we list for you may not be as in the course; if not, use the key words that are associated with the assignment to find alternative website links; however, in the process, you will discover many resources that are not listed in your training books. You will get a feel for what is useful; bookmark the good ones.

C. WHAT IS A PARALEGAL?

Paralegals perform tasks that require substantive and practical legal knowledge. A paralegal is best described as a legal assistant," a person competent in the area of substantive and procedural law. The term "paralegal," refers to a person sufficiently trained in law and legal procedures to assist an attorney in the delivery of legal services and/or directly to public.

According to the American Bar Association (ABA) a definition of a legal assistant or paralegal is *a person qualified by education, training or work experience, who is employed or retained by an attorney, law office, corporation, governmental agency or other entity who performs specifically delegated substantive legal work for which a lawyer is ultimately responsible.*

Initially, the paralegal profession developed in response to the need for legal professionals to fill a position between that of an attorney and a legal secretary. Thus, legal services could be provided to the public at a lower cost (than that of an attorney). The first paralegals were known as "legal secretaries," and as time went on, it naturally followed that more skills and abilities were acquired to assist attorneys in more substantive legal work.

The biggest differences between lawyers and paralegals are that lawyers can set fees, give legal advice, appear as counsel of record in court, and sign pleadings (and other court documents) in a representative capacity. If a paralegal attempts to do any of these acts, they could be in violation of the unauthorized practice of law statutes that exist in most U.S. states, as well as some other countries (though not the United Kingdom).

In the Canadian province of Ontario, a paralegal may set fees, give legal advice and represent others in court for the matters mentioned above. They are not allowed to represent for indictable offences or family law.

Other traditional differences between a paralegal and a lawyer (e.g. an attorney in the United States, a solicitor, barrister or legal executive in the UK or solicitor or advocate in India) is that:

1. Paralegal expertise/training tends to be more of a niche, whereas a lawyer has a much broader, longer, more formal and holistic training, and

2. The lawyer's primary job is to consider, analyze and strategize, whereas a paralegal's primary responsibility is to carry out the tasks arising from that consideration, analysis and strategy.

In the UK there are now over 4,000 government registered/regulated paralegal advisory firms offering services that would previously have been offered by lawyers. Similar results are found in Ontario, Canada, where again Paralegals are licensed by the same regulating body as lawyers.

Paralegals are found in all areas where United States lawyers work — in criminal trials, in real estate, in government, in estate planning. In the US, paralegals and legal document assistants (LDAs) are often mistaken for one another. In most other jurisdictions the latter profession is not yet developed enough to have a clear distinction between the two.

In Canada, paralegals are legal agents who have the ability to represent on many matters, including all Provincial Offences, work for Provincial Tribunals and Boards, as well as Summary Criminal Cases. They are not "law clerks" in the province of Ontario, Canada and considered to be a formal part of the legal system. Paralegals may become Commissioners, Notary Publics and act as a Justice of the Peace.

In the Province of Ontario, a paralegal is an officer of the court (*i.e.* considered a formal part of the legal system). Paralegals in Ontario are licensed and regulated by the Law Society of Upper Canada, which also regulates and provides licenses for all lawyers in Ontario. A paralegal license allows a paralegal to independently represent clients in provincial offences court, summary conviction criminal court, small claims court and administrative tribunals such as the Financial Services Commission of Ontario or the Workplace Safety and Insurance Board.

The role that a paralegal has in the United States is similar to the role of a law clerk or legal assistant in Ontario. Many paralegals in Ontario work in the areas of permitted practice for paralegals and also work alongside lawyers in areas of practice that are only permitted to be practiced by lawyers. It is illegal for paralegals in Ontario to independently practice in an area of law that is permitted only for lawyers. An example of this is family law, or an indictable offense in criminal law.

D. PARALEGAL RESPONSIBILITIES

As has just been discussed, paralegals actually do many of the same things attorneys do. What don't paralegals do might be an easier question to answer. Paralegals in the US are careful to avoid giving legal advice. They typically do not directly advise clients with respect to their legal obligations or rights, though it is sometimes difficult to pinpoint what constitutes "legal advice." There is a fine line between permissible and impermissible advice. To be on the safe side (and avoid potential liability for the *unauthorized practice of law* (UPL), a good rule of thumb is:

> Never advise a client or other person on any matter if the advice may alter
> the legal position or legal rights of the one to whom the advice is given.

According to United States law, there are five specific acts which only a licensed attorney can perform:

1. Establish the attorney-client relationship

2. Give legal advice

3. Sign legal papers and pleadings on behalf of a party

4. Appear in court on behalf of another (i.e. the client)*

5. Set and collect fees for legal services

Non-attorneys, including paralegals, can appear in a representative capacity in many types of administrative hearings (that is, hearings held by administrative agencies located within the executive branch, as opposed to courts formally organized as part of the judiciary).

Beyond the five acts above, the paralegal can perform practically any other task, including legal research, legal writing, factual investigation, preparation of exhibits, and the day-to-day tasks of case management. The key is that attorneys are entirely responsible for the actions of their paralegals, and, by signing and filing court documents drafted by paralegals (or law clerks), attorneys make those documents their own.

The paralegal phenomenon is a legal-economics argument in all jurisdictions - they exist precisely because they are not lawyers and thus can do the work much more inexpensively. Other than expertise, the main constraint on what work a paralegal can or cannot do tends to relate to local rules that reserve (i.e. give a monopoly to) particular activities to lawyers. Each jurisdiction tends to have its own "reserved activities list".

Typical duties include drafting and filing legal documents, calendaring and tracking important deadlines, assisting attorneys to prepare for trials, interviewing clients and witnesses, garnering relevant facts and information pertaining to a lawsuit, conducting legal investigations, organizing and maintenance of client files, providing legal research and using computers and related software as well as other reference materials to research and document law.

E. WHERE DO PARALEGALS WORK?

In the United States, the need for accredited qualifications and bar licensure limits the number of licensed attorneys. At the same time, there are many legal tasks for which a bar license is unnecessary but some amount of legal training is helpful. In order to lower costs, businesses may choose to employ paralegals to undertake such tasks instead of a more expensive lawyer. Paralegal time is typically billed less than what a lawyer charges, and thus to the paralegal has often assumed the substantive and procedural tasks which are too complex for legal secretaries (whose time is not billed) but for which lawyers can no longer bill. This in turn makes lawyers more efficient by allowing them to concentrate solely on the substantive legal issues of the case, while paralegals have become the "case managers."

The United Kingdom has gone one step further. Much legal work by lawyers for the poorer elements of society is legally aided, or paid for by the government. As overall costs have risen due to more people than ever engaging in law-related issues, the government has reduced its assistance for such legal aid. As a result the work has become economically less feasible for attorneys, and the paralegally trained are stepping in to fill the gap.

Increasing medical paralegal specialty: Some attorneys who practice in fields involving medical care have only a limited knowledge of healthcare and medical concepts and terminology. Therefore, in addition to Legal Nurse Consultants, a certain number of registered nurses have become fully trained as paralegals in the manner described above and assist behind the scenes on these cases, in addition to serving as expert witnesses from time to time. There is an extremely high demand for nurses to begin with, so the demand for nurses with paralegal skills is expected to remain very high in the near future. Expert witnesses command high fees for court appearances and related expenses.

So where and how are paralegals employed? Who uses their services? Attorneys do, and corporations, government agencies, insurance companies, banks, and, lots of them work for themselves. The demand for government paralegals is growing at an enormous rate. Many work for the Federal government in administrative agencies.

General categories:

- FREELANCE PARALEGALS - operate their own business and provide services to attorneys on a contractual basis. A freelance paralegal works under the supervision of an attorney, who assumes responsibility for the paralegal's work product.

- INDEPENDENT PARALEGALS - offer their services directly to the public or contract with law firms, and other entities, without the need for attorney supervision. In addition, they assist clients by supplying forms and procedural knowledge relating to relatively simple or routine legal procedures. Independents must be careful not to violate state statutes prohibiting practice of the law in and of itself.

- DIFFERENCES BETWEEN THE TWO - freelance paralegals are not to be confused with **independent paralegals**—often called legal technicians, who do NOT work under the direct supervision of an attorney and provide legal services directly to the public.

- SPECIALIZATION – Many opportunities exist for the paralegal to specialize in various types of law, real estate, criminal, family, personal injury, business, etc. These specialties are discussed in the course material.

F. CAREER OPPORTUNITIES

The potentials include positions in law firms, government agencies, legal services, corporations, professional and trade associations, banks, real estate organizations, publishing companies, as well as other public and private-sector businesses or institutions.

Employment of paralegals and legal assistants is projected to grow 22 percent between 2006 and 2016, much faster than the average for all occupations. Employers are trying to reduce costs and increase the availability and efficiency of legal services by hiring paralegals to perform tasks once done by lawyers. Paralegals are performing a wider variety of duties, making them more useful to businesses.

Demand for paralegals also is expected to grow as an expanding population increasingly requires legal services, especially in areas such as intellectual property, health care, international law, elder issues, criminal law, and environmental law. The growth of prepaid legal plans also should contribute to the demand for legal services.

Private law firms will continue to be the largest employers of paralegals, but a growing array of other organizations, such as corporate legal departments, insurance companies, real estate and title insurance firms, and banks also hire paralegals. Corporations in particular are expected to increase their in-house legal departments to cut costs. In part because of the range of tasks they can perform, paralegals are also increasingly employed in small and medium-size establishments of all types.

Paralegals and legal assistants held about 263,800 jobs in 2010. Private law firms employed 7 out of 10 (71%) paralegals and legal assistants; most of the remainder worked for corporate legal departments and various levels of government. Within the Federal Government, the U.S. Department of Justice is the largest employer, followed by the Social Security Administration and the U.S. Department of the Treasury. A small number of paralegals own their own businesses and work as freelance legal assistants, contracting their services to attorneys or corporate legal departments.

Clearly the economic benefits of utilizing paralegals becomes a welcome alternative to both the attorney and to consumers at large as specifically delegated and supervised legally substantive work is performed and distributed. Also, as attorneys realize that their own productivity and cost efficiency are maximized through utilizing paralegal services and legal transcription services, the demand has and will continue to increase, and new opportunities will open up for the paraprofessional. The independent paralegal status has become very popular too.

According to the findings of the National Federation of Paralegal Association (NFPA), the future of Paralegals is increasing rapidly with the projection being that by the year 2014 there will be between 150,000 and 176,000 new paralegals in this nation. Working in aspects such as law firms, corporations and corporate legal departments, financial institutions, insurance companies, real estate and title agencies, state and federal governmental agencies, courts, public defenders' and prosecutors' offices, public utility companies, publicly funded legal service projects and community legal service programs.

Recession Impact? To a limited extent, paralegal jobs are affected by the business cycle. During recessions, demand declines for some discretionary legal services, such as planning estates, drafting wills, and handling real estate transactions. Corporations are less inclined to initiate certain types of litigation when falling sales and profits lead to fiscal belt tightening. As a result, full-time paralegals employed in offices adversely affected by a recession may be laid off or have their work hours reduced. However, during re-cessions, corporations and individuals are more likely to face problems that require legal assistance, such as bankruptcies, foreclosures, and divorces. Paralegals, who provide many of the same legal services as lawyers at a lower cost, tend to fare *relatively better in difficult economic conditions.*

Earnings (Department of Labor):

Wages of paralegals and legal assistants vary. Salaries depend on education, training, experience, the type and size of employer, and the geographic location of the job. In general, paralegals who work for large law firms or in large metropolitan areas earn more than those who work for smaller firms or in less populated regions. Self-employed paralegals make more than salaried people According to the Bureau of Labor Statistics (BLS), the projected job growth for paralegals between 2010-2020 was 18%.

In May 2021, the median annual wage for paralegals and legal assistants was $56,230. The lowest 10% earned less than $36,410, and the highest 10% earned more than $88,640.

In May 2021, the median annual wages for paralegals and legal assistants in the top industries in which they worked were as follows:

Federal government	$69,680
Finance and insurance	$64,740
Local government, excluding education and hospitals	$58,300
State government, excluding education and hospitals	$49,350
Legal services	$48,270

In addition to earning a salary, many paralegals receive bonuses, in part to compensate them for sometimes having to work long hours. Paralegals also receive vacation, paid sick leave, a savings plan, life insurance, personal paid time off, dental insurance, and often reimbursement for continuing legal education and perhaps certification.

Related Occupations.

Other occupations to be considered with the paralegal training which call for a specialized understanding of the law, but that also do not require the extensive training of a lawyer are:

- Claims adjusters, examiners, and investigators
- Law clerks
- Occupational health and safety specialists
- Occupational health and safety technicians

- Title examiners, abstractors, and searchers

- Collection Agencies

Results from a recent Compensation in Legal and Law Related Jobs (non-law firms) survey conducted by Abbott, Langer & Associates stated the median salary for paralegals is $36,500, with 10% making over $51,000. Transcribers who contract for services charge an average of 6 to 10 cents per line with an average of 25 lines per page, thus the charge of $1.50 to $2.50 or more per page is possible, with the average of $24 per hour in the range of a qualified person.

The opportunities for expanding roles in your career are also furthered through continuing education, expanded experience, increased acceptance of responsibility and increased challenges and as standards for the paralegal profession -- qualifications, responsibilities and regulation -- are established and recognized, paralegal roles and responsibilities will be expanded. Furthermore, technological advances such as the Internet will create new roles for paralegals in assisting attorneys to conduct more cost-efficient research and produce more specialized presentations. These are dynamic times for the paralegal profession.

Technologically speaking supply and demand are what run the evolution and creation of new software, macros and research methods available. Currently the Internet is the paralegal's best friend in terms of research and technology, making the job easier to do. As for software, each attorney has his/her preference in terms of what is used for document creation, which can be anything from "Hotdocs," which is WordPerfect related to Legal Solutions, a program divided into modules depending on the field of practice. Finally, the macros and templates you create as you learn and as you gain experience will be priceless to you and to the work product that you produce.

A relatively recent addition to the opportunities paralegals may pursue is called *scoping*. Because of the advent of computerization in the courtroom, there is a growing industry of people all over the country who produce legal transcripts as a support service to court reporters. Many, if not most of them, work at home and use the Internet to advertise and deliver their product. These people are called *scopists*. Scopists take the legal testimony that is produced by court reporters in computerized shorthand and, using specialized software, translate the material into English. They then edit the text that results, inserting proper names and technical words that the computer's dictionary does not catch, proofread the finished result and format it to court specifications. Scopists work for individual reporters or groups of reporters. To be a scopist you must be efficient and have a good command of the English language. Medical scooping requires a medical background, so if that interests you, check out our medical terminology course for the training you will need. You should spell well, be familiar with the jargon of the legal profession and familiar with the format required for documents in a courtroom.

Scopists advertise their services in the publications produced by state court reporting associations and on court reporters' forums on the Internet. They can also do direct mailings from lists of court reporters that are sold by some of the state agencies that license court reporters.

As a paralegal (PL), you will find the work challenging and interesting, providing expanding job opportunities and careers in law and law-related applications, without the need for going to law school in a dynamic growth profession.

As a PL you'll learn how the law affects you in the process of everyday living – buying or selling a house, starting a business, understanding insurance coverage, what to do in a car accident, handling divorces and issues relating to children/support, aging parents and powers of attorney, etc.

Becoming a paralegal is an enjoyable and fulfilling occupation, and offers a broad spectrum of employment opportunities. In fact, you will be entering a growth profession and you can even move to further career planning. Don't forget the other potential occupations you may consider with the paralegal training, insurance claims adjusters, examiners, and investigators,

law clerks, nursing paralegal specialties, occupational health and safety specialists, occupational health and safety technicians, and title examiners, abstractors, and searchers, to name a few.

Famous Paralegals in film, television and literature.

Unlike nurses and physician assistants, paralegals have not caught the popular imagination and rarely are seen or mentioned in fictional or non-fiction legal television programs, or in legal fiction in print. There are however exceptions.

The most famous is probably Erin Brockovich, a real legal clerk whose participation in a toxic tort case became a major motion picture. In the movie *Eagle Eye* (2008) starring Shia LaBeouf and Michelle Monaghan, Monaghan plays a single mom who works as a paralegal.

Another notable exception is the character Della Street, from the *Perry Mason* novel, television and movie series. Although Mason identifies Della as "my confidential secretary", the projects he assigns her are entirely consistent with the law office work performed by experienced paralegals.

John Grisham includes many paralegals in his novels; for example, Rudy Baylor (the main character in *Rainmaker*) works briefly as a paralegal - and his associate Deck subsequently becomes Rudy's paralegal when he starts his own firm.

Harvey Birdman: Attorney at Law, an esoteric cartoon comedy, features a paralegal in the form of "Avenger," who is usually seen managing files, preparing and presenting documents to the attorneys, and drafting letters to clients. Avenger will usually accompany the charismatic, yet often under-prepared, Birdman into court, and whisper case information and advice into his ear. Despite not knowing English, he is by far the most competent employee of Sebben & Sebben.

The most current example is likely contained in FX's (TV network) *The Riches* in which Doug Rich, a con-artist played by Eddie Izzard, impersonates a lawyer at a cutthroat real estate development company. Rich's apparent lack of legal knowledge is often compensated by Aubrey McDonald, a highly-skilled paralegal who manages to help guide the under-educated anti-hero through more than a few sticky situations.

What kind of skills are useful in deciding whether you will make a good paralegal?

G. PERSONAL ASSETS AND SKILLS

The National Association of Paralegals provides an interesting outline of essential skills and attributes of character.

Paralegals perform substantive legal work that, absent the paralegal, would be performed by an attorney. The depth of knowledge and sense of responsibility that paralegals bring to the work environment make them a vital part of the legal effort. The following are basic fundamental skills and character traits that are essential for an effective paralegal:

Honesty: No one should be in this profession unless they are trustworthy. The practice of law is a fiduciary undertaking, for both the paralegal and the lawyer.

Loyalty: Like honesty, this trait emanates from character and is demonstrated over time.

Analytical Skills/Good Judgment: Analytical ability and good judgment are key qualities necessary to being an effective paralegal. Nowhere do we gain more insight into good judgment making than through our mistakes. Extreme care is crucial when it comes to making moral and ethical decisions regarding the paralegal's work.

Knowledge: A paralegal acquires knowledge through formal paralegal education as well as from professional experience. It is imperative to continue to learn and grow to achieve the highest standard of excellence in one's chosen practice area.

Communication: It is vital to communicate simply and clearly in concise and precise language, whether oral or written.

Organization: Lawyers depend upon their paralegals to provide organization of the case.

Attention to Detail: A paralegal must be detail-oriented. Minor details that are overlooked can spell disaster at a critical moment in a case.

Motivation: The paralegal must desire to be and to do the absolute best.

Empathy: Every paralegal must possess compassion for individuals, understand and respect the circumstances or problems which may confront each client, and commit themselves to professionally serve the client to the best of their ability.

The association also provides a useful outline of what employers look for in hiring a paralegal.

Employer Expectations

They want well-trained people. The goal of a paralegal educational program is to provide a student with the information and skills necessary to successfully function as a paralegal. They are hopeful that paralegal graduates know how to accomplish specific legal tasks mastered previously through practical school assignments.

Employers place a high priority on quick learning ability and flexibility. Qualified candidates must be able to adjust to continually shifting priorities and the rigors of legal "corporate culture."

The issue of professionalism is important to paralegal employers. Employers expect paralegals to be professional in both attitude and demeanor.

Excellent organizational skills are highly valued skills. Employers favor paralegals with initiative and self-motivation. Paralegals must anticipate attorney needs and have the ability to solve problems *without direct supervision.*

Mastery of personal computers and technology expertise has become essential for job market success. Most work environments are highly automated. Keeping abreast of technology is an ongoing challenge. While paralegal candidates may not know the specific software to be used, they must be familiar with similar or comparable software products. Successful applicants understand a computer as a tool for organization, research and communication.

A good attitude is essential! If a person is difficult to deal with, inflexible, unwilling to learn something new or lacks self-confidence, he/she should not pursue a paralegal career.

Let us talk a little more about skills.

- **ORGANIZATION**

A well-organized individual is a "plus," mainly because law offices are busy and sometimes very demanding. If you can answer phones, return phone calls, interview witnesses and at the same time file documents, create procedures and checklists, and other related tasks, you will keep things running smoothly. If organization is natural to you, then you will be ahead of the game. As a paralegal student, organizing your notebooks, tracking homework assignments, creating a study or work schedule and following directions will be a learning opportunity for you. Use your time wisely!

Remember the lawyers in the office will depend on the paralegal to organize every case.

- **ANALYTICAL SKILLS**

Analytical skills are used in tasks relating to trials, legal investigations, legal research, and oral and written communication. The word, "analysis," is defined as the separation of a whole into its constituents with a view to examination and interpretation, and a statement of the results of such a study. As a paralegal, analysis involves the ability to discern how the facts and opinions you have garnered fit together in patterns or sequences. You also determine how the facts fit into the legal strategy that you or your supervising attorney plans to pursue.

- **INTERPERSONAL AND COMMUNICATIONS SKILLS**

You need decision-making ability when meeting clients, attorneys and other office staff. It is important for the paralegal to master the ability to communicate and interact with clients, attorneys and other office staff. As you work closely with your attorney(s) and clients, a positive working relationship helps getting tasks done more effectively. There will be times when clients may be experiencing difficulties in their lives, such as divorce, serious accidents, injuries, or the death of a loved one. Be sensitive, and empathetic (putting yourself in their shoes) using tact and the ability to be polite and sensitive to the situations presented.

Though virtually every waking moment is spent listening or speaking to someone, the truth is most of us do not have the faintest idea of what we are really trying to achieve. How we sound, what we say, or whether we are good listeners are important elements we need to reassess. Scientific research verifies that when meeting someone for the first time, how you say something and what you look like when you say it are much more important than the words you actually speak.

Communication skills are rated highly as important factors in a paralegal's success! It has been said that the legal profession is a "communications profession," because effective legal representation depends to a great extent on how well a legal professional can communicate with clients, witnesses, court judges, juries, opposing attorneys, and others. Poor communication can obviously damage a case.

Speech needs to be precise and clear in communicating ideas or facts to others in both written and oral exchanges. For example, when you discuss facts learned in an investigation, your oral report must communicate exactly what you found. Any miscommunication or lack of clarity could result in serious consequences.

Be an "active," listener and follow instructions, prepare questions, and build on the foundation of what you have just heard, always listening carefully to what is being said and asking questions to clarify what you have heard and what you understand is important. Repeating instructions will not only ensure that you understand what was said, but also gives the attorney, client, or witness a chance to add anything that s/he may have forgotten. In the interviewing process, listening actively and clarifying what was said is also crucial.

- **COMPUTER SKILLS**

In the workplace today, computer skills are essential. As a paralegal, you must understand how to use computers, software and the various resources the web provides. Throughout this paralegal training, you will have to use the Internet for research relating to your studies. As computer technology continues to evolve, high-tech paralegals will be increasingly in demand. Technology is not only transforming the paralegal workplace but also creating new types of paralegal positions. The Internet has virtually replaced many hard book law libraries, so a skilled paralegal will fully understand and be able to use that tremendous knowledge base using all the tools (computers and software). The ability to use a variety of dictation equipment whether it is a simple cassette system, or a digital system accessed by a phone line (jack) and PC, a foot pedal and headset, or working on computerized courtroom recording equipment for court reporters, are skills you may find necessary to learn.

- **READING SKILLS**

Reading skills involve more than just being able to decipher the meaning of written words and letters, sentences, paragraphs, sections, or pages. As a paralegal you will need to be able to read, understand and interpret many different types of written material, including statutes and court decisions. As you become familiar with legal terminology and its concepts used in the evaluation and preparation of various documents, you will develop the ability to read so carefully that you do not miss important distinctions.

- **WRITING SKILLS**

Since virtually everything in the legal profession is ultimately reduced to writing, writing skills are important - letters, memoranda, witnesses' testimony, and the variety of legal documents produced in the legal process. Writing is an active thinking process, a way to develop new knowledge, and reinforcing the process of remembering it. You might be asked to draft a formal argument, perform a strategic analysis, or even write your own case study. As you write about a client's situation—describing the situation (facts) from as many angles as you can think of and comparing it to other facts, is an integral part of the process. The written record of your thinking then becomes part of your new knowledge, which is passed on to your supervising attorney.

- **FUNDAMENTAL KNOWLEDGE**

Throughout the process of learning, analyzing and processing you will discover that knowledge accumulates in astronomic proportions. Since this is a continual process, it is always interesting and exciting to add to your knowledge.

- **RESPONSIBILITY AND RELIABILITY**

To succeed in any career, you must be responsible, reliable, committed to hard work, objective, ethical, and considerate of others. These attributes define your personality, as well as character, and are important in the paralegal practice today. The practice of law involves helping people with their legal problems. Deadlines are critical. For instance, a certain document must be sent to the right party, or filed in the court by a specific date. Missing a deadline could result in the client losing his or her legal rights (with a possible lawsuit brought against the attorney).

- **COMMITMENT**

Of equal importance is commitment to your work and to the goals of your own business or those of your employer. Commitment and persistence work hand in hand and require your best effort.

- **OBJECTIVITY**

Avoidance of emotional biases aside, your sympathy for a client's plight should not prevent you from acknowledging factual evidence that is harmful to a client's position. Those who work on behalf of a client may dislike having to deal with one of your firm's overly aggressive business clients, for example, or even a criminal defendant charged with spousal abuse. Keep your mind clear of being defensive and judgmental and think only of the client's interests and your true function in any process in his behalf, avoiding involvement related to your personal views and assumptions.

- **CONFIDENTIALITY**

Of utmost importance is the ability to keep client information confidential. Under no circumstances are you allowed to disclose ANY information that may be detrimental to the client's legal affairs. You do not share any information except, of course, that related to the documents or testimony filed in conjunction with the case at hand, to anyone, family friends, spouse, family members, close friends or others unrelated to the case professionally. Discussing personal or confidential information on elevators, hallways, or other areas where others may overhear your conversation is prohibited. In fact, considerable liability is a definite problem should this breach of confidence be made.

The legal term used to describe the premises of confidentiality is "fiduciary." A lawyer (and a paralegal) is a fiduciary. The relationship with the client is one of trust and confidence. S/he represents the client's interest to the best of his/her ability and does not use that position of trust and confidence to further private interests. S/he never discusses the client's business with outsiders. So sacred is the relationship between lawyer and client that information given to the lawyer by the client is a privileged communication (also known as attorney client privilege), which, in legal terms, means a lawyer cannot be compelled to testify concerning the information provided.

The rule of evidence relating to confidential communications between a client and his/her attorney (pertaining to the professional relationship) requires the client's consent to disclosure.

- **MISCELLANEOUS**

Additional skills include the more obvious ones...accuracy, efficiency, attentiveness to detail, discretion, diplomacy, and the ability to work under pressure. When the pace of the work becomes frantic and deadlines must be met, it is sometimes difficult to meet the challenge. For example, it is 11 AM and you have to complete a brief by noon. When the pressure is on, it is important to remain calm, and focus on completing the work.

H. EDUCATION

Education is available from a variety of resources ... home study programs (which you are now pursuing in this course), vocational schools, and colleges, some of which provide certificates, associate, and bachelor's degrees. Two-year community colleges, universities, and business schools offer an associate degree program. Upon successful completion of 60-70 semester hours, a student earns an associate's degree. The curriculum usually consists of approximately one-half paralegal courses and one-half courses in general education and related areas. Baccalaureate Degrees in paralegal studies are offered by four-year colleges and universities, which have a paralegal major, minor, or concentration within a major. These programs are usually about 120 to 130 semester hours, including 30 to 60 semester units in paralegal and related courses. Certificate programs, including this one, are geared at a much faster learning pace (and generally, a much lower cost), and can be completed in a matter of months.

According to the American Bar Association (ABA), the paralegal profession is rapidly growing and the responsibilities are steadily increasing. Since the early 1970s, the ABA played an active role in paralegal education. By 1973, the ABA set the standards of paralegal education and training programs throughout the U.S. Today, the ABA has representatives from National Federation of Paralegal Associations (NFPA), the American Association for Paralegal Education (AAPE), and the National Association of Legal Assistants (NALA).

Paralegal educational programs include the study of both substantive law and procedural law.

- Substantive law is best described as "laws that regulate legal rights and obligations," (from either the constitution, legislative enactments [statutes] or case law) and "procedural law."

- Procedural law establishes methods of enforcing rights and obligations set by substantive law.

Substantive law refers to laws that define the rights and duties of individuals towards one another and, toward the state. For the "state," both Federal and State administrative agencies are authorized to promulgate rules and regulations.

Procedural law provides the ground rules for the way cases proceed through the court system. For the Federal Judicial System these rules are found in the "Federal Rules of Civil Procedure and the Federal Rules of Criminal Procedure." On the other hand, the Federal Rules of Evidence are a hybrid of both substantive and procedural law.

I. REGULATION, ETHICS & PROFESSIONAL RESPONSIBILITY

In preparing for a career as a paralegal, you must know what the responsibilities are, why they exist, and how they will or may affect you. Although attorneys are subject to direct regulation by the state, paralegals are not (although they may be in the near future, in the form of licensing requirements). Paralegals are regulated indirectly, both by legal ethical codes and by state laws that prohibit those who are not lawyers from practicing law. The American Bar Association, and State Bar Associations continue to issue guidelines that serve to directly and indirectly regulate the paralegal profession.

According to Webster's Dictionary, 'to regulate' means, "to control or direct in agreement with a rule." Who are the regulators? Beginning in the mid-1850, restrictions were placed on who could or could not, practice law and state statutes were enacted prohibiting the unauthorized *practice of law* (UPL). By the 1930s, virtually all states had enacted legislation prohibiting anyone but licensed attorneys from practicing law. The legal profession is regulated then through ethical codes and rules adopted by each state—in most states, by order of the state supreme court.

"Legal ethics" in the United States is generally understood to primarily apply to lawyers, while codes of professional responsibility also apply in a derivative sense (indirectly) to non-lawyers who work with lawyers, such as paralegals or private investigators. In the United States, the practice of law is regulated by the governments of the individual states and territories. As a whole, federal law does not control legal ethics.

Each state or territory has a code of professional conduct dictating rules of ethics. These may be adopted by the respective state legislatures and/or judicial systems. The American Bar Association has promulgated the Model Rules of Professional Conduct which, while formally only a recommendation by a private body, have been influential in many jurisdictions. The Model Rules address many topics which are found in state ethics rules, including the *client-lawyer relationship*, duties of a lawyer as *advocate* in adversary proceedings, dealings *with persons other than clients, law firms and associations, public service, advertising*, and *maintaining the integrity of the profession*. Respect of client confidences, candor toward the tribunal, truthfulness in statements to others, and professional independence are some of the defining features of legal ethics.

The *regulators* and oversight for attorneys are:

1. **BAR ASSOCIATIONS** - Lawyers themselves determine the requirements for entering the legal profession and the rules of conduct each must follow.

2. **STATE SUPREME COURTS** - Typically, the state's highest court is the ultimate regulatory authority for that state.

3. **STATE LEGISLATURES** - Regulate the legal profession by enacting legislation affecting attorneys—statutes prohibiting the unauthorized practice of law.

4. **UNITED STATES SUPREME COURT** - Occasionally, the United States Supreme Court decides issues relating to attorney conduct.

5. **SELF-REGULATION** - The regulation of the conduct of a professional group by members of the group themselves. This usually involves the establishment of ethical or professional standards of behavior with which members of the group must comply as in "1" here, bar associations (self-regulatory).

Paralegal Ethical Codes

Paralegals have established their own Ethical Codes and also use the indirect regulation provided through attorney ethical codes. The two major national paralegal associations in the United States—are NFPA, and the NALA which were formed to define and represent paralegal professional interests on a national level.

NALA'S Code of Ethics sets forth "canons" as listed below.

A paralegal must adhere strictly to the accepted standards of legal ethics and to the general principles of proper conduct. The performance of the duties of the paralegal shall be governed by specific canons as defined herein so that justice will be served and goals of the profession attained.

The canons of ethics set forth are adopted by the National Association of Legal Assistants, Inc., as a general guide intended to aid paralegals and attorneys. The enumeration of these rules does not mean there are not others of equal importance although not specifically mentioned. Court rules, agency rules and statutes must be taken into consideration when interpreting the canons.

Canon 1. A paralegal must not perform any of the duties that attorneys only may perform nor take any actions that attorneys may not take.

Canon 2. A paralegal may perform any task which is properly delegated and supervised by an attorney, as long as the attorney is ultimately responsible to the client, maintains a direct relationship with the client, and assumes professional responsibility for the work product.

Canon 3. A paralegal must not: (a) engage in, encourage, or contribute to any act which could constitute the unauthorized practice of law; and (b) establish attorney-client relationships, set fees, give legal opinions or advice or represent a client before a court or agency unless so authorized by that court or agency; and (c) engage in conduct or take any action which would assist or involve the attorney in a violation of professional ethics or give the appearance of professional impropriety.

Canon 4. A paralegal must use discretion and professional judgment commensurate with knowledge and experience but must not render independent legal judgment in place of an attorney. The services of an attorney are essential in the public interest whenever such legal judgment is required.

Canon 5. A paralegal must disclose his or her status as a paralegal at the outset of any professional relationship with a client, attorney, a court or administrative agency or personnel thereof, or a member of the general public. A paralegal must act prudently in determining the extent to which a client may be assisted without the presence of an attorney.

Canon 6. A paralegal must strive to maintain integrity and a high degree of competency through education and training with respect to professional responsibility, local rules and practice, and through continuing education in substantive areas of law to better assist the legal profession in fulfilling its duty to provide legal service.

Canon 7. A paralegal must protect the confidences of a client and must not violate any rule or statute now in effect or hereafter enacted controlling the doctrine of privileged communications between a client and an attorney.

Canon 8. A paralegal must disclose to his or her employer or prospective employer any pre-existing client or personal relationship that may conflict with the interests of the employer or prospective employer and/or their clients.

Canon 9. A paralegal must do all other things incidental, necessary, or expedient for the attainment of the ethics and responsibilities as defined by statute or rule of court.

Canon 10. A paralegal's conduct is guided by bar associations' codes of professional responsibility and rules of professional conduct.

J. LICENSING REQUIREMENTS

A government's act of licensing is an "official granting of permission to an individual," (such as an attorney or paralegal) bestowing on the attorney the right to practice law, and this is accomplished at the state level. Each state has different requirements individuals must meet before they are allowed to practice law and give legal advice.

Are paralegals required to become licensed? One of the major issues facing legal professionals and other interested groups today is whether paralegals should be subject to direct regulation by the state through licensing requirements. Current issues relating to licensure include general versus limited licensing.

Paralegals, legal assistants, and paralegal organizations are taking note. Both the National Federation of Paralegal Associations (NFPA) and the National Association of Legal Assistants (NALA) have released statements on the topic. NALA asserts that state regulation is unnecessary, but stands behind third-party education, testing, and professional improvement efforts. NFPA endorses certain regulation efforts that would allow paralegals to provide certain additional tasks to the public.

As mentioned, a license is something that gives one the right to practice a particular profession. It is usually done to make sure that whoever is performing a line of work has met the minimum qualifications for it. *Regulations* are the requirements imposed on people performing a particular trade under a particular license.

The debate over whether to implement paralegal licensing efforts is a hot-button issue among the entire profession. There are two schools of thought on the licensing and regulation issue.

Some believe that licensing will enhance the work a paralegal will be able to perform and provide access to legal services for those that can't currently afford it. Others are against licensure because they feel that the profession was created to assist attorneys, not replace them, and that licensing will establish their relative independence. They argue that attorneys are already licensed, and because paralegals work for attorneys, there is no need for a double layer of licensure.

Limited licensing has also been suggested wherein the licensing requirements would apply only to those paralegals (independent paralegals or legal technicians) that wish to provide specified legal services directly to the public. With limited licensing, qualified paralegals would be authorized to handle routine legal services traditionally rendered only by attorneys.

K. CERTIFICATION

In the United States, there is no such thing as a *licensed* paralegal; rather, paralegals can be "registered," "certificated," or *certified*. While certification or registration is voluntary in most states, it prepares a paralegal to enter the profession; in many places it may increase the likelihood of a paralegal's hire or promotion, and serves to identify a person as capable of work that is on par with certain standards.

As we have already discussed, there are two major national organizations that offer designations to paralegals who meet *voluntary* regulation standards: the National Association of Legal Assistants (NALA) and the National Federation of Paralegal Associations (NFPA).

NALA offers its Certified Legal Assistant examination, a comprehensive 2-day examination that awards the paralegal the "CLA" or "Certified Legal Assistant" or "CP" Certified Paralegal" designation. Both the "CLA" and "CP" designations are proprietary trademarks owned by NALA, paralegals who have attained further education and received a paralegal certificate are referred to as "Certificated" unless they have passed the examination and been awarded the "Certified" designation. Additionally, those paralegals who receive the "Certified Paralegal" designation then have the opportunity to earn the "Advanced Certified Paralegal" designation.

The NFPA offers the Paralegal Advanced Competency Exam, which is a four-hour exam on a variety of legal topics; those who pass that exam can call themselves PACE-Registered Paralegals and display the "RP" designation. NFPA's core purpose is to advance the paralegal profession and is committed to the profession's Code of Ethics.

Graduation from a certificate or degree program does not, technically, certify a paralegal; in most states, passing an exam administered by a recognized entity is the only benchmark. Many states, such as Florida, have started to legislate licensing requirements for paralegals in an effort to maintain quality and to determine who can call themselves paralegals.

ON-LINE ASSIGNMENTS/RESEARCH

On any on-line research assignments, just make your taking notes and keep them in a physical or digital notebook. Scores for the on-line research assignments are not included in your quiz cumulative totals, but are obviously important in your educational process. Since website s come and go, you may occasionally run into a reference in this material that no longer exists. If you wish to pursue the subject matter related to that reference, just key the related words into a search engine and see what you can find. That is very good practice for future research.

QUESTIONS – CHAPTER 1

1. Why is the legal profession regulated?

_____

_____

2. Who are the regulators?

_____

_____

3. What are the major national paralegal associations called?

_____

_____

4. How is the paralegal profession related to attorney ethical codes?

_____

_____

5. What is privileged communication?

_____

_____

6. What does UPL stand for?

_____

_____

7. What does "licensing" actually mean?

_____

_____

8. Go to www.paralegals.org , the home page for the NFPA.

Click on any subject matter that interests you and read what they have to say.

9. A highly respected and experienced legal secretary decides to open a business, for the purpose of delivering certain legal services directly to the public. Her services include: Legal document preparation, divorce and adoption cases. She holds briefing sessions during which she gives detailed instruction regarding trials and hearings (questions most likely asked by family court judges) along with responses that her "clients," should give to the court. Jane decides to advertise her services in a local newspaper, holding herself out to be an "expert in family law," along with a "do-it-yourself" divorce kit. Her charge for this service is no more than $50.00. Many of her clients are either indigent or illiterate.

The bar association in her state charged her with the _unauthorized practice of law_. A former client gave testimony in Jane's court hearing that she advised her to lie about the date of her second marriage. Another former client testified that when he found out that his wife was abusing their children, he was advised he should not try to change the petition for divorce to seek custody of the minor children but should leave it to the state agency to handle abuse and custody issues.

Was the state bar association's filing of unauthorized-practice-of-law charges against Jane legitimate?

RESEARCH ASSIGNMENTS

1. Name and describe five types of organizations that hire paralegals.

2. Research assignment: Go online and find anything in a search engine about the case _Oregon State Bar Association v. Smith_, 149 Or.App. 171, 942 P.2d 793 (1997). Answer these questions.

    a. Who is Robin Smith, and what was she accused of?

    b. What is an injunction? Why, and against whom was an injunction issued in this case?

    c. What does "enjoined," mean? What was the Peoples' Paralegal Service, Inc, enjoined from doing?

    d. Did these activities constitute the unauthorized practice of law?

    e. How did People's Paralegal Service, Inc, argue against the injunction?

3. The American Bar Association website has the Model Rules of Professional Conduct published. Go to their website at https://www.americanbar.org/ then click ABA groups in the top right. From there click Professional Responsibility. Scroll down to "You look out for your clients. We look out for you." And click "View- MODEL RULES"

Review the topics, then select the very first one:

> Model Rules of Professional Conduct

> Client-Lawyer Relationship

> Rule 1.1 Competence

The first rule, 1.1, Competence, notes:

A lawyer shall provide competent representation to a client. Competent representation requires the legal knowledge, skill, thoroughness and preparation reasonably necessary for the representation.

You may click on any of the rules on the list to learn more.

.

Answers are provided starting on Page 259

CHAPTER 2
The Law

In this Chapter, we will discuss:

A. The Origins of American Law

B. Case Law and Common Law Tradition

C. U.S. Constitution – The Law of the Land

Law is the "dynamic force for maintaining social order and preventing chaos in society." Lawmakers, courts and other officials of the law help to preserve a harmonious society. American law and the legal system used in the United States are based on the British system. English law was gradually adopted and became generally accepted in this country by the time of the American Revolution. The principles derived from the common law system of England formed the basis of the legal rights of the American people, and are the foundation for the laws governing this nation.

The law is not a body of static rules to be obeyed by all citizens subject to its sanctions, rather, it is a dynamic process by which rules are constantly being adopted and amended to fit the current problems of our evolving society.

Three branches of the government are closely related to the law, the legislative, executive, and judicial. Administrative agencies of federal, state and local government perform the lawmaking and administering functions.

A. ORIGINS OF AMERICAN LAW

"Law "literally means a rule, or a body of rules established by an authority, society or custom. It also may be a judicial system or its workings, and an avowed or undisputed authority. The science, philosophy or study of such rules is called "jurisprudence." *Justicia*, the root word for *just / ice* means "moral or absolute right, upholding what is just, fair treatment and due reward in accordance with honor, standards or law, and most importantly, the administration and procedure of law." *Judicum* in Latin means "judgment" and is also the root for "judge," one who passes judgment upon in a court of law.

The basic precepts of law were derived from "common law," the elements of which are based on custom and precedent, established from a judicial decision. Though many cultures probably made a major contribution to the philosophy of common law, it historically has been attributed to the events of judgment in medieval England. Today, it still prevails in most English-speaking nations, including the U.S. (except Louisiana, which adheres to civil law).

The formality and inflexibility of early common law often led to injustice. In 15th century England, the chancellor issued the first of many decrees to restore equity (fairness), which then integrated into the process. This was the beginning of the modern body of *equity law* (legal principles and rules), which later merged with the common law in many jurisdictions. The relatively slow progress of common law processes led to the adoption of numerous statutes that superseded common law, notably in the fields of commercial, administrative, and criminal law.

Moral right and justice – a significant number of laws are based on a society's religious beliefs. For example, both supporters and opponents of the death penalty contend the Bible supports their position. Indeed, Western civilization's earliest written laws or rules of conduct are found in the Ten Commandments. At times playing by the rules hasn't been a popular idea, and certainly that is true in some respects today. There is obvious distaste for authority and a prevailing sense of aimlessness in both individual and corporate ways. The confusion and hopelessness relate directly most often to the lack of agreement as to what principles or rules to live by. Whose rules do we follow anyway?

Some believe that almost all concepts of right or justice grow out of current culture. These theorists believe justice is an evolving concept which society is constantly redefining. To determine whether there are any instinctual notions of right and justice, universalists attempt to locate, in all cultures, shared and unchanging beliefs about justice. Some of the activities related to cultures have been considered by those outside those cultures to be "right" or "wrong." For example, think about common practices among other cultures, incest, patricide, infanticide, marriage and bigamy.

Natural Law. The ancient concept of natural law is rooted in Aristotle, who defined natural law as "true law," as right and reason unaffected by passion or desire. That definition has had a growing influence in American jurisprudence. In other words, jurisprudence is the philosophy of law or the science on which the principles of legal rules are based. Proponents of this theory argue that certain overarching and instinctive impulses guide men and women, and that laws should not be enacted that infringe on these impulses. Generally, natural law theorists argue that all people in their natural state are guided by the notion of self-preservation, and that society should enact laws that will preserve the freedom of self-preservation.

The **Declaration of Independence** describes some of those rights as life, liberty, and the pursuit of happiness. Natural law theorists contend that any law infringing on a person's right to "pursue happiness" is inappropriate, even as to elements of livelihood. Because minimum wage laws limit both the employer and employee's ability to contract freely, how our natural rights are infringed, makes for a great discussion.

You now have an idea about the complexities involved with making, interpreting and enforcing law.

B. CASE LAW AND COMMON LAW TRADITION

1. Case Law – Rules of Law and Decisions Rendered By Judges

Case law consists of Rules of Law and decisions rendered by judges in cases that have come before the court. Common Law tradition originated in medieval England, and with that colonial heritage, much of American law is based on the English legal system. After the United States declared its independence from England, American jurists continued to be greatly influenced by English law and English legal writers. Indeed, much of American law pertaining to areas of contracts, torts (civil wrongs), property, and criminal law derives in large part from the English legal system.

Case law is the largest single body of law in existence. It is interpreted and set forth by appellate courts or courts of review. Appellate courts are charged with hearing appeals from decisions made by lower or trial courts to determine whether prejudicial error was committed, which requires reversal of the decision or judgment reached in a lower court.

"Precedent" is a term for a court decision that furnishes an example of authority for deciding subsequent cases in which identical or similar facts are presented. The *Doctrine of Stare Decisis* is a flexible doctrine of the courts, recognizing the value of following prior decisions (precedents) in cases similar to one currently before a court, allowing the court's practice to be consistent and uniform with prior decisions based on similar facts.

Often, a court will depart from the rule of precedent if it decides that the precedent should no longer be followed. In the case – *Brown v. Board of Education of Topeka* (decided in 1954), the United States Supreme Court expressly overturned precedent when it concluded that separate educational facilities for whites and African Americans were unconstitutional. In this case, a tremendous amount of publicity prevailed, and ultimately, as people began to realize the ramifications of this change in the law, the Civil Rights Movement, was initiated. You have doubtlessly heard the many claims and the bases for racial discrimination as a direct result of this case.

To learn how the Supreme Court justified its departure from precedent in the Brown decision, you may access the court's opinion at https://www.findlaw.com/. Click the magnifying glass in the top right corner of the screen, click search legal topics above the search window and key in

Brown v. Board of Education

Select the first link 'Brown v. Board of Education of Topeka (1954)'

That will give you some idea of what is available on the website. The case is discussed in several different articles. Plan to spend thirty minutes at Findlaw reading about the Brown case, a landmark in U.S. history.

2. Judicial Branch and Common Law

As we discussed earlier, the most ancient and historically significant source of American law is the common, or judge-made, law (you can see where the word judgment came from). More than any other source, the importance of common law can be traced to our colonial ties with England. In contrast to other European countries, such as France and Germany, the English legal system developed primarily in the courtroom, rather than in a legislative body.

Although the English parliament still promulgated several statutes, English judges in response to actual disputes first developed certain areas of private law, such as property, torts, and contract. The subsequent written opinions of judges, containing the reasoning supporting the decision, were collected in bound volumes. As a result, when similar disputes arose, judges referred to the disposition of the earlier case and applied the reasoning of that case to the disputes before them. In doing so, judges followed the precedent of the earlier cases.

This practice of deciding new cases with reference to previous decisions is called *Stare Decisis*, a Latin term meaning "to stand on decided cases." Generally, judges, in applying common law concepts are obligated to follow this doctrine. The failure to do so could result in the reversal of their decisions by an appellate or reviewing court. The *Doctrine of Stare Decisis*, or following precedent, is critical to society—it helps ensure that law is predictable and stable.

What happens when there is a dispute before a judge and there is no precedent to follow, or in other words, the case is one of *the first impression*? Here is an example:

> **Jane v. Tarzan**
>
> *The year is 1905, and automobiles are more frequently being driven in cities. However, at this time, local governments have not yet enacted any traffic laws, and autos must share the streets with pedestrians, trolleys, and horses. Jane, a pedestrian, was crossing the street at a crosswalk when an automobile driven by Tarzan, hit her. Jane sues Tarzan, arguing that Tarzan was liable for her injuries. Research by the attorneys representing Jane and Tarzan, as well as the judge, reveal that this is the first time the court has ever addressed the issue of a pedestrian being hit by an automobile in a crosswalk.*

Because this is a *case of first impression*, the judge has the opportunity to create new common law. In resolving Tarzan and Jane's dispute, the judge will attempt to articulate a sound legal principle regarding the rights and obligations of both pedestrians and drivers in crosswalks. The judge, in her opinion, decides in favor of Jane on the grounds that automobiles should yield the right of way to pedestrians in crosswalks, and because Tarzan did not do so, he is liable to Jane for her injuries.

In subsequent and similar cases, judges will rely on the decision in *Jane v. Tarzan* and, following precedent will hold drivers failing to yield the right-of-way to pedestrians liable for any subsequent injuries.

Notice how the common law, or judge-made law, works in this scenario. The principle that a driver must yield to a pedestrian and that if a driver fails to do so s/he will be held liable for any resulting injuries, does not come from a statute or regulation, but rather from a decision by a judge.

3. Cases of First Impression

When deciding cases or when there are conflicting precedents, courts may consider several factors, including legal principles and policies underlying previous court decisions or existing statutes, fairness, social values and customs. A government policy known as "public policy," is based on widely held societal values and concepts drawn from the social sciences.

Judges strive to be free of subjectivity and personal bias in deciding cases. However, each judge has his or her own unique personality, set of values or philosophical leanings, and intellectual attributes—all of which frame the decision-making process.

> **CASE IN POINT:**
>
> Plessy v. Ferguson, 163 u.s. 537, 16 s. ct. 1138, 41 l.ed. 256 (1896). In the Plessy case, the United States Supreme Court upheld a Louisiana statute, which provided separate railway cars for whites and African Americans. The court held that the statute did not violate the U.S. Constitution, which mandates equal protection under the law. Because the statute provided for equal facilities for African Americans, lower courts interpreted this decision to apply to other types of facilities as well, and the "separate-but-equal doctrine" prevailed until the Brown decision in 1954.

4. Law and Equity

The distinctions between equity and law apply to the remedies of common law, which were frequently inadequate to give the wronged party a fair deal. The case would then be taken to the king's chancellor, who tempered the strict letter of the law with fairness. As a result, chancery courts, in which equity is practiced, were established, presided over by a chancellor instead of a judge. A few states still have courts of chancery, while others do not separate cases in equity from cases at law, but instead, apply equity principles when appropriate. In most states, equity and law are organized under a single court, which has two dockets (an entry of the proceedings in a court), one in equity and one in law.

Courts of equity often supplement the common law by making decisions based on considerations of justice and fairness. Today, the same court can award both legal and equitable remedies so plaintiffs may request both equitable and legal relief in the same case. Yet judges continue to be guided by so-called equitable principles and maxims when deciding whether to grant equitable remedies. Maxims are propositions or general statements of rules of law that courts often use in arriving at a decision. These maxims are:

MAXIMS AND REMEDIES

1. HE WHO SEEKS EQUITY MUST DO EQUITY. If you seek the return of property you were induced to sell through fraud, you must offer to return the purchase price.

2. HE WHO COMES INTO EQUITY MUST COME WITH CLEAN HANDS. If you are induced to breach a contract and make one with someone else instead, then you breach the contract with the first entity, and a court of equity will not compel specific performance of the new contract.

3. EQUITY WILL PRESUME THAT TO BE DONE WHICH SHOULD HAVE BEEN DONE. If someone unlawfully takes possession of your cow, a calf from that cow will belong to you, because a court of equity will presume that the cow was being held for you.

4. EQUITY AIDS THE VIGILANT, NOT THOSE WHO SLUMBER ON THEIR RIGHTS. Where a statute of limitations has not run, but a claimant has delayed unreasonably in bringing suit, a court of equity may bar the claim by reason of the delay.

5. EQUITY FOLLOWS THE LAW. Except where the common law is clearly inadequate, equity follows the precedents of the common law and the provisions of the statutes. Thus, if a deed is void by common law or statute, the mere fact that a holder has given valuable consideration for it will not make the deed valid in equity.

6. EQUITY REGARDS SUBSTANCE RATHER THAN FORM. Common law is normally governed by legal form. Corporations, for example, are regarded in law as artificial beings, separate from stockholders, directors and officers. To accomplish justice, equity may disregard the corporate fiction and examine the substance of a dispute. For example, several men sell out a fish business and agree not to go into the same business in the same area. They immediately form a corporation to carry on a fish business in direct competition with the purchaser or the former business. The Court ignores the corporate entity and grants an injunction against the violation of the agreement not to compete.

7. SPECIFIC PERFORMANCE (remedy). Requires the performance that was specified in a contract; usually granted only when money damages would be an inadequate remedy and the subject matter of the contract is unique (real property is one example).

8. RESCISSION (remedy). Is an action to undo a contract—to return the parties to the positions they occupied prior to the contract. If the money has already changed hands, rescission would also involve restitution, wherein each party would be returned money or other items of value that had been exchanged by the parties previously.

9. INJUNCTION (remedy). Is a court decree ordering a person to do or refrain from doing a certain activity. For example, an injunction may be obtained to stop a neighbor from burning trash in his or her yard or to prevent an estranged husband from coming near his wife. Those who violate injunctions are held in contempt of court.

Ordinarily, law actions have for their object the assessment of damages, but a court of equity goes further and attempts to prevent the wrong itself, or to give the complainant (the one who is complaining) what he bargained for. Among the more common equity actions are injunction suits, specific performance, partition suit, rescission of a contract, reformation of a contract, and all matters relating to trusts and trustees.

PROCEDURAL DIFFERENCES BETWEEN AN ACTION

AT LAW AND AN ACTION IN EQUITY

PROCEDURE	ACTION AT LAW	ACTION IN EQUITY
Initiation of lawsuit	A complaint is filed	A petition is filed
Decision	By judge or jury	By judge (no jury)
Result	Judgment	Decree
Remedy	Monetary damages	Injunction, decree of specific performance, or rescission

C. THE UNITED STATES CONSTITUTION

1. Supreme Law of the Land

Without a doubt, the U.S. Constitution is the Supreme Law of the Land, a significant source of American law. The Constitution provides that government be divided into three equal, independent branches—the legislative (congress), the executive (president), and the judicial (courts). This principle is set forth in Article VI of the Constitution, which provides that the Constitution, laws, and treaties of the United States are indeed the Supreme Law of the Land. This provision is commonly referred to as the "supremacy clause." You can find a transcript of the Constitution here:

https://www.archives.gov/founding-docs/constitution-transcript

The Federal Constitution and the Constitutions of the 50 states formed the framework of our government. Clearly defined as basic organization it limits the power of the three branches of government (executive, legislative, and judicial), and additionally, sets forth the basic rights of the citizens. In 1791, the written declaration of rights of the individual became known as the "Bill of Rights," (10 amendments to the constitution embodying a series of protections for the people). They include:

a. The First Amendment guarantees freedom of religion, speech, the press, and rights to assemble peaceably and petition the government.

b. The Second Amendment guarantees the right to keep and bear arms.

c. The Third Amendment prohibits, in peacetime, the lodging of soldiers in any house without the owner's consent.

d. The Fourth Amendment prohibits unreasonable searches and seizures of persons or property.

e. The Fifth Amendment guarantees the rights to indictment by grand jury with due process of law, prohibiting self-incrimination and double jeopardy. In addition, the Fifth Amendment prohibits the taking of private property for public use without just compensation.

f. The Sixth Amendment guarantees the accused in a criminal case the right to a "speedy trial," by an impartial jury and the right to counsel.

g. The Seventh Amendment guarantees the right to a trial by jury in a civil case involving at least twenty dollars.

h. The Eighth Amendment prohibits excessive bail and fines, as well as cruel and unusual punishment.

i. The Ninth Amendment establishes that people have rights in addition to those specified in the Constitution

j. The Tenth Amendment establishes that those powers neither delegated to the federal government nor denied to the states are reserved for the states.

You are hopefully somewhat familiar with many of the amendments and how they relate to law. One of the most common references you hear on the cop shows or court TV is the Miranda Law. Read about this popular hearing before the U.S. Supreme Court - http://www.findlaw.com - (or key in Miranda rights and you will discover information on the case), search for the U.S. Supreme Court's case Miranda v. Arizona 384 U.S. 436 (1966). In this particular case, Miranda (defendant) was in police custody, totally cut off from the outside world, and was questioned by police officers. No rights were afforded to this defendant. The outcome of this case made way for what we now call "Miranda Rights."

In the same vein, you will have likely heard comments about the Fifth Amendment relating to the right of the person. You have doubtlessly heard this expression, "I plead the Fifth!" Under this amendment, no person shall be held to answer for a capital, or otherwise infamous crime, unless on a presentment or indictment of a "grand jury," except in cases arising on the land or naval force (Maritime Law), or in the militia.

To ensure that no branch became too powerful, the Constitution made certain it contained a system of "checks and balances." A good example can be found in Article II, section 4 that provides that, "The President, Vice President and all civil officers of the United States, shall be removed from Office on Impeachment for, and Conviction of, Treason, Bribery, or high Crimes and Misdemeanors."

Next, visit https://www.learner.org/series/democracy-in-america/ and review the video that discusses the Constitution https://www.learner.org/series/democracy-in-america/the-constitution-fixed-or-flexible/ (Democracy in America).

Click on the VoD icon. Fifteen related topics are available. The videos are well done and informative so explore as many as possible before moving on. Plan to spend several hours on that series.

Congress and State Legislatures

Article 1 of the Constitution delegates to Congress the authority to pass federal laws. "All legislative Powers herein granted shall be vested in a Congress of the United States" (Constitution, Article 1, Section 1). Since 1900, the legislature has been the major source of American law. Their purpose is to *legislate* which in Latin means "to make laws or statutes."

At each level of government are found legislatures. At the federal level is Congress (the House of Representatives and the Senate). Each state has its own legislature and cities and counties have legislative bodies, such as city councils or a county board of supervisors. The purpose of each is to enact statutes, or, in the case of local governmental bodies, initiate ordinances, which relate to public policy.

A good example of statutes and ordinances is the Federal Tax Code (which created a whole new industry of law specialty and work for accountants and attorneys) and has a complex series of statutes, collected together, that govern all aspects of taxation (and enforcement provisions) on individuals, corporations, and other organizations. As a paralegal you may transcribe or research the applicability of certain tax deductions for a client. One of the items in that code allows a person to deduct interest paid on a home loan. However, good research need not end with that discovery. Statutes are enacted to promote social goals. What social goal do you believe Congress was attempting to encourage with this statute? Obviously, it was home ownership, and to promote that goal, Congress enacted legislation designed to encourage people to secure mortgages and purchase homes. Having made that discovery, you may wish to explore other provisions of the tax code that deal with home ownership. Often, legal research requires you to go beyond the plain language of the statute to attempt to ascertain its purpose. Remember, that the law is supposed to be based on logic.

Congress is made up of two chambers

> (1) House of Representatives, or the lower house, and

> (2) Senate, or the upper house. The Constitution outlines the duties of and differences between these two houses.

Both houses of Congress can propose legislation, as can the president, but only the House of Representatives can *originate* a bill. The House consists of 435 representatives, and the number of representatives that each state has is based proportionately on its population. In contrast, each state is entitled to two senators, regardless of its population or size.

As a result, in the House, states with large populations have significant influence, whereas all states have equal representation in the Senate. For example, in the House, California has as many members as have Alaska, Arkansas, Delaware, Hawaii, Idaho, Montana, Nebraska, Nevada, New Hampshire, New Mexico, North Dakota, Rhode Island, South Dakota, Utah, Vermont, Wyoming, West Virginia, Oregon, Maine, and Oklahoma combined. But in the Senate, California has the same number of senators as does Wyoming, the least populous state.

Most state governments are patterned after Congress, with a lower house, usually called the House of Delegates or House of Representatives, and an upper house, the State Senate.

2. The United States Supreme Court

The final interpreters of the law are the Justices of the Supreme Court. Doubtless you are familiar with the importance of the Supreme Court decisions and their influence on American law and policy (as noted in the Miranda Law, Civil Rights Laws, etc.). It is often critical in preserving or altering numerous landmark judicial decisions. In the case <u>Roe v Wade,</u> the Supreme Court legalized abortions. In the Gore/Bush election debacle, this court made the final determination as to who would be president.

The Supreme Court consists of the Chief Justice of the United States and such number of Associate Justices as may be fixed by Congress. The number of Associate Justices is currently fixed at eight (28 U. S. C. §1). Power to nominate the Justices is vested in the President of the United States, and appointments are made with the advice and consent of the Senate. Article III, §1, of the Constitution further provides that "[t]he Judges, both of the supreme and inferior Courts, shall hold their Offices during good Behavior, and shall, at stated Times, receive for their Services, a Compensation, which shall not be diminished during their Continuance in Office."

Constitutional Origin. Article III, §1, of the Constitution provides that "[t]he judicial Power of the United States, shall be vested in one supreme Court, and in such inferior Courts as the Congress may from time to time ordain and establish." The Supreme Court of the United States was created in accordance with this provision and by authority of the Judiciary Act of September 24, 1789 (1 Stat. 73). It was organized on February 2, 1790.

Jurisdiction. According to the Constitution (Art. III, §2): "The judicial Power shall extend to all Cases, in Law and Equity, arising under this Constitution, the Laws of the United States, and Treaties made, or which shall be made, under their Authority;-to all Cases affecting Ambassadors, other public Ministers and Consuls;-to all Cases of admiralty and maritime Jurisdiction;-to Controversies to which the United States shall be a Party;-to Controversies between two or more States;—between a State and Citizens of another State;-between Citizens of different States;—between Citizens of the same State claiming Lands under Grants of different States, and between a State, or the Citizens thereof, and foreign States, Citizens or Subjects.

"In all Cases affecting Ambassadors, other public ministers and Consuls, and those in which a State shall be Party, the supreme Court shall have original Jurisdiction. In all the other Cases before mentioned, the Supreme Court shall have appellate jurisdiction, both as to Law and Fact, with such Exceptions, and under such Regulations as the Congress shall make."

Appellate jurisdiction has been conferred upon the Supreme Court by various statutes, under the authority given Congress by the Constitution. The basic statute effective at this time in conferring and controlling jurisdiction of the Supreme Court may be found in 28 U. S. C. §1251 et seq., and various special statutes.

Rulemaking Power. Congress has from time to time conferred upon the Supreme Court power to prescribe rules of procedure to be followed by the lower courts of the United States. See 28 U. S. C. §2071 et seq.

The Term. The Term of the Court begins, by law, on the first Monday in October and lasts until the first Monday in October of the next year. Approximately 10,000 petitions are filed with the Court in the course of a Term. In addition, some 1,200 applications of various kinds are filed each year that can be acted upon by a single Justice.

Supreme Court justices are appointed for life.

The United States Supreme Court has an excellent website describing basic function, procedure, biographies and photographs of the justices, as well as the history of the Supreme Court building.

<u>https://www.supremecourt.gov/</u> Go there now to have a look.

As you will discover later in the course, there are various rules which are codified relating to how and where lawsuits are filed. The Supreme Court may hear arguments on matters related to such general items as changing the rules. Here is an example of a rule change, Federal Rules of Evidence, Section 2072, United States Code (USC). The Court has approved the change and it is now submitted to Congress.

DOCUMENTS ON FILE, SUPREME COURT & LIBRARY OF CONGRESS

RULE CHANGE 804

April 28, 2010

Honorable Nancy Pelosi

Speaker of the House of Representatives Washington, D.C. 20515

Dear Madam Speaker:

I have the honor to submit to the Congress the amendment to the Federal Rules of Evidence that has been adopted by the Supreme Court of the United States pursuant to Section 2072 of Title 28, United States Code.

Accompanying this rule are excerpts from the report of the Judicial Conference of the United States containing the Committee Notes submitted to the Court for its consideration pursuant to Section 331 of Title 28, United States Code.

Sincerely,

/s/ John G. Roberts, Jr.

April 28, 2010

Honorable Joseph R. Biden,

President, United States Senate Washington, D.C. 20510

Dear Mr. President:

I have the honor to submit to the Congress the amendment to the Federal Rules of Evidence that has been adopted by the Supreme Court of the United States pursuant to Section 2072 of Title 28, United States Code.

Accompanying this rule are excerpts from the report of the Judicial Conference of the United States containing the Committee Notes submitted to the Court for its consideration pursuant to Section 331 of Title 28, United States Code.

Sincerely,

/s/ John G. Roberts, Jr. April 28, 2010

SUPREME COURT OF THE UNITED STATES

ORDERED:

1. That the Federal Rules of Evidence be, and they hereby are, amended by including therein an amendment to Evidence Rule 804.

[See infra., pp. .]

2. That the foregoing amendment to the Federal Rules of Evidence shall take effect on December 1, 2010, and shall govern in all proceedings thereafter commenced and, insofar as just and practicable, all proceedings then pending.

3. That THE CHIEF JUSTICE be, and hereby is, authorized to transmit to the Congress the foregoing amendment to the Federal Rules of Evidence in accordance with the provisions of Section 2072 of Title 28, United States Code.

AMENDMENT TO THE FEDERAL RULES OF EVIDENCE

Rule 804. Hearsay Exceptions; Declarant Unavailable

* * * * *

(b) Hearsay exceptions. — The following are not excluded by the hearsay rule if the declarant is unavailable as a witness:

* * * * *

(3) Statement against interest. — A statement that:

(A) a reasonable person in the declarant's position would have made only if the person believed it to be true because, when made, it was so contrary to the declarant's proprietary or pecuniary interest or had so great a tendency to invalidate the declarant's claim against someone else or to expose the declarant to civil or criminal liability; and

2 FEDERAL RULES OF EVIDENCE

(B) is supported by corroborating circumstances that clearly indicate its trustworthiness, if it is offered in a criminal case as one that tends to expose the declarant to criminal liability. * * * * *

D. ADMINISTRATIVE, STATUTORY LAW & LEGISLATIVE ENACTMENTS

Administrative law consists of rules, orders, and decisions of administrative agencies at all levels of government.

Every law enacted by the legislature begins as a bill, which is given a number. When the bill is passed by the legislature and becomes law it is known as a *statute*. Laws passed by the federal Congress and the various state legislatures are also called *statutes*. Statutory law includes local "ordinances." Ordinances commonly have to do with city or county land use, for example, zoning, building and safety codes. Persons who violate ordinances may be fined or jailed, or both. No state statute or local ordinance may violate the U.S. Constitution—due to the supremacy clause.

As a paralegal, you may often deal with cases that involve violation of statutory law. Here are just a few examples of the areas in which you might work which are governed extensively by statutory law:

STATUTORY LAW EXAMPLES

Corporate Law	State statutes
Patent, copyright, trademark law	Federal statutes
Employment Law	Federal statutes (as to discrimination, workplace safety, labor unions, pension plans, Social Security). States handle unemployment laws/taxes, insurance on a state level
Antitrust Law	Federal statutes
Consumer Law	State and federal statutes
Wills and Probate, administration	State statutes – relating to transfer of property on the property owner's death

Legislative enactments are also known as *statutes*. The federal government and most states organize statutes by subject matter and publish them as "codes," known as *Annotated Codes.* Each code has its own index as well as a comprehensive or general index covering all of them. Federal statutes are found in the United States Code (U.S.C.). In Utah, the codes are known as Utah Code (U.C.A.). These codes are the state laws as amended each year through the legislature. They include both annotated and unannotated editions. To learn more about the United States Code –

Go online to: http://uscode.house.gov/

The Office of the Law Revision Counsel of the U.S. House of Representatives prepares and publishes the United States Code pursuant to section 285b of title 2 of the Code. The Code is a consolidation and codification by subject matter of the general and permanent laws of the United States.

The Code does not include regulations issued by executive branch agencies, decisions of the Federal courts, treaties, or laws enacted by State or local governments. Regulations issued by executive branch agencies are available in the Code of Federal Regulations. Proposed and recently adopted regulations may be found in the Federal Register.

Look at the website= page referred to above, and click on Search the U.S. Code. The next page is a search page with the blanks for the criteria. Insert in the first category, *evidence*. Then click "search." You will see over 3000 documents listed. You can see why you must narrow your search somewhat. Please look at the second item on the list, USC - The Declaration of Independence – 1776, one with which you will certainly be familiar if you live in America. Click on it and read it once more since it is an amazing document.

1. Federal Agencies

The Constitution established three co-equal branches of government

- the legislative

- the judicial

- the executive branches

Under the Constitution, the President, as the Chief Executive Officer, is charged with executing the laws of the United States, commanding the armed forces, and, with the advice and consent of the Senate, entering into treaties and appointing judges and ambassadors. Review Article II of the Constitution, which describes the President's powers.

https://www.archives.gov/founding-docs/constitution-transcript

Obviously, the President does not personally oversee the execution of each law Congress passes. That particular responsibility is delegated, either by statute or regulation, to the executive branch departments or to administrative agencies. Most agencies have two primary tasks - to promulgate and enforce regulations. Due to the growing influence of federal and state agencies in areas as diverse as financial, securities, environment, workplace safety, energy, Social Security, commodities, agriculture, banking, and commerce, administrative law represents an enormous part and continuing growth in legal interpretation and action, and is often the most complex part of American law.

In administering regulations, federal agencies must follow administrative rulemaking procedures. Agencies can engage in rulemaking if authorized by Congress through either the agency's enabling legislation, which created the agency, or by a statute the agency is authorized to administer.

For example, the Clean Air Act specifically authorizes the EPA to promulgate regulations for its enforcement (setting penalties), as well as its implementation (establishing specific clean air standards). The Occupational Safety and Health Act known as OSHA enables and grants to the agency its broad authority to make rules regarding workplace safety standards. In addition, OSHA provides information about how it has implemented its enabling legislation, the Occupational Safety and Health Act.

To ensure public participation in the rulemaking process, federal agencies must publish in the Federal Register a notice describing any proposed regulation. Following publication of the notice, the agency must permit public comment on the proposed rule and its potential effects. After it receives and evaluates comments, the agency publishes the final rule in the Federal Register. The final rule may incorporate suggestions submitted by the public during the comment period. It will later be compiled, by subject matter, into the Code of Federal Regulations (CFR).

Enforcement Process

The Big Chemical Company is dumping toxic waste into a nearby stream in violation of an EPA regulation. On receiving this information, investigators determine whether Big Chemical is indeed illegally polluting the stream. Search warrants and subpoenas are issued by government enforcement agencies. The process may also involve collecting and reviewing thousands of documents and interviewing potential witnesses.

Upon completion of the investigation, if it is determined that The Big Chemical Company has violated relevant regulations, the EPA will issue an administrative complaint against Big Chemical. Unless the parties settle, an administrative trial will be conducted before an Administrative Law Judge (ALJ). After holding a hearing, the ALJ will in turn, issue an order or decision that either party may appeal to an EPA appellate board. Further appeals from the administrative appellate board can be lodged with an appropriate federal court.

Congress creates federal administrative agencies because it cannot possibly oversee the actual implementation of all the laws it enacts. Tasks are therefore delegated for issues relating to highly technical areas, such as air and water pollution. Congress, however, does monitor indirectly particular areas or agencies.

These agencies then exist to assist the executive and congressional branches in carrying out their responsibilities. Notable executive agencies include: the Federal Bureau of Investigation (Justice Department), the U.S. Customs Service (Treasury Department), the Food and Drug Administration and the Social Security Administration (Health and Human Services).

In order to create an administrative agency at the federal level, Congress passes enabling legislation, which specifies the name, purpose, composition, and powers of the agency being created. Federal agencies fall into two basic categories: independent and executive. Independent agencies are created by Congress to assist in exerting regulatory control or to carry out government administration. Agencies, therefore, perform a vital function in areas where specific expertise is a requirement in order to perform a governmental function or regulate a specific business. Independent federal agencies include: Central Intelligence Agency, the Environmental Protection Agency, the Equal Employment Opportunity Commission, the Federal Communications Commission, and the Interstate Commerce Commission.

If you work for a law firm that has many corporate clients, you may be involved extensively in transcribing information relating to agency regulations and their applicability to certain business activities. Paralegals in the field become very familiar with the administrative process when preparing documents for clients to obtain benefits from state or federal administrative agencies. To locate such agencies and discover the purpose and administrative origins you may go to this website:

http://www.usa.gov

Please bookmark it as it is in an upcoming assignment.

Enabling acts are important sources of information in researching legal matters involving administrative agencies. The Federal Trade Commission (FTC) for example, prohibits unfair and deceptive trade practices.

When visiting websites or researching otherwise, be sure to check out the stage of adjudication (the act of resolving a controversy and rendering an order or decision based on a review of the evidence). Also, the legislative rule legally binds a law enacted by legislature, and the Delegation Doctrine authorizes Congress to delegate some of its lawmaking authority to administrative agencies.

The "Administrative Process" is a procedure used in the administration of law. "Rulemaking" is an action undertaken by administrative agencies when formally adopting new regulations or amending old ones, and enforcement or rather, investigations regulate entities to monitor compliance with agency rules.

Go to the website for *The Code of Federal Regulations* and the *Federal Register* at the following site:

https://www.govinfo.gov At that website, you may research regulations. Key in any subject matter in the window to see if regulations (old or new) have been adopted. On the left side of the page, choose, "Search Tips" for ideas on what you may look for.

2. State Agencies

State agencies were implemented to regulate and provide vital services not under the direct control of the federal government. States use agencies to assist with such matters as the administration of workers' compensation, social services, tax collection (department of revenue), etc. Either the state legislature or the state's chief executive officer (the governor) creates them.

Whatever form negotiations take relative to the state or federal agency enforcement process may be, their purpose is to rectify the problem to the agency's satisfaction and eliminate the need for additional proceedings. If a settlement cannot be reached, the agency may issue a formal complaint against the offending party and adjudicate the dispute. The case will then be heard before an Administrative Law Judge (ALJ).

As a paralegal, you may find yourself working with a state or a federal agency, simultaneously. Not all states publish agency regulations in a compiled form, as the federal government does, which makes it difficult to research state regulations in those states. However, many states have administrative codes, which make it easier to locate the rules and regulations of specific agencies.

E. NATIONAL LAW

National law refers to the law of a particular nation. The elements of the common law system exist in several countries, including India and Canada, to name a couple. In contrast to Great Britain and the common law countries, most of the other European nations base their legal systems on Roman civil law, or "code law." The term civil law refers to "codified law," a grouping of legal principles enacted into law by a legislature or governing body. In a civil law system, the primary source of law is a statutory code, and case precedents are not as judicially binding as they normally are in a common law system. Judges in a civil law system are not obligated to follow precedent to the same extent as in a common law system. The *Doctrine of Stare Decisis* does not apply.

As well as the countries noted above, the civil law system is not only used by continental European countries, but in Latin America, Africa and Asia. In the U.S., the State of Louisiana, because of its historical ties to France, uses in part a civil law system. The legal systems of Puerto Rico, Quebec, and Scotland are similarly characterized as having elements of a civil law system.

F. INTERNATIONAL LAW

International law is the law that governs relations among nations, a body of written and unwritten laws observed by independent nations. In essence, no independent nation can be compelled to obey a law external to itself, so nations can and do voluntarily agree to be governed for the purpose of facilitating international trade and commerce.

Traditional sources of international law include the customs that have been historically observed by nations with treaties. For example, the U.S. Constitution requires approval by two-thirds of the Senate before a treaty executed by the president will be binding. On the other hand, a bilateral agreement occurs when two nations form an agreement that will govern commercial exchanges. Multilateral agreements are formed by several nations. The United States is a member of more than one hundred multilateral and bilateral organizations to include at least twenty through the United Nations alone.

Well, now that you fully understand the basics about law, we'll move on.

CHAPTER 3

The Court System

In this Chapter, we will discuss:

- Jurisdiction

- Venue

- Standing to Sue

- Judicial Procedures

- Choosing a Court

- Alternative Dispute Resolution

- Selection Process

Introduction

The Latin term for law is *lex*, and is a system of written or unwritten law for a given jurisdiction. A "lexicon" is a dictionary of legal terms. If you do not know the meaning of a legal term, you can look up the term in a lexicon. The codebooks contain the laws that have been created by state and federal legislatures. The *Corpus Juris Secundum* (corpus=body, juris=pertaining to the law, secundum=second or small part) is an encyclopedia of laws. The *Corpus Juris Secundum* is commonly used as a legal reference by lawyers.

The philosophy or science of law is known as "jurisprudence." Jurisprudence deals with the principles of law and legal relationships. A statute is a law created by a state or federal legislature. The violation of a statute will usually result in a legal proceeding in a court of law.

All members of the legal profession are collectively referred to as the "bar." Attorneys follow a code of ethics established by the American Bar Association (ABA), and may be censored by the bar association if they are found guilty of misconduct in their profession. We have formerly discussed information about ethics. Attorneys are regulated by the American Bar Association and the code of ethics is available at their website for review.

http://www.abanet.org **or** http://www.paralegals.org to read about the code.

A judge presides over and administers the law in a court of justice. A court of law may also be referred to as the "bench." Also, the bench may mean the seat occupied by the judge or a commissioner (includes family court jurisdiction for adjudicated youth). A "jurist" is a person who has a thorough knowledge of the law and who has written extensively on legal subjects. Do not confuse a jurist with a "juror" (one who sits on a jury).

When a statute has been violated, the judge will hear the case as presented by the prosecuting and defense attorneys. In juvenile court, the judge, a commissioner, or an attorney general, conducts criminal investigations relating to the "respondent" (the juvenile) and the public defender tries a case in court on behalf of the juvenile offender. In an adult court, the prosecuting attorney conducts criminal prosecutions on behalf of the state or the "people," whereas the defense attorney tries a case in court on behalf of the one who is charged with the crime. If you were charged with a criminal act and you did not want the assistance of a defense attorney, you could appear in court in *propria persona*, or in *pro per* or *pro se*. Someone who is in *propria persona*, or in *pro per*, or *pro se*, is acting in his or her own behalf and does not have the assistance of an attorney.

The title "Esquire," is sometimes written after an attorney's surname. The word "esquire" is usually abbreviated to Esq., and a personal or professional title is not prefixed to the name, for example, Abraham Lincoln, Esquire, since he was a practicing attorney.

As we have discussed, the American system of justice is based on the elements of English common law. Add to that, the Constitution of the United States, state constitutions, statutes passed by federal and state legislatures, administrative law, case decisions and legal principles that form common law, as well as laws of other nations and international law.

Several different types of courts exist that interpret and enforce the American system of justice. There are fifty-two court systems, one for each of the fifty states. Federal courts are not superior to state courts but are an independent court system derived from Article III, Section 2, of the Constitution.

A. JURISDICTION

Certain requirements must be met before bringing a lawsuit before a court. Generally, a court can exercise personal jurisdiction (*in personam* jurisdiction) over residents of a certain geographical area. A state trial court, for example, has jurisdiction over residents within the state or within a particular area of the state. A state's highest court is known as the State Superior Court, which has authority over all residents within that state.

A "long arm statute" permits a state to obtain jurisdiction over nonresident individuals and corporations. Under this statute, one must demonstrate that s/he is a nonresident of that state and had sufficient contacts within the state to justify the jurisdiction. For example, if a Maryland citizen committed a wrong within the state of Delaware, such as causing an automobile injury, a Delaware state court usually exercises jurisdiction.

Jurisdiction over subject matter limits the types of cases a court can hear. Within the state and federal court systems are courts of general jurisdiction and courts of limited jurisdiction. For example, probate courts—state courts that handle only matters relating to the transfer of a person's assets and obligations on that person's death, including matters relating to the custody and guardianship of children - have limited subject-matter jurisdiction, whereas, bankruptcy courts handle only bankruptcy proceedings as they are governed by federal bankruptcy law, allowing debtors to obtain relief from debts when they have financial difficulty.

Jurisdictional determination also is related to whether the case is being heard for the first time. Courts having original jurisdiction are courts of the "first instance or "trial courts" (where lawsuits begin, trials take place, and evidence is presented). Case in point: Any court having original jurisdiction is known as a "trial court." Courts having *appellate* (root word is appeal) jurisdiction are known as reviewing courts, or "appellate courts."

Generally, cases can be brought before them only on appeal from an order or judgment of a trial court or other lower court.

Jurisdiction of the Federal Courts is limited. As it states in Article III of the U.S. Constitution, Section 2 "[t]he judicial Power shall extend to all Cases, in Law and Equity, arising under this Constitution, the Laws of the United States, and Treaties made, or which shall be made, under their Authority."

Exclusive versus concurrent jurisdiction occurs when both federal and state courts have the power to hear a case. When cases are tried only in federal courts or only in state courts, exclusive jurisdiction exists. Federal courts have exclusive jurisdiction in cases involving federal crimes, bankruptcy, patents, trademarks, and copyrights; State courts have exclusive jurisdiction in subject matters, such as divorce, adoptions, and probate matters.

Before a dispute is brought to a court, one must research not only the merits of the action, but also which court—state or federal, general or specialized—a claim may be prosecuted.

> EXAMPLE
>
> Subject Matter and Personal Jurisdiction Options
>
> On a rainy afternoon, George was driving his car when it slid and hit Rachel's van in downtown Wilmington, Delaware, causing $50,000 in damages (to the van plus the medical expenses). George is a resident of Delaware, and Rachel of New Jersey. Because vehicular accidents do not raise a federal question, the dispute is not based on the Constitution or a federal statute, thus, the Delaware state court would possess subject-matter jurisdiction over Rachel's action against George. However, because there is "diversity of citizenship," (each party is resident of a different state), and the amount in controversy is over $50,000, Rachel could very well invoke the federal district court's diversity jurisdiction to entertain this case, if she believes that she may be more successful against George in that court.

1. State Courts

Each state has various levels of courts. In some states there are two levels, and in others, three. Generally, a state's highest court is called the Supreme Court, but that is not always true, for example, in New York, the Supreme Court is the state's lowest court.

In Latin, as was noted earlier, *juris* means "law," and *diction* means, "to speak." Before any court can exercise personal or in Latin, *personam* jurisdiction, it must be determined whether a person is a resident of a certain geographical area. A state trial court, for example, normally has jurisdictional authority over residents within the state or within a particular *area* of the state.

In some cases, under the authority of a long arm statute, a state is permitted to obtain jurisdiction over nonresident individuals and corporations. Therefore, under a long arm statute, it must be demonstrated that the nonresident had sufficient contacts (minimum contacts) within the state to justify the jurisdiction. Similarly, federal courts have authority to entertain suits against residents of each of the federal districts.

2. Federal Courts

Because the federal government is a government of limited powers, the jurisdiction of the federal courts is limited. Article III of the U.S. Constitution established the boundaries of federal judicial power. Article III, Section 2 states that "(t)he judicial Power shall extend to all Cases, in Law and Equity, arising under this Constitution, the Laws of the United States, and Treaties made, or which shall be made, under their Authority.

Federal district courts can also exercise original jurisdiction over cases involving diversity of citizenship. Under Article III, Section 2, a basis for federal court jurisdiction over certain disputes, includes disputes between citizens of different states.

Assume that the following events have taken place:

> **CASE SCENARIO**
>
> Maria Ramirez, a citizen of Florida, was jogging near Collins Avenue in Miami, Florida, when a large crate flew off a passing truck and she sustained serious injuries. She incurred as a result, numerous medical expenses and could not work for six months. Maria decided to sue the trucking company for $50,000 in damages. The trucking company's headquarters are located in Georgia, even though the company does business in South Florida.

In this situation, Maria could bring suit in a Florida court because she is a resident of Florida. The trucking company clearly does business in South Florida since that is where the accident occurred. She could bring suit in a Georgia court, because a Georgia court could exercise jurisdiction over the trucking company since it is in Georgia. She could also bring suit in the appropriate Florida court since that is where the accident happened.

Exclusive versus concurrent jurisdiction allows both federal and state courts to hear a case, as is true in suits involving diversity of citizenship (such as is Maria's case), where concurrent jurisdiction exists.

On the other hand, when cases can be tried *only* in federal or state courts, exclusive jurisdiction exists. Therefore, federal courts have exclusive jurisdiction in cases involving federal crimes, bankruptcy, patents, trademarks, and copyrights, and matters of admiralty law (transportation) on the seas and ocean waters. States also have exclusive jurisdiction in certain subject matters—divorce and adoption, probate, etc.

B. VENUE

If you have watched any of the plethora of legal themes on TV, you have probably heard the word, "venue." Venue is defined as "the locality where a crime is committed, or a legal action occurs." It becomes the geographical district where an action is tried and from which a jury may be selected. Venue is concerned with the most appropriate location for a trial.

Basically, the concept of venue reflects the policy that a court trying a suit should be in the geographic neighborhood (usually the county) in which the incident leading to the lawsuit occurred or in which the parties involved in the lawsuit reside. For example, a change of venue from Oklahoma City to Denver, Colorado, was ordered for the trials of *Timothy McVeigh* and *Terry Nichols* after they had been indicted in connection with the 1995 bombing of the Alfred P. Murrah Federal Building in Oklahoma City. If a question exists as to the impartiality of the person(s) to be involved in judging the suit, a change of venue may be requested. In the McVeigh case, that is exactly why a change of venue motion was made since it is certainly doubtful that with all the publicity and the feelings generated from that tragic event, would have made it difficult to have a fair trial in Oklahoma City or its environs.

C. STANDING TO SUE

To bring a lawsuit before a court, a party must have "standing to sue," which means the individual must have a sufficient stake in a controversy before s/he can bring a lawsuit. Assume an individual was injured in an auto accident caused by defective brakes. The individual would have standing to sue the automobile manufacturer for damages since s/he would certainly have a stake in the event the brakes failed.

D. JUDICIAL PROCEDURES

From the moment a lawsuit is initiated until the final resolution of the case, it must follow specifically designated "procedural rules." The procedural rules for federal court cases are set forth in the <u>Federal Rules of Civil Procedure</u>. State rules which are often similar to the federal rules, vary from state to state—and even from court to court within a given state. Legal transcriptionists need to be familiar with the procedural rules of the relevant courts.

Do a web search for "federal rules of civil procedure" and read up on what you can find for jurisdiction and subject matter jurisdiction.

E. CHOOSING A COURT

When an attorney is working on a case, s/he must decide which court is the proper one for a given action. That determination includes:

- Review the jurisdiction of each court

- Evaluate the strengths and weaknesses of the case

- Evaluate the remedy sought

- Evaluate the jury pool available for each court (if seeking a jury trial)

- Evaluate the likelihood of winning in each court

- Evaluate the length of time it will take each court to decide the case

COURTS AND THE LEGAL SYSTEM

TERMINOLOGY AND DEFINITIONS

LEGAL TERM	DEFINITION
U.S. Supreme Court	The highest court in the federal judicial system. Composed of a chief justice and eight associate justices. This court has final jurisdiction in matters tried in the lower federal courts and can also hear certain cases on appeal from the highest courts in the state systems if a constitutional question of federal law is involved.
U.S. Court of Appeals	An appellate court. Reviews cases from lower federal courts. There are currently 13 judicial circuits, each of which has a U.S. Court of Appeals.
U.S. District Court	A federal trial court or a federal court of original jurisdiction. The court in which a case is first tried in the federal court system.
Special courts	There are several special U.S. courts that have limited jurisdiction, including the Court of Claims, the Court of Customs and Patent Appeals, and the Tax Court.
Supreme court	The highest court in most state court systems. Certain cases decided in a state supreme court may be appealed to the U.S. Supreme Court if a constitutional question of federal law is involved.
Court of appeal	A court that reviews cases from the trial courts or lower courts. The highest court in states not having a supreme court.
Appellate court	Same as court of appeal. A court that reviews cases that are appealed from a lower court.
Trial court	A court of original jurisdiction. Hears a case the first time it is tried in court.
Probate court	A court that deals with the probate of wills and the settlement of estates. Also, may be called orphan court or surrogate court. In some states the probate court has jurisdiction over the estates of minors and the appointment of guardians.

F. ALTERNATIVE DISPUTE RESOLUTION

Generally, litigation in court is a last resort. Because of the growing backlog in the court system, many individuals and business entities use "Alternative Dispute Resolution" (ADR), in fact, it is now included in a number of legal contracts as a first alternative, and is increasingly used in medicine relating to care issues and reimbursement of medical services and claims.

ADR methods for settling disputes outside the court system include:

- negotiation
- mediation
- arbitration.

Negotiation is where disputing parties, with or without the assistance of attorneys, meet informally to resolve the dispute out of court.

Mediation is a method of settling disputes outside court using the services of a neutral third party, who acts as a communicating agent between the parties. This method of dispute settlement is less formal than arbitration. A mediator need not be a lawyer. Mediation usually results in the quick settlement of a dispute.

Arbitration is a more formal method of ADR. In arbitration, the third party hearing the dispute normally makes the decision, wherein the arbitrator becomes a private judge.

Arbitration clauses and statutes are frequently used in commercial matters, and are beginning to enjoy great popularity in medical applications. An arbitration clause in a contract provides that, in the event of a dispute, the parties will determine their rights by arbitration rather than through the judicial system. Most states have statutes under which arbitration clauses are enforced. At the federal level, the "Federal Arbitration Act" (FAA) of 1925 enforces arbitration clauses in contracts relating to interstate commerce between two or more states.

The first step in the arbitration process is the submission agreement where the parties agree to submit the dispute for arbitration. In most states an agreement to submit a dispute for arbitration must be in writing. The second step is the hearing process. In a typical hearing, the parties begin as they would at a trial by presenting opening arguments to the arbitrator and stating the desired remedies. Witnesses may be called and after all evidence has been presented, the parties give closing arguments. After each side has had an opportunity to present evidence and to argue its case, the arbitrator(s) reaches a decision. The final decision of the arbitrator is called an "award."

The role of the courts in the arbitration process is limited. When a dispute arises as to whether the parties have agreed in an arbitration clause to submit a particular matter to arbitration, one party may file suit to compel arbitration. The court before which the suit is brought will not decide the basic issue or controversy, but must decide whether the dispute is arbitrable (whether the matter can be resolved through arbitration).

You can read more about ADR on this website: www.fjc.gov

G. SELECTION PROCESS

- Review the jurisdiction of each court

- Evaluate the strengths and weaknesses of the case

- Evaluate the remedy sought

- Evaluate the jury pool available for each court (if seeking a jury trial)

- Evaluate the likelihood of winning in each court

- Evaluate the length of time it will take each court to decide the case

QUESTIONS – CHAPTER 2 AND 3

1. What is judicial review?

   _____

2. Identify the *constitutional amendment* being violated in the following hypothetical situations.

   a. Ann's supervisor threatens to fire her if she does not work on Sunday even though that is when she attends worship services

   _____

   b. The county proposes an ordinance requiring that anyone caught stealing, be punished by having his or her hand cut off for the first offense and the other hand cut off for the second offense

   _____

   c. Because Robert's house is located in a drug-infested neighborhood, the police decided that he must be a drug dealer. The police burst in and tear the place apart searching for drugs. They find nothing

   _____

   d. The federal government bans all advertising of cigarettes

   _____

   e. A man accused of a crime is held in jail pending charges for 30 days

   _____

   f. A woman accused of murder refuses to take the stand to answer questions

   _____

3. In an employment discrimination case, attorney Jane Brady decides to meet with a new client, Jan. Jan briefly describes her former employer and the events leading up to her being fired. In essence, Jan wants to sue for gender discrimination. Attorney Brady feels that Jan has a strong case. Several of Jan's former co-workers have agreed to testify that they heard the employer say on many occasions that he would never promote a woman to

a managerial position. The mere mention of "woman to a managerial position," sparked an interest in this case.

a. In what court should her action be filed and why?

_____

_____

b. Do both state and federal laws prohibit gender discrimination?

_____

4. Explain the function of the courts of general jurisdiction

_____

_____

5. What is a long arm statute?

_____

6. Do the words subject matter have any relevance to the types of a cases a court can hear?

_____

7. Is the power of the federal court limited?

_____

8. What does the word "law" mean?

_____

9. The American legal system was derived primarily from what country?

_____

10. What is common law?

_____

11. What is case law?

_____

12. What does "precedent" mean?

_____

13. Does the "Doctrine of Stare Decisis" relate to precedents?

    _____

14. What was the case cited which was used to depart from the rule of precedent related to the ultimate civil rights movement?

    _____

15. Explain the distinction between law and equity

    _____

16. List 3 of the 6 Equitable Principles and Maxims

    _____

    _____

    _____

    _____

    _____

    _____

    _____

    _____

    _____

    _____

    _____

    _____

17. What 3 remedies are related to equity?

    _____

    _____

18. Ordinarily, law action objectives relate to assessment of damages, but a court of equity can go further to provide the complainant

    _____

19. Legislative bodies enact statutes and

    _____

PARALEGAL PRACTICE: COMPLETE COLLEGE-LEVEL COURSE, VOLUME 1 | JARI DAVIS

20. What type of law do state and federal agencies operate under?

    _____

21. Can a state or municipality enact a statute or ordinance which may violate the Constitution?

    a._____

    and what clause would relate to that premise?

    b._____

22. Under whose jurisdiction to the following statutory matters fall?

    a. Corporate law _____

    b. Patent law _____

    c. Employment law _____

    d. Will and probates _____

23. Name three Federal agencies _____

24. If a federal or state agency attempts to enforce a rule or law, and compliance is not obtained from the offender, subsequent proceedings are adjudicated by

    _____

25. If the agency prevails in the process noted in #24, does the offender have rights remaining after a final determination Y_____ N _____. If you answer yes, what are the rights?

    _____

ASSIGNMENT

26. Go to the Supreme Court website,

https://www.supremecourt.gov/oral_arguments/oral_arguments.aspxClick on Oral Transcripts and choose the 08-1371 numbered argument, 4-19-2010 (or search for it with the information in the table below).

Argument Session: April 19, 2010 - April 28, 2010	Date Argued
08-1371[1]. Christian Legal Soc. Chapter of Univ. of Cal., Hastings College of Law v. Martinez	04/19/10

Read the argument. It relates to charges about discrimination.

27. Go to **www.usa.gov**.

   a. Look up on the alpha federal list at least 4 different agencies

   b. At the top of the page on subject matter, click on "find government agencies," and review the options.

   c. Click on state government, input your state and explore the subject matter there.

You're not done yet – do the assignment next

---

[1] https://www.supremecourt.gov/oral_arguments/argument_transcripts/2009/08-1371.pdf

ONLINE ASSIGNMENT:

1. Locate a website referred to earlier related to the Constitution, find the Fifth Amendment (rights of persons), and read the annotations relating to

- Indictment by Grand Jury

- Double Jeopardy

- Development and Scope

- Supreme Court Review

- Procedure in the Trial Courts

2. Use the website dedicated to the United States Supreme Court, located at https://www.supremecourt.gov/ - review the role of the justices of the Supreme Court (click on About the Court and follow links regarding the Chief Justice, Associate Justices, Retired Justices, and Court Officers).

3. In addition to the FindLaw's home page at **www.findlaw.com** to see if you can locate anything on your state court system, or go to the National Center for State Courts website: https://www.ncsc.org/ .

Check the information on the federal court system at **www.uscourts.gov** - trial courts a good state court directory here). Opinions of U.S. circuit courts www.law.cornell.edu/opinions.html.

These sites offer links to many of the federal and state sources of law that you have read about in the Introduction to American Law. When available, select pages related to your state. As you browse through, find answers to the following questions and make notes here – no answers are provided since this is an assignment to familiarize you with resources.

a. Were you able to access the text of your state's constitution?

b. Did the site include your state's code, statutes and administrative regulations?

c. What other primary research materials were available at the site?

d. Search through "Primary Materials" sites for three other states. Compare your state's website to others you found in terms of comprehensiveness and ease of use?

CHAPTER 4
Civil Litigation

In this Chapter, we will discuss

A. Substantive & Procedural Law

B. Commencement of a Lawsuit

C. Early Stages of a Suit

D. Middle Stages of Suit

E. Trial (Final Stage)

A. SUBSTANTIVE AND PROCEDURAL LAW

Much of the law in the U.S. is devoted to making rules that regulate behavior in various situations. For instance, *tort law* governs the rules that make it wrong for a drunk driver to destroy your car. *Contract law* requires a tenant to pay rent as agreed and may make a roofing contractor liable for the damage caused by his poor workmanship. These are prime examples of rules of *substantive law*.

Substantive rules or laws are useless unless there is some way of enforcing them. It will be of little help if the law prohibits drunk driving if it is not enforced. Therefore, substantive rules are meaningless without "remedies." *Procedural law* is the means by which a problem is *remedied.*

Law then is divided into these two main types - *substantive law and procedural law.* Substantive law is the actual law itself, whereas procedural law entails the legal process. Substantive law deals with the act itself, the relevant legal elements, and what makes an act legal or illegal. To learn the difference you must first go over some examples of each category mentioned.

Our legal system uses two main weapons to enforce its rules on behavior: Criminal punishment and civil lawsuits. Criminal punishment is intended to deal with offenses, which damage society as a whole. Only the government can bring a criminal prosecution (action). While criminal law focuses on punishing or rehabilitating the wrongdoer, it does not compensate a victim. Civil lawsuits are designed to do just that, and they are the second weapon. Civil actions are used to get satisfaction and to restore the aggrieved party some measure of his/her loss.

If Phil intentionally kills Will, Phil will likely be charged with murder. The elements of murder are compared to Phil's *actions (*classifications of Common Law Murder) with Intent-to-kill being the most common. The intentional, unlawful killing of another human being is considered the most serious criminal offense. Phil was found to have committed murder. This is known as *substantive law analysis*—that is, looking at what the actual law may be.

Procedural law deals with the whole legal process; the rights a person has during arrest, trial, imprisonment, sanctions (punishment), the right to sue, to name a few. If Phil is arrested, he will have the right to an attorney, the right to a jury trial, and the right to be deemed innocent until proven guilty. These are known as types of procedural law. They deal with the legal process that comes into play after an actual act.

Civil litigation is the law of remedies. Litigants (those involved in the lawsuit) deal with the details dictated by <u>The Federal Rules of Civil Procedure.</u> Plaintiffs in civil actions are seeking damages, injunctions, or specific performance. Plaintiffs may be natural persons, entities, estates, or political subdivisions. In the adjudication of a matter, we have discussed how a court must have proper jurisdiction. Lawsuits are initiated when the plaintiff files pleadings with the clerk of the court and serves the defendant with a *complaint*. Lawsuits revolve around issues of fact (resolved by the trier of fact) and issues of law (resolved by judges).

Issues of fact require the introduction of testimonial and documentary evidence at trial in addition to issues of law that are brought to the court's attention when one of the parties files a motion.

During the pre-suit phase prior to a lawsuit being filed, the attorneys conduct investigations, attempt negotiations, and prepare strategies. The lawsuit begins officially when a complaint is filed. Discovery however, consumes most of the time and effort in preparing for trial, and this process occurs subsequent to the filing of pleadings and is the stage where the majority of evidence is presented.

1. Standard of Proof

In a civil trial, the defendant must be found guilty (liable) by a preponderance of evidence. In terms of reasoning, the defendant must be over 50 percent liable in order to render a favorable verdict. In criminal law, the standard of proof is much more stringent. The defendant cannot be found guilty simply by means of a "preponderance of evidence," but has to be guilty beyond a "reasonable doubt." Generally, proof of guilt requires much more than going beyond the 50 percent preponderance standard. The court utilizes mitigating and aggravating circumstances as well (prior criminal history) and adds to these elements the questions of reasonable doubt.

2. Legal Reasoning

In the U.S., the ideal reflects a set of values called the "rule of law." As a matter of principle Americans tend to believe that law should limit the coercive powers of government. What do you think? Relating back to the good old "Constitution," where "no person shall ... be deprived of life, liberty, or property, without due process of law." Much of what the government does, of course, deprives people of life, liberty, or property. For example, a court's judgment may require one person to pay money or transfer property to someone else, may incarcerate a person or otherwise restrict personal freedom, and, as harshly as it may sound, "the death penalty," may be the final judgment assessed to a perpetrator. In any instance, the rule of law requires coercion to be used by state or federal officials only when and as authorized by the standards of law.

Consequently, people want to know by what right someone sitting behind a bench or standing behind a badge uses the state's power to deprive one of life, liberty, and the pursuit of happiness. In most instances, we may confront a legal problem with conflicting instincts. On the other hand, we may try to solve it as required by the formalistic version of the rule of law. At the same time, we may rely on whatever intuitions and former experience we have mustered regarding non-legal causes of legal decisions.

Case in point: Legal laws do not describe regularities in the behavior of any one person or thing. Rather, they prescribe human conduct. How are people to act? What is appropriate behavior? That's what the process tries to decide. The "scales of justice," must be weighed. For example, in a criminal case with "mitigating" and "aggravating," circumstances, the court must decide what sanctions – various levels of punishment under which a perpetrator will be sentenced.

The chief feature of legal reasoning is that it is used in the process of anticipating or settling important disputes. Every society develops methods for settling persistent disputes among its members. Therefore, different methods are employed by different societies in different times and places. Important disputes in developed societies can be settled, if need be, by appealing to judges to apply the law. Generally, this method is better than the alternatives (cutting off hands for theft, deporting people, etc.) so that disputes may be settled with finality in peaceful and/or justifiable ways. Dispute settlement by law is more peaceful than a duel, or a feud. The adjudication is more public, accountable and revisable in cases of error. Obviously, then the law and the reasoning process itself enable judges to reach final, peaceful, and justifiable dispute settlements.

"Deductive legal reasoning" is most closely associated with reasoning from enacted law (usually consists of general rules). These rules are found in a variety of official legal documents, such as constitutions, statutes, codes, regulations, and executive orders.

Deductive legal reasoning differs from "analogical legal reasoning" in a number of ways. First, reasoning starts from a rule, not a case. Rules are enacted before cases governed by the rule have materialized. Secondly, the principle of "legislative supremacy" generally requires judges to play a subordinate role to the more democratic branches of government. Courts however, have no authority to reformulate enacted rules as the case law interpreting the rules unfolds. Thirdly, the static statement of enacted rules leads legal reasoning from such rules to focus heavily on problems of "rule interpretation."

Casting legal arguments in their deductive form serves a number of valuable functions. Legal rules establish the framework of law within a legal system, setting up an elaborate classification scheme that specifies the conclusions that judges might reach in determining their decision. Reasoning from settled rules makes law manageable, simply by transforming vague questions of what is "just" into more concrete questions that are often uncontroversial.

On the other hand, deductive legal reasoning can be highly misleading; it may seem that the rules dictate the result in a case when they should not do so. Both analogical legal reasoning and deductive reasoning do not avoid the importance of the need to judge.

Commencement of Lawsuit

a. Overview

What happens when a person wants to sue another person? Do you simply call the court and make an appointment to stop by later that day to discuss your problem with the judge relating to the other person/entity? No. Do you call your local state troopers to administer justice? No. In order to utilize the system of justice, a person must follow certain procedures. In order to bring an action (sue someone), you must complete, file and serve "pleading," which is the initial document along with all of the subsequent documents, related to your gripe, and these are the documents involved in a lawsuit. There are numerous types of pleadings.

The gripes you have are known as allegations. Each allegation (a statement declared or asserted to be true) of the complaint is generally contained in a separately numbered sentence. Generally, the first sentences set forth the relief sought (punishment or what is desired from the party being sued) along with the type of lawsuit.

The *plaintiff,* is the griper. The person/entity against whom the gripe is filed is the *defendant.* The defendant responds to the complaint by filing an *answer* in which s/he admits or denies the statements or allegations made in the complaint. The complaint and the answer are called *pleadings.*

In some jurisdictions, the aggrieved party must file a demand letter, before beginning a lawsuit. This letter informs the defendant that a lawsuit is imminent, providing the parties an opportunity to discuss settlement before a complaint is filed.

After the first pleadings are filed, the parties file additional documents to learn the elements of the other side's case. This process is known as *discovery*. Discovery reveals facts and legal theories relied on by the parties; it also exposes strengths and weaknesses of each party's case. For example, the parties can file written questions, called *interrogatories*, to be answered under oath by the opposing side. At that point, other relevant documents may be requested, and other parties asked questions under oath or *deposed*.

The discovery process is controlled by a special set of rules written by courts or legislatures. Other rules control the entire litigation process including evidentiary matters. Evidence may include a single piece of information (a paper, contract, receipt, etc.) or a collection of documents and testimony used at trial to try to prove a case. Evidence from a reliable source is relevant to the case and is admitted by the judge at trial, proving or disproving a fact in issue.

We will go through a brief process of describing the way it all works, but more detailed information will be available through the various chapters dealing with law specialties.

Caption – [see subsequent samples] is the "heading" setting forth the parties, (plaintiff, defendant), the court where filed – all in a specific format, usually a standard one used by the court. Each court may have its own different style or format. Plaintiff - Dave Clark files a complaint against Defendant Phil Collins as follows:

CASE SCENARIO

On January 6, 2014 Plaintiff Clark and Defendant Collins entered into a contract. Collins was a contractor for Clark. The contractor (Collins) required a certain amount of money to complete the scope of work in the amount of $5,000. Clark paid Collins $5,000, and in so doing performed all of his obligations under the contract. Collins failed to complete the construction of Clark's home, as he was required under contract. Additional sentences in the legal complaint describe what happened in that process thus far. Finally, the actual relief is requested, either for Collins to finish the work for instance, or to pay back the money. These are known as "damages." A request for a jury trial may also be made. The issues to be tried may be decided by a judge, or by a jury. If decided by a jury, the judge serves only as the "referee," guiding and monitoring the process. Depending on the case, a plaintiff may want his or her fate or the issues at stake to be in the hands of a legal professional (a judge) or several people from all walks of life (a jury).

The complaint is then served on the defendant (delivered to him/her/it). Often, the complaint and the summons are combined into one document, the "Summons and Complaint." The complaint becomes effective only when it is accompanied by a summons. You will see a sample of a summons and complaint in the "Early Stages of a Lawsuit" section, which follows.

Service of a summons and complaint may be made in various ways (by hand, by mail, or by other notice), depending on the particular procedural laws of the jurisdiction. Generally, it is best to serve the opposing party (the defendant) by hand. In all cases, law requires *proof* of such service. There is no substitute for face-to-face acceptance. Personal service also avoids such excuses, as "it must have gotten lost in the mail." Once service has been properly made, the defendant has a specific amount of time in which to answer the complaint (tell his side of the story). Depending on both the jurisdiction and method of service, the amount of time will vary. Service of a summons and complaint may be made in various ways (by hand, by mail, or by other notice), depending on the particular procedural laws of the jurisdiction. Generally, it is best to serve the opposing party (the defendant) by hand. In *all* cases, law requires proof of such service. There is no substitute for face-to-face acceptance. Personal service also avoids such excuses, as "it must have gotten lost in the mail." Once service has been properly made, the defendant has a specific amount of time in which to answer the complaint (tell his side of the story). Depending on both the jurisdiction and method of service, the amount of time will vary.

TERMS

The words most commonly used in a lawsuit are:

ADMISSIBLE	Can be admitted
ABOVE-NAMED	Previously mentioned in caption
ACKNOWLEDGEMENT	Formal statement made before an authorized person acknowledging that the document was executed of one's own free will
AFFIANT	Person who makes an affidavit.
AFFIDAVIT	Written declaration made under oath
ANSWER	A written response to a complaint
CAPTION	Heading on a court document, style and format, noting the court, parties to the suit, case number, judge and type of pleading
CASE LAW	Body of law relating to decisions made by judges that have come before a court
CERTIFICATE OF SERVICE	Written declaration that a copy of a pleading has been served (by mail or by hand) on either party or counsel of a lawsuit
CITATION	Providing a source for the law being quoted (or being cited for an infraction of law)
COMPLAINT	Initiation of lawsuit description of what the party bringing it complains of
COUNTERCLAIM	Motion (defensive) claiming the defendant has a claim against the party bringing the initial suit
COURT DOCKET	Number assigned to a case (is on all of the documents related to a suit)
ENDORSEMENT	Information as to the nature of a legal document written on the back of same

ETALIUS	Latin for "and others," most often abbreviated as et al
IN RE	Regarding
JURAT	Clause written at end of an affidavit stating when, where, and notary before whom an affidavit was sworn
JURISDICTION	Right/authority of a court to hear and adjudicate lawsuit
PARTY	Either of the individuals, entities involved in a lawsuit (plaintiff v defendant, etc.)
PRAYER	Closing paragraph of a pleading stating relief sought
VENUE	Geographical location where a lawsuit is tried
VERIFICATION	Signed statement at end of a document alleging statements of fact in the document are true

b. Litigation Process

A. Time Limitations

Every state has its own *statute of limitations*, which delineates the legal time limit for filing a lawsuit, after the date of the infraction, injury, breach, accident, etc. The length of time in Delaware is two years. In California, Kentucky, Louisiana, Tennessee, Maine and North Dakota it ranges anywhere from one year to six years. You will have to learn the time limitations in your state.

Often, very short notice requirements rule when a claim may be made against a state, city, or county. It may be necessary to file a formal "Notice of Claim," in as little time as 30-60 days after a motor vehicle accident, for instance. Therefore, it is essential that anyone with an auto accident claim seek legal advice as to the statute of limitations and notice requirements that will apply in that particular case. Waiting too long can mean losing all one's rights to make a claim for injuries.

B. Legal Representation

Do you have to have an attorney to file a lawsuit? No, an attorney is not required. However, a number of things must be considered if one represents oneself. One needs to be certain that all possible defendants can be named and located, and that all possible causes of action are clearly defined and used, e.g., the driver information from the operator of the vehicle that injured one, (there may be a claim against the driver's business, or the owner of the car, as well as a tavern where the driver had been drinking), insurance information, and as much other information as may be reasonably obtained.

If the defendant had insurance, that insurance company may hire an attorney to oppose the lawsuit, and can make it difficult to maneuver through the complex litigation process on one's own. It is not smart for someone inexperienced in these matters to decide when it is appropriate to sign off or settle and for how much.

C. EARLY STAGES OF THE LAWSUIT

1. Drafting a Complaint

The complaint itself may be no more than a few paragraphs long, or it may be many pages in length, depending on the complexity of the case. The complaint will include the following

- Caption

- Jurisdictional statement (that the court filed in has appropriate jurisdiction)

- General allegations (body of the complaint)

- Prayer for relief

- Signature

- Demand for a jury trial

 SAMPLE (caption and complaint)

The caption – as mentioned - identifies the court in which the action is being filed, (For example, IN THE SECOND JUDICIAL DISTRICT COURT, IN AND FOR DAVIS COUNTY, STATE OF UTAH), names of the parties in the lawsuit (Plaintiff, and Defendant), the file or case number, also known as the docket, Name of the Judge, and the Plaintiff's attorney.

Type of document (for example; COMPLAINT AND DEMAND FOR JURY TRIAL), Jurisdictional: Allegations (for example; a party's statement, claim or assertion made in a pleading to the court.), title and section numbers in the United States Code (For example; *Diversity of Citizenship under 28 U.S.C. 1332*). It would look something like this (the format depending upon which court it is filed):

SAMPLE (FOR CAPTION MATERIAL)

JULIE EDWARDS

Attorney at Law

2330 North Main

Layton, Utah 84040

801-555-5555

IN THE SECOND JUDICIAL DISTRICT COURT, IN AND FOR

DAVIS COUNTY, STATE OF UTAH

JODI MC CALL,

	:	COMPLAINT
Plaintiff,	:	Civil No. 0060304EV
vs.	:	Judge Thomas L. Ray
JOHN DOE and MARY DOE,	:	
Defendants.	:	

GENERAL ALLEGATIONS This is where the items complained of appear)

That on _____ (date) at approximately (time – if applicable), the PLAINTIFF did (whatever is complained of) and after that listing is complete, the pleading closes with what is known as a

PRAYER FOR RELIEF

WHEREFORE, the Plaintiff prays for the following relief:

1. That the Plaintiff be awarded appropriate compensatory damages,

2. That the Plaintiff be awarded an amount deemed fair and just by a Jury to compensate the Plaintiff for damages sustained as presented by the evidence in this case.

SIGNATURE OF PLAINTIFF'S ATTORNEY

The signature, date and law firm are then listed.

Accompanying the complaint in this case is an **Affidavit**, which describes from the plaintiff's perspective what transpired. Sometimes the affidavit has the same caption as the complaint; however, this one is just a simple affidavit.

SAMPLE AFFIDAVIT (filed with complaint)

JULIE EDWARDS

Attorney at Law

2330 North Main

Layton, Utah 84040

801-555-5555

IN THE SECOND JUDICIAL DISTRICT COURT, IN AND FOR

DAVIS COUNTY, STATE OF UTAH

JODI MC CALL,

	:	AFFIDAVIT IN SUPPORT OF COMPLAINT
Plaintiff,	:	Civil No. 0060304EV
vs.	:	Judge Thomas L. Ray
JOHN DOE and MARY DOE,	:	
Defendants.	:	

THE UNDERSIGNED, Jodi McCall, under penalty of perjury, residing at 1234 South XYZ Street, Layton, Utah, is of legal age, has personal knowledge of all matters set forth in this Affidavit, and hereby swears and affirms that the following is true and accurate, to the best of her knowledge and belief:

1. That I was injured in an accident, blah, blah, blah.

2. That as a consequence, I was an inpatient in the hospital, in serious condition, and

   under sedation and breathing support to the extent that I was blah, blah, blah.

3. I still suffer blah, blah, blah.

Dated this 1st day of April, 2014.

Jodi McCall

_____

Jodi McCall, Affiant

VERIFICATION: this is at the end of documents requiring a notary.

[**Verification**]: Then a notary signs as:

State of Utah)
              : SS
County of Davis)

Sworn and subscribed before me this 1st day of April, 2014

Matilda Jones

_____
Notary Public
My commission expires: 2/2/2015

2. Filing the Complaint

Once the complaint has been prepared, it is carefully checked for accuracy, and signed by the attorney. The complaint is then filed with the court in which the action is going to take place. The complaint is hand delivered to the clerk of the court, along with the filing fee (check payable to the court). Each court has its own set filing fee. The original is filed with the court and the needed copies include one for the office.

The court clerk will then file the complaint by stamping the date on the document, assigning the pleading a case number (*docket number*) and subsequently assigned to a particular judge.

Alternatively, under the <u>1993 revision of Rule 5(a) of the FRCP</u> provides that federal courts may permit filing by fax or computer. To find out whether a particular court permits documents to be filed electronically, go to this website: http://www.findlaw.com and click on state or federal courts.

After the complaint has been filed, a specified period of time is permitted for the defendant to answer the complaint. During the process of the litigation, the court may consult with the attorneys for both sides, often through a "scheduling conference." Following the meeting, the judge will enter a scheduling order that sets out the time limits within which pretrial events take place. For example; pleadings, discovery, and final pretrial conference, under *FRCP 16(b)*, the scheduling order should be entered "as soon as practicable and in no event more than 120 days after the complaint is filed."

3. Service of Process

At the time the complaint is filed, a summons is then prepared and personally delivered (Service of Process) to the defendant(s) of the lawsuit. You prepare a summons by filing out a form similar to the one presented here. You will also prepare a cover sheet for the case, which is required by federal courts and in some state courts.

SAMPLE SUMMONS

JULIE EDWARDS

Attorney at Law

2330 NORTH MAIN

Layton, Utah 84040

801-555-5555

IN THE SECOND JUDICIAL DISTRICT COURT, IN AND FOR

DAVIS COUNTY, STATE OF UTAH

JODI MC CALL,		
	:	SUMMONS
Plaintiff,	:	Civil No. 0060304EV
vs.	:	Judge Thomas L. Ray
JOHN DOE and MARY DOE,	:	
Defendants.	:	

THE STATE OF UTAH TO THE ABOVE-NAMED DEFENDANT:

You are hereby summoned and required to file an answer in writing to the attached Complaint with the Clerk of the above-entitled Court, and to serve upon or mail to Plaintiff's attorney, a copy of your Answer within ___ days after service of this Summons upon you.

If you fail to do so, judgment by default will be taken against you for the relief demanded in said Complaint , which has been filed with the Clerk of said Court and a copy of which is hereto annexed and herewith service upon you.

Then the signature line.

4. Waiver of Notice

In Federal courts, the 1993 revision of the FRCP added *Rule 4(d)*, allows for a simpler and less costly alternative to service of process. Under this rule, a plaintiff's attorney is permitted to notify the defendant directly, through the mails or "other reliable means," of the lawsuit. After the complaint has been filed, attorney Edwards will probably ask her paralegal to follow the procedures outlined in FRCP 4(d). As a paralegal you must comply with FRCP 4(d) in that you will need to fill out two forms, Form 1A, which is entitled "Notice of Lawsuit and Request for Waiver of Service of Summons." It is imperative that this form is signed by attorney Edwards, requesting defendant to waive the requirement that he be notified of the lawsuit by having a summons served on him. Subsequently, as the paralegal, you will fill out Form 1B, entitled "Waiver of Service of Summons." Once these forms are filled out and attorney Edwards has reviewed and signed, you will send to the defendant, a packet containing the following contents:

- Two copies each of *Form 1A*, and *Form 1B*.

- Copy of the *Complaint*

- A pre-addressed, self-stamped envelope for the defendant, to use when returning Form 1B

If defendant agrees to waive service of process, s/he will need to sign and return the waiver to attorney Edwards within thirty days after the waiver form was sent by Attorney Brown. For defendants located in a foreign country, the time period is extended to sixty days.

The reason for using *FRCP 4(d)* purely eliminates the costs associated with service of process, as well as cooperation among adversaries. If a defendant does not agree to waive service then a complaint and summons must be served personally. On the other hand, to encourage defendants to agree to the waiver of service, *FRCP 4(d)(3)* provides that defendants who return the required waiver are not required to respond to the complaint for sixty days (ninety days outside the United States). Under *FRCP 12* the defendant must respond to the complaint within twenty days after process is served.

Next, is a sample of how this is handled in some states.

JULIE EDWARDS

Attorney at Law

2330 NORTH MAIN

Layton, Utah 84040

801-555-5555

IN THE SECOND JUDICIAL DISTRICT COURT, IN AND FOR

DAVIS COUNTY, STATE OF UTAH

JODI MC CALL,	:	ORDER FOR SERVICE BY POSTING & CERTIFIED MAIL
Plaintiff,	:	Civil No. 0060304EV
vs.	:	Judge Thomas L. Ray
JOHN DOE and MARY DOE,	:	
Defendants.:		

Upon reviewing the Affidavit of Jane Catchem filed herein, it satisfactorily appears to the Court therefrom that a Cause of Action exists for Plaintiff against Defendant, and that Plaintiff has been unable to obtain personal service. Defendant is a necessary and proper party of this action, and the Court being otherwise fully advised in the premises, and good cause appearing therefore.

IT IS HEREBY ORDERED that the Summons and Complaint in this matter be served by means of posting the Summons and Complaint on the property and by mailing a copy regular and certified mail.

THIS ONE IS SIGNED BY THE COURT (JUDGE)

5. Defendant Response (Answer or Reply)

Once a defendant receives the plaintiff's complaint, the defendant must respond either via mail or through service of process. If the defendant fails to respond within the allotted time frame, the court, on the plaintiff's motion, will enter a default judgment against the defendant. The defendant will then be liable for the entire amount of damages that the plaintiff is claiming and will lose the opportunity for defense against the claim in court or settle the issue with the plaintiff out of court.

Most cases are settled out of court before they go to trial. Even if defendant's attorney suspects that an out-of-court settlement might be financially preferable to a trial, as the paralegal you will still draft a response to plaintiff's claim. You know that if the defendant does not respond to plaintiff's complaint within the proper time frame, the court will enter a default judgment against defendant.

Because a defendant's answer must include the response to the claims mentioned above against the defendant, the mechanism for response to the allegations is known as the REPLY.

ANSWER OR REPLY

A defendant's answer must respond to each allegation in the plaintiff's complaint. *FRCP 8(b)* permits the defendant to admit or deny the truth of each allegation. Defendant's attorney may advise defendant to admit to some of the allegations in the plaintiff's complaint.

The answer may contain one or more of the following:

- A general denial of the claim

- Admissions (admitting on an item by item basis) that most of the allegations in the complaint are true, and others are not (For example, a defendant might admit that he hit the plaintiff's car, but deny that the plaintiff was injured)

- An "affirmative defense," is a claim that plaintiff was also at fault in causing the accident or that the statute of limitations had run out before the complaint was filed

- A "counterclaim," may be made by the defendant against the plaintiff; in affect, a counter-claiming defendant is now going to counter sue the plaintiff

- A "cross-claim," is a claim against another defendant, maybe a tire company or some such related to this action in some way

- A "third-party claim," is a claim against another person or company who was not originally named in the lawsuit

6. Motion to Dismiss

A "Motion to Dismiss," is a procedural request presented to the court by an attorney on behalf of the client. When one party files a motion with the court, they must also send to, or serve on the opposing party a Notice of Motion. This notice of motion informs the opposing party that the motion has been filed and indicates when the court will hear the motion. In addition, it gives the opposing party an opportunity to prepare for the hearing and argue before the court why the motion should not be granted.

The Motion to Dismiss requests that the court dismiss the case for reasons listed in the motion. The defendant's attorney could file a motion to dismiss if there is any belief that his/her client had not been properly served, or that the complaint had been filed in the wrong court, statute of limitations had expired, or the complaint did not state a claim for which relief could be granted.

If defendant's attorney decides to file a motion to dismiss, s/he may want to attach one or more supporting affidavits, which are sworn statements, indicating certain facts that may contradict the allegations made in the complaint. As the paralegal, your supervising attorney may want you to draft a memorandum of law (in some states, this is called a brief).

The memorandum of law is submitted along with the motion to dismiss and the accompanying affidavits. The memorandum presents the legal basis for the motion, citing any statutes and cases that support the claim. The supporting affidavit gives actual support to the motion to dismiss, while the memorandum of law provides the court with the legal grounds for the dismissal of the claim.

                    SAMPLE MOTION TO DISMISS

JULIE EDWARDS

Attorney at Law

2330 NORTH MAIN

Layton, Utah 84040

801-555-5555

IN THE SECOND JUDICIAL DISTRICT COURT, IN AND FOR

DAVIS COUNTY, STATE OF UTAH

JODI MC CALL		
	:	ANSWER AND MOTION TO DISMISS
Plaintiff,	:	Civil No. 0060304EV
vs.	:	Judge Thomas L. Ray
JOHN DOE and MARY DOE,	:	
Defendants.	:	

Comes now the Defendant and moves the Court to dismiss the Plaintiff's Complaint, and answers as follows:

1. Responding to each of the items complained of (allegations) – each is numbered so the answers follow the numbering).

WHEREFORE, Defendants Doe move the Court for:

1. Dismissal

2. Judgment in favor of the Defendant

3. For such other and further relief as the Court deems fit.

7. Amending the Pleadings

In the event the attorney did not have sufficient time to become familiar with the facts of the case, the complaint or answer may be amended to account for newly discovered facts or evidence. Amendments may also be advantageous when circumstances determine a different legal theory or defense.

8. Motion for Judgment Pleading

After the pleadings are closed, the court then decides the issue without proceeding to trial. The motion will be granted only if no facts are in dispute. In addition when it appears from the pleadings that the plaintiff has failed to state a cause of action for which relief may be granted. The only concern is how the law applies to a set of undisputed facts.

9. Motion for Summary Judgment

A motion requesting the court to enter a judgment without proceeding to trial is based on evidence outside the pleadings and will be granted only if no facts are in dispute. The issue of concern is how the law applies to a set of undisputed facts.

To support a motion for summary judgment, one party must submit evidence obtained at any point prior to trial (including during the discovery stage). A motion for summary judgment is particularly appropriate if plaintiff had previously signed a release waiving the right to sue defendant on the claim. In this situation, defendant's attorney would attach a copy of the release to the motion and file it with the court. Defendant's attorney would argue that the execution of the waiver barred plaintiff from pursuing the claim against defendant.

The burden would then shift to plaintiff's attorney, Edwards. She would have to argue that the release was invalid or otherwise not binding using such defenses as whether the release had been voluntarily signed by plaintiff. If she fails, then the judge could very well grant the motion for summary judgment in defendant's favor. If successful, and she convinces the judge that the release signed by plaintiff was procured by coercive or fraudulent practices, the judge would deny the motion for summary judgment and schedule the case to go to trial.

D. THE MIDDLE STAGES OF THE LAWSUIT

1. Discovery

Discovery is the process by which each side finds out much and the nature of the information the other side has. It is a formal investigation wherein each side gathers evidence to prepare its case. The days of "trial by ambush," in which neither side knew what the other was going to do until trial actually begins are pretty well gone forever.

Even before the trial begins, the parties can use a number of procedural devices to obtain information and gather evidence about the case. For example, the plaintiff's attorney wants to know how fast the defendant was driving his car the time of the accident, whether s/he had been drinking, the nature of the conditions where the accident took place, etc. Discovery simply means "to obtain information about the opposing party from any source, including witnesses." The reason for discovery is to get to the truth by making sure that both sides have all the information available regarding the accident (or whatever) and any resulting events.. Many times settlement of a claim is possible after the discovery process is complete. It forces everyone involved to accurately evaluate the strengths and weaknesses of a case.

The process of discovery is governed by local rules of court procedure (every jurisdiction may be different). Early on, the idea is to obtain evidence from witnesses who might not be available at the time of the trial or whose memories will fade as time passes. It can also pave the way for summary judgment if both parties agree on all of the facts, as well as on an out-of-court settlement.

Even if the case goes to trial, discovery prevents surprises by giving parties access to evidence that might otherwise be hidden, thereby allowing each to learn as much as possible in terms of what to expect at trial.

Discovery then includes access to witnesses, documents, records, and other types of evidence. Among the rules governing discovery are making sure that a witness or a related party is not unduly harassed, that privileged information (communications) may not be disclosed in court and also safeguarding that only matters relevant to the case are discoverable.

Traditional discovery procedures include depositions, interrogatories, requests for production of documents, requests for admissions, requests for medical records, and independent medical examinations, to name a few.

2. Depositions

Depositions are the testimony of various parties and witnesses taken before the trial. The plaintiff, defendant, observer, or expert witness (doctor, psychiatrist) is sworn to tell the truth, and is examined (questioned under oath) by the attorney(s) in the presence of a court reporter who records the testimony either with a voice recorder or a shorthand machine (computerized shorthand). The court reporter also administers the oath to the witness. Later, the court reporter will prepare the written transcript of the testimony. The judge, however, is not involved at this stage.

The rules of civil procedure allow any party to a lawsuit to take depositions (FRCP, Rule 30). Most often, a deposition is held in a conference room at the office of the attorney who will do the questioning. In addition, lawyers for the opposing party appear in order to assist the witness being interrogated by listening and making appropriate objections (FRCP, Rule 30(c)).

The deposition is useful because it helps the trial lawyers prepare by giving them an idea about what to expect from each *deponent* (one who is deposed) when they actually testify as a witness. Secondly, under appropriate circumstances, the transcript itself, the written record of what the witness said at the deposition, can and will be used as evidence at the trial. This is routinely done when a witness gives an answer at the trial that is different from the answer the witness gave in a deposition.

Trial lawyers often discredit (impeach) the opposing party's witnesses by trying to catch them in discrepancies of testimony. The lawyer will, on occasion, walk dramatically over to counsel's table, pick up a deposition transcript, gave it back to the witness, read the question and the witness's previous answer from it, and ask, "Isn't it a fact that you gave that response (a different answer) to the to the same question at your deposition?"

As you may well expect, witnesses do not always want to appear for depositions, just as they do not always want to appear and give testimony in a trial. In both circumstances, the court will issue a *subpoena.* A subpoena is an order of the court directing the witness to appear at a specified time and place and give testimony. The judge can punish a disobedient witness who fails to comply with that court order with fines, court costs or even jail (contempt of court). The subpoena is another routine order that a clerk of the court issues without having to consult or obtain the signature of a judge.

Here is a sample of what you might write or transcribe. The lines at the left are actual preprinted (or software-produced) so that in subsequent depositions or in trial testimony, they can be referred to by line number.

 SAMPLE TRANSCRIPT (EXCERPT)

67   Q: Where were you at the time of the accident?

68   A: I was on the southwest corner of the intersection.

69   Q: Are you referring to the intersection where Route 7 and State Road 40 cross?

70   A: Yes.

71   Q: How fast were you driving?

72   A: About 35 miles an hour

73   Q: Describe the events, which led to the accident?

74   A: Well, I was driving along, minding my own business, when, er, um, a, I reached over the turn the station on the radio because some dumb commercial was going on, and, uh, when I looked up – I mean I really didn't take my eyes off the road for a minute, you know, uh, ... etc. etc.

A really fun example of the interesting responses you might hear are reproduced next for your review. They are things people actually said in court, word for word, recorded and transcribed by court reporters who had the torment of staying calm and not laughing out loud while these exchanges were actually taking place. Brackets are around the ones not answered with some editorial license within them.

Q: What is your date of birth?

A: July fifteenth.

Q: What year?

A: Every year

Q: What gear were you in at the moment of the impact?

A: Gucci sweats and Reeboks.

Q: This myasthenia gravis, does it affect your memory at all?

A: Yes.

Q: And in what ways does it affect your memory?

A: I forget.

Q: You forget. Can you give us an example of something that you've forgotten?

Q: How old is your son, the one living with you?

A: Thirty-eight or thirty-five, I can't remember which.

Q: How long has he lived with you?

A: Forty-five years.

Q: What was the first thing your husband said to you when he woke up that morning?

A: He said, "Where am I, Cathy?"

Q: And why did that upset you?

A: My name is Susan.

Q: Do you know if your daughter has ever been involved in voodoo or the occult?

A: We both do.

Q: Voodoo?

A: We do.

Q: You do?

A: Yes, voodoo.

Q: Now doctor, isn't it true that when a person dies in his sleep, he doesn't know about it until the next morning?

A: [Whaaaatt?? Would you restate that one please?]

Q: The youngest son, the twenty-year old, how old is he?

A: [???]

Q: Were you present when your picture was taken?

A: [??????]

Q: So the date of conception (of the baby) was August 8th?

A: Yes

Q: And what were you doing at that time?

A: [wouldn't that one have been fun?]

Q: She had three children, right?

A: Yes.

Q: How many were boys?

A: None.

Q: Were there any girls?

A: [Duh]

Q: How was your first marriage terminated?

A: By death.

Q: And by whose death was it terminated?

A: [Duh]

Q: Can you describe the individual?

A: He was about medium height and had a beard.

Q: Was this a male, or a female?

A: [Duh]

Q: Is your appearance here this morning pursuant to a deposition notice, which I sent to your attorney?

A: No, this is how I always dress when I go to work.

Q: Doctor, how many autopsies have you performed on dead people?

A: All my autopsies are performed on dead people.

Q: All your responses must be oral, OK? What school did you go to?

A: Oral.

Q: Do you recall the time that you examined the body?

A: The autopsy started around 8:30 p.m.

Q: And Mr. Dennington was dead at the time?

A: No, he was sitting on the table wondering why I was doing an autopsy.

Q: Doctor, before you performed the autopsy, did you check for a pulse?

A: No

Q: Did you check for blood pressure?

A: No.

Q: Did you check for breathing?

A: No.

Q: So, then it is possible that the patient was alive when you began the autopsy?

A: No.

Q: How can you be so sure, doctor?

A: Because his brain was sitting on my desk in a jar.

Q: But could the patient have still been alive, never the less?

A: Yes, it is possible that he could have been alive and practicing law somewhere.

THOSE TAKE FIRST PRIZE!!

OK, now back to work. To get a person to appear for a deposition requires a formal process. The invitation to appear would look something like the following:

United States District Court

FOR THE EASTERN DISTRICT OF UTAH

Plaintiff

File No. 00-506

Judge _____

Vs.

Defendant

Attorney for the Plaintiff

Attorney for the Defendant

TO: Defendant's Attorney

NOTICE OF TAKING DEPOSITION

PLEASE TAKE NOTICE, that (Plaintiff's name) by and through his/her attorneys, will take the deposition of (Defendant's name) on _____Date at (time)_____ at the law offices of the (defendant), (address), pursuant to the Federal Rules of Civil Procedure, before a duly authorized and qualified notary and (court reporter) stenographer.

Dated: _____Law Office Name _____

Attorney's Name _____

DEPOSITION SAMPLES

This is the cover page for the actual deposition when transcribed.

 DEPOSITION (title page)

TITLE PAGE

STATE OF DELAWARE		*	SUPERIOR COURT
		*	Civil Action
	Plaintiff	*	Docket/Case No. CV-00-04
		*	
VS		*	
	Defendant	*	

DEPOSITION of _____, taken pursuant to notice dated
_____, 2014, at the law office of MASON & MASON, 2600 Litigant Drive, The
Suites, New Castle, Delaware 19720, on _____, 2014, commencing at 1:50 P.M.
before Geraldine Ford, a Notary Public in and for the County of New Castle.

State of   Delaware

APPEARANCES

For the Plaintiff: JANICE MASON, ESQ
                                               MASON & MASON ATTORNEYS-AT-LAW
                                               2600 Litigant Drive, The Suites
                                               New Castle DE 19720
For the Defendant: LORIE SAUERS, ESQ
                                               SAUERS & MADDOX
                                               555 Collins Boulevard, The Barristers
                                               Newark   DE 19702

INDEX PAGE
INDEX OF TESTIMONY

DEPONENT: Russell Curtis
Examination   by   Attorney Williams
Examination   by   Attorney Hendrix

INDEX OF EXHIBITS

Deposition

Exhibit No.	DESCRIPTION	MARKED
1	Invoice # 1645	10
2	Annual Report for 2014	98

3. Interrogatories

Another word for questioning or examining a witness is *interrogate*. That is the root word for interrogatory. Interrogatories are written questions that must be answered in writing by the parties to the lawsuit and then signed by the parties under oath. Normally, the legal transcriptionist drafts the interrogatories for the attorney's review and approval. It is customary to prepare interrogatories in the form of a court paper, with a caption, and leaving space after each question for the answer to be written or typed. The interrogatories are served on the party whose answers are desired, usually by mailing or delivering them to the opposing party's attorney. The process of preparing written interrogatories and submitting them to another party to be answered is called "propounding interrogatories;" the party who is asking the questions is the "propounding party," and the party who is required to answer them is the "responding party." The set of interrogatories would have the same heading as in the previous pleadings.

Can one take the deposition of the responding party instead? The answer is "yes," parties may be deposed and almost always are. However, each procedure has its own strengths and weaknesses. Depositions allow greater flexibility, but the nature of the process costs more, and typically witnesses are only deposed once. Sending interrogatories is less expensive and can be done as often as needed. Many courts place limits on the total number of interrogatories that may be propounded without court permission. According to FRCP, Rule 33(a), 25 is the limit in federal court.

The transcript of the deposition has numbers at the left hand margin of the document so that the testimony may be referred to quickly in the event it is subsequently used in court to nail specifics or address discrepancies. "Q" represents the question, and "A," the answer.

NOTE: An important difference between interrogatories and depositions is that any witness may be deposed, but only parties to the suit can be made to answer interrogatories. Interrogatories make an acceptable, documented record.

A sample of the first set of interrogatories (remember, there may be several involved) follows.

SAMPLE INTERROGATORIES

United States District Court

FOR THE EASTERN DISTRICT OF DELAWARE

Plaintiff   File No. 00-080

    Vs   Judge

Defendant

Attorney for the Plaintiff

PLAINTIFF'S FIRST INTERROGATORIES TO DEFENDANT

PLEASE TAKE NOTICE that the following Interrogatories are directed to you under the provisions of Rule 26(a)(5), and Rule 33 of the Federal Rules of Civil Procedure. You are requested to answer these Interrogatories and to furnish such information in answer to the Interrogatories as is available to you.

You are required to serve integrated Interrogatories and Answers to these Interrogatories under oath, within thirty (30) days after service of them upon you. The original answers are to be retained in your attorney's possession and copies of the answers are to be served upon Plaintiff's counsel.

The answers should be signed and sworn to by the person making answer to the Interrogatories.

When used in these Interrogatories the term "Defendant," or any synonym thereof, is intended to and shall embrace and include, in addition to said Defendant, all agents, servants and employees, representatives, attorneys, private investigators, or other who are in possession or who may have obtained information for or on behalf of the Defendant.

These Interrogatories shall be deemed continuing and supplemental answers shall be required immediately upon receipt thereof if Defendant, directly or indirectly, obtains further or different information from the time answers are served until the time of trial.

1. Were you the driver of an automobile involved, in an accident with plaintiff on the _____day of _____, 2014, at about _____o'clock _____A.M. at the Intersection of _____ and _____, in the city of _____in the county of NEW CASTLE, state of DELAWARE? If so, please state the following.

   (a) Whether your name is correctly spelled in the complaint in this cause of action.

   (b) Any other names by which you have been known, including the dates during which you have used those names.

   (c) Your Social Security number and place and date of birth.

   (d) Your address at the time of the accident,

   (e) The names, addresses, and phone numbers of your present and former spouses (if any) and all of your children, whether natural or adopted, who are residing with you at the time of the accident (if any)

2. Please list your places of residence for the last five years prior to your current residence, including complete addresses and telephone number.

3. Please tell us every minute detail of what transpired between the date you were born and the current time.

Dated: _____ Law Offices of Plaintiff

4. Request for Production of Documents

Various documents may be required to try the case. Procedures used to obtain documents are labeled "Request for Production of Documents." This is the process to obtain copies of various related documents (police reports, speeding tickets, driving records, insurance policies, correspondence related to the accident medical records, medical bills), which are once again served on the responding party. This request specifies the time and place to which the responding party must appear and produce documents (often can be done by mail). The responding party must also file a written response listing the items produced and attached.

Requests for production can only be used to obtain documents from other parties to the suit. What happens if you need documents from someone who is not a party? They can be obtained using a *subpoena duces tecum*, (sounds like dew-ses tea-come) which is a subpoena to appear, and order the witness to bring specific listed documents or items. Both Requests for Production and *Subpoenas Duces Tecum* can be used to obtain physical objects other than paper documents when necessary. The "Request for Entry upon Land for Inspection," is used to obtain entry to a location (for example, the location of the accident) under another party's control (personal property issue).

5. Request for Admissions

This element of the process is to get the respondent to admit or deny certain statements. As you can see, a typical lawsuit involves a great many items in the discovery process. For example, one of the elements of damages will be the cost of the plaintiff's medical bills. The plaintiff's attorney will have to prove that each one of the medical bills is genuine, and are directly related to treatment for the injuries related only to this accident and not some unrelated or historic medical problem. Must we really spend trial time going through clerical details, which are relatively acceptable by both parties in the discovery process? For instance, we can short-cut some of the relative tedium by using the facts that the opposing party does not seriously dispute and get her/him to admit to them in advance of trial. Thus, if the opponent has already admitted a fact, we no longer need to take up trial time proving it. <u>FRCP, Rule 36</u>, provides a procedure for such admissions of fact within the Request for Admissions. This request is a court paper, similar in appearance to a set of interrogatories, listing facts that we want to establish and at the same time, asks the opposing party to admit or deny them.

In effect the finished product looks something like this.

   REQUEST FOR ADMISSIONS

(It has all the same headings-captions as the other material related to the lawsuit.)

1. Admit or deny that you were driving on such and such date.
2. Admit or deny that your driver's license had expired.
3. Admit or deny that your car is a 1992 Pontiac.

The responding party must answer each question in a form in which it is stated, "admit, deny," only without detailed explanations.

1. Admit.
2. Admit.
3. Admit.

6. Discovery of Expert Opinion

Expert witnesses give opinions on specialized subjects that jurors might not be able to grasp on their own, or add credibility to the various party's facts. They are people who are experts in their field; e.g., a psychiatrist summarizing the mental condition of a patient. Although expert witnesses are expected to be impartial in their opinions, lawyers naturally try to find experts whose "impartial" opinions will help the most in their cases.

7. Independent Medical Examinations

Often, lawsuits involve physical injuries and the legal process helps assess the amount of money to be obtained relating to how severe and permanent the injuries are. Proving physical injuries requires testimony by professionals, doctors or other medical providers). FRCP, Rule 35, allows a party to file and serve a "Notice of Independent Medical Examination" (also termed as "IME") on the party whose medical condition is the issue in the suit. This notice is usually a single page court paper instructing the person to be examined and to appear at the specified doctor's office at the date and time stated.

8. Role of Paralegal in Discovery

Although preparing a discovery request may be quite routine, responding to one is a time-consuming task that is delegated only to someone with thorough training, and good judgment. Assembling and organizing the required documents and information often involves considerable client contact. Most paralegals find this aspect of discovery quite rewarding and challenging.

The paralegal may be asked to analyze the information received from the opposing party in response to discovery. In document-intensive litigation (securities and antitrust cases) it is not all unusual to be confronted with a room full of file boxes that must be inspected and evaluated page by page, indexed, and incorporated into a litigation support computer database. Having it all done by attorneys would be rather expensive. Clerks and secretaries often lack the training and legal judgment necessary to recognize the evidentiary materials.

E. THE TRIAL - LAST STAGE OF A LAWSUIT

1. Trial Date

At some point in the middle stages, a trial date will be assigned. The case will then be placed on the court calendar. The court calendar documents a list of dates on which cases are ready for trial. The date of trial may be several months away, or even a year or two, depending on what county (jurisdiction) your case was filed. Each jurisdiction is different when it comes to assigning trial dates (depending a lot on how busy the calendar [how many cases awaiting due process]). It could be as little as six months from the time your complaint is filed to actually begin trial of your case, up to as years in some large urban areas.

2. Trial Preparation Checklist

(A) TWO MONTHS BEFORE THE TRIAL

_____ —	Review the status of the case and inform the attorney of any depositions, interrogatories, or other discovery procedures that need to be undertaken prior to trial
_____ —	Interview witnesses and prepare witness statements
_____ —	Review deposition transcripts, summaries, and answers to interrogatories, witness statements, and other information obtained about the case. Inform the attorney of any further discovery procedures that should be undertaken prior to trial
_____ —	Begin preparing the trial notebook

(B) ONE MONTH BEFORE THE TRIAL

_____ —	Make a list of the witnesses who will testify at the trial for the trial notebook
_____ —	Prepare a subpoena for each witness, and arrange to have the subpoenas served
_____ —	Prepare any exhibits that will be used at trial, and reserve any special equipment (for example, VCR) that will be needed.
_____ —	Draft *voir dire* questions and perhaps prepare a jury profile
_____ —	Prepare motions and memoranda.
_____ —	Continue assembling the trial notebook

(C) ONE WEEK BEFORE THE TRIAL

_____ _	Check the calendar and call the court clerk to confirm the trial date.
_____ _	Complete the trial notebook
_____ _	Make sure that all subpoenas have been served
_____ _	Prepare the client and witnesses for trial
_____ _	Make the final arrangements (housing, transportation etc.) for the client or witnesses, as necessary
_____ _	Check with the attorney to verify how witnesses should be paid (lost wages, travel expenses, etc.)
_____ _	Make final arrangements to have all equipment, documents, and other items in the courtroom on the day of the trial.

(D) ONE DAY BEFORE THE TRIAL

_____ _	Meet with others on the trial team to coordinate last-minute efforts
_____ _	Have a final pretrial meeting with the client

3. Trial Notebook

In order to present the plaintiff's case effectively, the attorney will need all relevant documents in the courtroom. S/he will need to be able to locate them quickly. To accomplish both of these goals, the paralegal prepares a trial notebook. This notebook contains copies of the pleadings, interrogatories, deposition transcripts and summaries, pretrial motions, a list of exhibits and when they will be used, a witness list, and the order in which each witness will testify and relevant cases or statutes the attorney plans to cite.

On court TV, you see the attorneys packing big cardboard boxes of stuff; sometimes the trial notebook really is what's in all those big boxes they lug around.

4. Jury Selection

Before the trial gets under way, if a jury has been requested, a panel of jurors must be assembled. The clerk of the court usually notifies local residents by mail that they have been selected for jury duty. The process of selecting the names of these prospective jurors varies, depending on the court. Most often the jurors are selected at random by the court clerk from lists of registered voters or those within a state to whom driver's licenses have been issued.

Once the persons have been selected, they report to the courthouse on the date specified in the notice. At the courthouse, prospective jurors are gathered into a single pool of jurors, and the process of the final selection is initiated. Traditionally, juries are made up of twelve individuals, although many courts now use six jurors.

Both the plaintiff's attorney and the defendant's attorney have some say into the make-up of the jury. Each attorney will question prospective jurors in a proceeding known as *voir dire*. *Voir dire* is a proceeding in which attorneys for the plaintiff and the defendant ask prospective jurors questions to determine whether any of the members are biased or have any connection with a party to the action or with a witness. They are also asked whether they can be fair and impartial. The judge and the attorneys for each side have the right to question jurors and may ask that a juror be excused "for cause" if they feel they are biased and as such cannot fairly decide the case. In addition, each side has certain "peremptory challenges" which permit them to excuse a limited number of jurors without giving any reason. Information about this process may be obtained at website:

Jury Research Institute - https://www.juryresearchinstitute.com/

5. Opening Statements

After selection of the jury, each attorney has the opportunity to make an opening statement to the jury. This statement describes what the case is about, gives a preview of what evidence will be presented, and basically outlines the nature of the argument.

6. Presentation of Evidence

The presentation of evidence begins following the opening statements. Plaintiff's attorney will present evidence first, followed by the defense. Evidence consists of the testimony of witnesses and exhibits which have been described thus far in this chapter and which the court allows into evidence. Complex rules of evidence govern what is legally admissible, and the trial judge resolves disputes between the attorneys. If you watched the O.J. Simpson trial, you saw lots of "sidebars," which addressed these disputes.

Two types of evidence are presented. Testimony is oral evidence on any relevant matter given by a witness who is under oath. Physical evidence includes all other types of evidence such as medical records, x-rays, and photographs, which the trial judge allows the jury to consider.

Online examples of court procedures may be found at:

www.courttv.com/

7. Motion for a Directed Verdict

After the attorney has presented the case for plaintiff (the evidence), then counsel for defendant may decide to make a motion for a "directed verdict." With this motion, the attorney is saying to the court that the plaintiff's attorney has not offered enough evidence to support a claim against the defendant. If the judge agrees to grant the motion, then a judgment will be entered for the defendant. The case will be dismissed and the trial will be over.

 SAMPLE MOTION FOR JUDGMENT (directed verdict)

MOTION FOR JUDGMENT AS A MATTER OF LAW

The Defendant _____ at the close of the Plaintiff's case moves the court to withdraw the evidence from the consideration of the jury and to find the Defendant not liable.

As grounds for this motion, defendant _____ states that:

(1) No evidence has been offered or received during the trial of the above-mentioned cause of action to sustain the allegations of negligence contained in Plaintiff _____complaint.

(2) No evidence has been offered or received during the trial proving or tending to prove that Defendant _____ was guilty of any negligence.

(3) The proximate cause of Plaintiff _____ injuries was not due to any negligence on the part of Defendant

(4) By the uncontroverted evidence, Plaintiff _____was guilty of contributory negligence, which was the sole cause of the Plaintiff's injuries.

Date: _____ Attorney for the Defendant

8. Closing Arguments

In the closing arguments a summation is made which includes all of the major points that support the parties' cases. Shortcomings of the opposing party's case are pointed out for emphasis. Jurors often view a closing argument with some skepticism. Neither attorney wants to focus too much on the other side's position, but the elements of the opposing position do need to be addressed and their flaws highlighted. This is a final attempt to influence the jury's verdict by reviewing the evidence and by using the art of persuasion. In most states, the plaintiff argues first, then the defendant argues, and then the plaintiff only is allowed a rebuttal.

9. Jury Instructions

After the summations, the judge will instruct the jury following the attorney's closing arguments, setting forth the rules of law that the jury must apply in reaching its decision or verdict. The jury's role is to serve as the fact-finder though they may disregard the facts as noted in the charge. However, they are not free to ignore the statements of law. The charge contains a request for findings of fact. Charges are also called "jury instructions," and are drafted by the attorneys before the trial begins. An attorney's trial strategy will be linked to the charges. Most often the legal transcriptionist drafts the charge for the attorney's review. The judge however, has the final decision as to what charge will be submitted to the jury.

This jury might have been instructed to answer the following questions (charges):

Was the defendant negligent? Answer: (yes or no) _____

If your answer to question (1) is "yes," then you must answer this question: Was the defendant's negligence a proximate (direct) cause of the plaintiff's injuries? Answer: (yes or no) _____

Was the plaintiff negligent? Answer: (yes or no) _____

If your answer to question (3) is "yes," then you must answer this question: Was the plaintiff's negligence a proximate (direct) cause of the accident and injuries that were suffered? Answer: (yes or no) _____

If your answer to either question (1) or question (3) is "yes," then answer the following: Taking 100% as the total fault causing the accident and injuries, what percentage of the total fault causing the accident and injuries do you attribute to:

_____ the defendant

_____ the plaintiff

(If you find that a party has no fault in causing the accident, then attribute zero percentage of the fault to that party)

Regardless of how you answered the previous questions, answer this question: Disregarding any negligence or fault on the part of the plaintiff, what sum of money would reasonably compensate the plaintiff for claimed injury. Answer: $ _____

10. The Verdict

Following the above, the jury begins its deliberations. Once it has reached a decision, the jury issues a verdict in favor of one of the parties. If the verdict is in favor of the plaintiff, the jury will specify the amount of damages to be paid by the defendant. Subsequently, after the announcement of the verdict, the jurors are discharged immediately.

To find information pertaining to jury verdicts in assorted trials, go to this website www.morelaw.com

11. Appealing the Verdict

If attorney for the defendant's post-trial motions are unsuccessful of if they decide not to file them, an appeal can still be filed. The purpose of the appeal is to have the trial court's decision either reversed or modified by an appellate court. The appellate court will review the trial court's proceedings to decide whether the trial court made a mistake in applying the law to the facts of the case.

In point of fact, the decision of the appellate court may be appealed even further. A state appellate court's decision may be appealed to the state supreme court. A federal appellate court's decision may be appealed to the United States Supreme Court. At each level of the appeal process, it is up to the higher court to decide whether it will review the case. A sample follows.

SAMPLE MOTION FOR JUDGMENT OR...

United States District Court

FOR THE <u>EASTERN</u> DISTRICT OF <u>DELAWARE</u>

<u>Caption goes here</u>

<u>MOTION FOR JUDGMENT AS A MATTER OF</u>

<u>LAW OR, IN THE ALTERNATIVE,</u>

<u>MOTION FOR A NEW TRIAL</u>

The Defendant _____moves this court, pursuant to *Rule 50 (b) of the Federal Rules of Civil Procedure,* to set aside the verdict and judgment entered on _____, 2014, and to enter instead a judgment for the Defendant as a matter of law. In the alternative, and in the event the Defendant's motion for judgment as a matter of law is denied, the Defendant moves the Court to order a new trial.

The grounds for this motion are set forth in the attached *memorandum*

Date: _____

Attorney for defendant:_____

CHAPTER 4 - QUESTIONS

1. A person bringing a lawsuit is the _____

2. A person being sued is the _____

3. Most legal conflicts (lawsuits) result in:

    (a) litigation

    (b) appeals

    (c) settling out of court

    (d) large amounts of damages paid

4. The legal power to try or adjudicate a case is

    (a) appellate decision

    (b) litigation

    (c) trier of fact

    (d) jurisdiction

5. The *Code of Federal Regulations (CFR)* contains

    (a) Federal statues

    (b) administrative laws

    (c) federal cases

    (d) state statutes

6. Lexis and Westlaw are

    (a) manual research services

    (b) legal encyclopedias

    (c) computerized research services

    (d) judges

7. The cause of action is set forth in a

    (a) summons

    (b) proof of service

    (c) notice of garnishment

    (d) complaint

8. Failure by the defendant to answer a complaint within the allotted amount of time may result in

    (a) a new complaint must be issued

    (b) a subpoena must be issued

    (c) dismissal of the lawsuit

  (d) default judgment

9. A jury is selected by the plaintiff's attorney T / F

10. What role does the paralegal play in preparing witnesses, exhibits, and displays for trial?

   (a)_____

   (b) What does the trial notebook include, list at least 4 of the items

   _____

   _____

11. Explain the meaning and purpose of a pretrial conference

   _____

12. How are jurors selected? _____

13. What role does the attorney play in *selecting jury members*?

   _____

14.   Explain the meaning of *jury instructions or charge?*

   _____

15. What is discovery? _____

16. What is the final step of the attorneys in a trial

     (a) opening statement

     (b) cross-examination of witnesses

     (c) closing statement

     (d) appeal

17. The judge usually instructs the jury regarding

     (a) what facts to believe or not

     (b) which party has the best case

     (c) the law relative to the decision they will make

     (d) all of the above

18. What is an appeal? _____

19. What is the difference between trial courts and appellate courts?

   _____

20. What is the purpose of interrogatories?

   _____

21. What is a deposition? _____

22. As a paralegal, your supervising attorney has asked that you draft a Motion for Judgment as a Matter of Law or Motion for a New Trial. Write the introductory paragraph

_____

_____

_____

_____

23. Ethical decisions are most often made as a paralegal, and in these following cases; you must make ethical decisions based on the guidelines given you by your supervising attorney.

(a).You are attending a trial with your supervising attorney. All of a sudden you need to leave the courtroom to meet with a witness. On your way down the hall, you happen to run into the defendant in the case. The defendant asks, "You work for the plaintiff's attorney, don't you? I have a question for you regarding the contract that your attorney offered into evidence." As the paralegal, should you answer the defendant's question? Yes or No _____

(b).During a lunch break in the course of a trial, you are washing your hands in the ladies rest room. One of the members of the trial jury approaches you and say; "I don't understand what negligence is, can you explain it to me?" How should you answer this question?

_____

24. Witnesses who are requested to appear at a trial are often served with

_____

25. Which court hears the case first?

(a) _____

(b) And if you don't like the decision, where do you do about it?

_____

26. What are interrogatories? _____

26. What is a memorandum? _____

SPECIAL ASSIGNMENTS / no answers for these

INTERNET RESEARCH ON COURT TRIALS

1. Go online to http://www.courttv.com Choose a court case, at the same time look up that state's court rules and find out how many challenges for cause are allowed, during *voir dire.*

2. When assisting your supervising attorney in a litigation case, you may be asked to do some research on jury verdicts in similar cases. One site that offer this type of research is Morelaw at http://www.morelaw.com. Once you have accessed the site; spend some time browsing through what they have to offer. Choose a large state, such as Texas, and answer the following questions.

    A. How many cases/verdicts were listed for that state?

    B. Now, choose five cases and, for each case, describe briefly what it was about, who "won" the case (the plaintiff or the defendant), and if the plaintiff won, what amount of damages were awarded.

    C. After selecting the case of your choice, describe in further detail the entirety of the lawsuit? Who was the defendant? What general area of law was involved (torts, product liability, contracts, to name a few). How did the jury decide the issue? Did the jury award damages? If so, what amount? Were punitive damages also awarded?

3. The mother of a minor child filed a complaint for paternity and child support against the alleged father. The case eventually went to trial, and a jury was selected. Thirty-six potential jurors were assembled, twelve males, and twenty-four females. Three jurors were excused for cause, and ten of the remaining prospective jurors were males. The mother's attorney then used nine of her ten peremptory strikes to remove male jurors, and the attorney for the alleged father used all but one of his challenges to remove female jurors. As a result, the jury was all female. The jury found the alleged father to be the child's father and ordered him to pay child support. The father appealed, claiming that the plaintiff's use of peremptory challenges to exclude men from the jury was unconstitutional. What arguments might the alleged father's attorney make to support this claim? How might the mother's attorney respond?

[HINT: See *J.E.B. v. Alabama ex rel. .B., 511 U.S. 127, 114 S. Ct. 1419 L.Ed.2d 89 (1994).]*

GOVERNMENT WEBSITES OF INTEREST

House of Representatives   www.house.gov

The Senate   http://www.senate.gov

C-SPAN   http://www.c-span.org/

Code of Federal Regulations   https://www.govinfo.gov/help/cfr

Federal Law Information   http://www.alllaw.com/law/federal_law/

Georgetown University   http://www.ll.georgetown.edu/library

Materials on Federal Courts

Federal Statutes   https://www.washburnlaw.edu/ (click on Library, then click
          on Research, and Databases, then look for Governmental and scroll to the Federal
          Register – Code of Federal Regulations)

Washburn University

International Law   http://www.abanet.org/intlaw/home.html

ABA materials

United Nations   http://www.un.org

Department of State   http://www.state.gov

U.S. Trade Representative   http://www.ustr.gov

Emory University   http://library.law.emory.edu/

International law materials

Legislation   https://caselaw.findlaw.com/

Findlaw materials

Securities Regulations   http://www.sec.gov

State Statutes   https://www.washburnlaw.edu/ (click on Library, then click
          on Research, and Databases, then look for Governmental and scroll to State Session
          Laws or Subject Compilation of State Laws) Washburn University

CHAPTER 5

The Law Office

In this Chapter, we will discuss

A. Types of Law Offices

B. The Legal Team

C. Code of Ethics – Clients

D. Billing – Fees

E. Marketing

F. Policies and Procedures

G. File Systems, Libraries

A. OVERVIEW – TYPES OF LAW OFFICES

The law office usually has an attorney or a group of attorneys who practice the legal profession assisted by various support professional, receptionist, secretary, office manager, or paralegal. The office is a place of business.

Two broad areas of operation govern law office management. Practice management determines the type of work to be accepted and how to organize the workload in order to accomplish the tasks at hand. Administrative management is concerned with hiring and firing policies, finances of the business, and inventory control (making sure that all necessary supplies and materials are available).

Organizational structure of a law office affects law office management in determining the structure of the practice. There are at least seven types of law practices.

1. Sole Practitioner

First, let us look at the sole practitioner - an attorney practicing law on her/his own, with or without the aid of a support person(s).

2. Small Firm

A small firm law office is generally defined as a group of no more than 25 attorneys practicing law collectively for their mutual benefit. The advantage of practicing law in a small firm is that responsibility is shared among all of the attorneys in a particular office. The negative side of a small firm law office is that decisions must be made jointly, and therefore may take more time to implement than if left to the discretion of a single attorney. Generally, small law firms have a support staff of moderate size, usually supervised by an office manager. The office manager is responsible for all administrative decisions affecting the office, such as hiring and managing support staff, ordering supplies, and controlling the budget.

3. Large Firm

The large law firm may have as many as 75 attorneys or more. Large law firms are likely to have management committees that make the practice management decisions. The committee may be composed of several attorneys in the firm, plus a director, who is in charge of the office's administrative management. A financial director is in charge of all financial concerns. The personnel director is responsible for hiring and firing of staff. The financial director will have a staff of bookkeepers and junior accountants to help manage the firm's money, and the office may also have a director of marketing who is responsible for finding new business for the office. A paralegal coordinator if often employed who is in charge of all of the office's legal assistants.

4. Boutique Practice

A boutique practice is a law office of any size that specializes in only one area of law.

5. Corporate Attorneys

Corporate attorneys are considered "in-house" counsel. They work exclusively for a corporation. The corporate legal department has its own support staff of law clerks, legal assistants, and secretaries. The corporation makes all management decisions.

6. Government

Federal, state, and local governments all hire attorneys to represent the government's interests. Each agency has an in-house legal staff, headed by an attorney known as the general counsel. Government law offices employ all of the same support staff as a corporate law entity, but the attorneys are government employees. Management decisions are made by the government agency.

7. Legal Clinic

Legal clinics are categorized as nonprofit attorneys, such as the public defenders, (appointed by judges to defend those who can't afford representation), legal aid (agencies or volunteer groups who provide legal knowledge or representation for those who cannot afford an attorney), and public interest research groups. As you can see, the services of these types of attorneys are only available to a limited group of clients, specifically indigents or persons who cannot afford legal representation.

B. THE LEGAL TEAM

The legal team consists of partners, shareholders, staff attorneys, law clerks, law students, paralegals, administrative and support staff, and general clerks.

Because the law office is a service industry, its ability to perform and produce is naturally dependent on the ability of its personnel, as is the case with any other business.

A major ethical concern arising out of the work of the legal team is the unauthorized practice of law. Legal advice may only be given by licensed attorneys, and no one else in the office ethically offers a legal opinion, regardless of how conversant s/he may be with the particular area of law. Clients pay for legal opinions, which – if interpreted incorrectly – may become subject to litigation. Malpractice-type insurance is purchased by most lawyers to insure against suits relating to misinterpretation of the law as an opinion and other elements relating to typical problems of practicing law.

C. CODE OF ETHICS – CLIENT RELATIONSHIPS

The rules relating to confidentiality are set forth in an actual "Code of Ethics," plus there are unwritten rules, and principles an attorney and a paralegal must follow. As you now know, the attorney-client privilege is the right of a client to expect that all information divulged to an attorney in the strictest of confidence.

Because of the nature of the legal profession, interpersonal relationships between the law office, potential, and current clients, is important. A good reputation creates a good public image and certainly dominates the practice's ability to attract and retain clients.

D. BILLING

Billing and accounts receivable management is a fundamental financial requirement of every business, including law offices. If you are the paralegal in the office, your duties may or may not include that responsibility. Billing may appear to be pretty straightforward. In fact, there are several types of different billing arrangements that all law firms utilize. Once the appropriate fees have been agreed upon with the client, the office must allocate its expenses between those that may be directly billed to the client, and those items that represent overhead, which is the expense for general office operations. Keep in mind that the overhead is the expense that must be met before any profit can be made. Simple accounting provides the information to categorize that expense. Of course, the office must attempt a strict control over the budget, and a part of that process includes generation, and maintenance of timekeeping records.

Once the fee has been determined and established, the office must create procedures for sending bills to clients. In addition, a law office has certain ethical considerations that must be taken into account. Under the American Bar Association's Model Rule of Professional Conduct 5.4 (a), a lawyer may not share a legal fee. Sharing a legal fee is known as "fee splitting." This means that a lawyer may only bill for legal work actually performed personally or by her/his firm, and s/he may not pay or receive a fee simply for recommending a client to another attorney. An attorney is also prohibited from sharing a legal fee with a nonlawyer, such as an accountant or doctor, who may refer a client to the law office. Legal fees are paid exclusively for legal work actually performed.

1. Fees

A. Retainers

Retainers are the most traditional method of billing clients and represent fees paid prior to the commencement of legal representation of the client. Retainers fall under two classifications: Those that are unearned, and those that are earned. An unearned retainer is a sum of money that the client pays, which is placed into a trust account. As the attorney performs work for the client, the attorney bills the client, and withdraws the appropriate amount from the trust account. This type of unearned retainer is known as a "cash advance retainer," and represents money paid by the client against future billing. It is considered unearned because the attorney only has the right to the funds once the legal work is performed. With this type of billing the attorney is guaranteed that there will be funds available for the work performed, and for the expenses of the process (filing fees, travel, phone and fax, etc.).

An earned retainer is a prepayment, which is an advance payment, but is immediately available for use by the law office, and no trust account is established. There are three types of earned retainers

- PURE RETAINER

This is a sum of money paid by a client to ensure that the attorney will be available to the client throughout a pre-agreed period of time, and that the office will not accept any client whose interests may be conflictive or are adverse to those of the client who paid the retainer. It is a method of ensuring the availability of legal representation.

- CASE RETAINER

This payment is a nonrefundable fee that a client pays as an inducement to perform legal work for the client. It is a "bonus" paid to convince the provider to accept the client.

- CONTINGENCY FEE

A method of payment in which the attorney's fee is a percentage of the ultimate award granted to the client. If the client loses, the attorney receives no fee. The plaintiffs in most personal injury cases hire lawyers under a contingency fee arrangement.

Under Model Rule 1.5(a), all contingency fee agreements must be in writing. A contingency fee agreement does not cover actual expenses, such as court costs, transcription fees, and filing fees. The client is responsible for those costs. Generally, the attorney will advance these costs against the ultimate outcome, but if the client loses, s/he remains responsible for those expenses. Additionally, states place maximum percentages on the amount paid as the contingency fee. The written contingency agreement alerts the client to these guidelines. Rule 1.5(a) prohibits contingency fee arrangements in criminal or domestic relation matters.

———➡   SAMPLE

CONTINGENCY FEE AGREEMENT

The Undersigned, residing at _____, hereby retains _____, having offices at _____

who represents the Undersigned in a claim arising from _____ on the _____ day of _____, 2014 against _____. The Undersigned hereby gives _____the exclusive right to take all legal steps to enforce the said claim and hereby further agrees not to settle this action in any manner without _____'s written consent. In consideration of the legal services rendered and to be rendered, the Undersigned hereby agrees to pay and hereby authorizes _____to retain out of any moneys that may come into hand by reason of the above claim Thirty-three and one-third (33-1/3) percent of the sum recovered, whether recovered by suit, settlement or otherwise. Such percentage shall be computed on the amount recovered after deducting from said amount expenses and disbursements for expert testimony and investigative or other services properly chargeable to the enforcement of the claim on prosecution of the action. In computing the fee, the cost as taxed, including interest upon a judgment, shall be deemed part of the amount recovered. For the following or similar items there shall be no deduction in computing such percentages: liens, assignments or claims in favor of hospitals, or for medical care and treatment by doctors and nurses.

Signed: _____   Signed: _____
                Attorney   Client

• FLAT OR FIXED FEE

This particular fee is a set dollar amount that the client is charged for a specific legal service. Typically, items such as drafting a will, or a contract, or representation in a fairly small and straightforward problem, are billed on a flat rate. Generally, clients prefer flat fees because they know what their entire legal cost will be. Law offices have to be careful that when they establish a flat fee as whatever the charge quoted must cover the actual time involved in resolving the legal problem.

- HOURLY FEE

This is a billing method for all time actually spent, and accrued, or charged by the hour on the client's legal problem. The more time spent, the greater the fee. This is, in fact, the most common method currently used, and requires careful and detailed time record keeping. The client however, receives regular itemized bills for work performed, including expenses. Payments made by the client are simply credited to the total amount billed.

If an hourly fee is utilized, the attorney indicates a specific hourly rate for each attorney, law clerk, and paralegal in the office. Keep in mind, each person's contribution to the overall process may be different, so the total for each billing period will depend not only on the amount of work performed but on who performed the work.

A client hourly rate is a set hourly fee the client is billed regardless of who performs the work. Under this method a paralegal's time and a senior partner's time are billed at the same rate.

A blended hourly rate establishes an hourly rate for each category of professional. Regardless of the hourly rate of any one particular professional, the client is billed by class rather than by person. Here are some examples of blended hourly billing.

> - 300.00 per hour for all partners
> - 250.00 per hour for all associates
> - 100.00 per hour for all law clerks and paralegals

2. Timekeeping

Keeping track of the actual time spent by the members of the legal team for each client problem helps the office determine whether the hourly fee charged represents an appropriate return for the time spent, making sure that a flat fee, for instance, actually covers the costs of doing the work, or whether a contingency fee truly compensates the office for the work performed. Factors in timekeeping:

- Billable time spent directly benefiting a particular client

- Non-billable time is general office time - breaks, staff meetings, and so forth.

- Pro bono work

Pro bono or *pro bono publico*, translated from the Latin means "for the public good." This term, and the service it entails, is a fundamental part of the actual provision of volunteer legal services for the indigent (one that cannot afford legal services). Attorneys and paralegals may devote several hours per week to pro bono work. This is charitable, non-billable time the staff spends to provide legal services for indigents or for public causes. This work is still recorded on the timesheets with indications that it represents those charitable efforts.

Most state bar associations have adopted either voluntary or compulsory pro bono participation by their memberships. The rules of professional conduct that govern attorneys in most states include public-service obligations as one of the ethical requirements. These services are a necessary part of the legal professional's life.

Many private law firms, and corporate legal departments have implemented a specific pro bono policy or program. Generally, these policies or programs state the firm's commitment to pro bono work and encourage the firm's attorneys and paralegals to participate in these activities for the common good of the community, firm or organization.

3. Accounting

Preparing and maintaining accurate financial records for a law office is imperative. The paralegal plays an important role in the preparation of these documents. The legal assistant may be required to input all pertinent data to maintain the books of the firm in preparation of the general ledger (balance sheet, operating statement - the accounting documents, which show the gross picture of the practice, income, assets, depreciation, liabilities, net worth), and the profit and loss statements (income, expense and net).

The accountant is usually the sole recipient of cumulative entries or calculations necessary to create the ledger or balance sheet. The advent of software made both the bookkeeping process and the accounting much simpler. Quicken, Peachtree Accounting, MYOB (Mind Your Own Business), to name a few, are now used to improve the formerly manual processes. The operator simply keys in the checks, deposits, expenses, etc., onto the system on a periodic basis. The monthly, quarterly, and annual reports are produced from these entries. A billing system is either independent or integrated into the financial reporting process. It bills the client according to whatever the framework requires, hours, copies, filing fees, etc.

A clear understanding of how these documents are prepared, and how the software works, will assist paralegals in their role in the firm. Periodically, the paralegal may be called on to assist the attorney in reading and interpreting financial documents for a client as part of a legal problem. Keep in mind, a basic knowledge of accounting can be of great help in the legal field.

E. MARKETING

Selling one's goods or services is an inherent part of any business. Without some kind of advertising and marketing effort, most businesses could not survive. The same is true of professionals.

Historically, attorneys were prohibited from advertising their services. However, the courts eventually decided that attorneys could advertise. The American Bar Association (ABA) promulgated guidelines for attorneys to follow. They are:

Model Rule of Professional Conduct 7.1 states that an attorney may not make any false or misleading statements in any aspect of marketing. The rule is designed to protect the public from being lured to use the services of a particular office based on fraudulent, false, or misrepresentative statements.

Model Rule of Professional Conduct 7.2, the ABA affirmatively states that attorneys may advertise; however, several caveats are attached to the rule. First, all advertisements, meaning all printed material, plus anything that can be reduced to a tangible physical object such as tape, must be retained by the advertising attorney for a period of at least two years in case a problem arises with respect to the ethics or legality of what was presented in the advertisement. Secondly, the advertisement must indicate the name of at least one attorney who will be legally responsible for whatever statements appear in the copy, and, finally, an attorney may not compensate someone for recommending the attorney's services, since this might be considered fee splitting, which is strictly prohibited.

A basic concept of marketing is name recognition. Both the American Bar Association and state bar associations place certain prohibitions on an attorney's ability to market and advertise their services, so the marketing must be done in a conforming fashion.

The people or companies in need of legal assistance have to be aware of the specific services the office provides and the expertise of each member of the legal team. Telephone yellow page, newspaper and television ads are common. The Internet has paved the way to a larger marketing perspective. You have by now become familiar with http://www.findlaw.com which source allows for a new attorney to utilize its "net browsers." It only takes a couple of clicks of the mouse to get you where you want to go online. Many attorneys have their own websites, informing the public of their services.

In conjunction with the directories and the web, name recognition might include a listing in a directory of lawyers known as Martindale-Hubbel.

You may visit their website . http://www.martindale.com

This publication is used primarily by professionals and lawyers to find other lawyers in different cities with different specialties. Other websites for paralegals are also becoming more common.

Word of mouth advertising is common. If fully satisfied with the firm's or an individual's performance, existing clients or former clients will refer a law office to other potential clients. To assist in that helpful event, follow-up can be done with newsletters and brochures. These newsletters and brochures create contact with the clients and assure them that the firm is interested in keeping them informed and connected to the office.

F. POLICIES AND PROCEDURES

Many law offices, whether public or private, use at least minimal and sometimes more formal written policies and procedures related to employment. They describe what the employer expects, and what the worker may expect if s/he complies, and what to anticipate if s/he does not. They describe the procedures the employee is to follow, and may include a job description. They may be used to clarify ethical concerns that may arise with respect to the office administration, and set the boundaries for benefits, termination, stock options, bonuses, etc. The P&P essentially underpins the way the employment agreement is anticipated to work for both parties. It is effective as soon as the employment contract is signed. If it is updated periodically, and staff is given a copy of the changes in order that they can comply.

The American Bar Association has created a sample manual that may be used by a law office, titled Law Practice Staff Manual 2d ed. You may visit their website at abanet.org and review it.

For computerized offices, Greenleaf Software has created a form staff manual on a floppy disk, titled "Cadence Poly and Procedure Manual," which may be loaded onto an office computer, and tailored to fit a particular office.

G. DOCUMENT MAINTENANCE AND FILE SYSTEMS

Abanet provides legal offices with recommendations on a variety of subjects, one of which is office file systems. An organized, uniform filing system signals competence and can help a law firm avoid malpractice claims by lessening the chance that documents will be misplaced or lost, says Todd C. Scott, author of "The Basics of Client Files: File Organization". Search the web for "todd scott the basics of client files".

In recent years, digital technology has become more available and a significant part of everyday work, making it more affordable than ever as an option for retaining client files.

While the specific electronic tool to create a digital filing system may differ depending on a law firm's size and budget, there are options for every practice that can mean a significant reduction in space and use of paper.

Whether electronic or not, Scott provides several tips for effective filing systems. Among them, he suggests making one person within a law firm responsible for opening files with new client information and physically organizing the files. This promotes consistency as well as avoids the likelihood of duplicative entries.

Within each file, the use of standardized subfile categories can ease document identification. Such categories may include, but are not limited to, legal research, attorney notes, client documents and discovery pleadings. Each category can also be color-coded so they are more readily identified.

Organizing client files by last name or sequential numbering is common, but these systems reveal very little about clients or their matters. Scott recommends more elaborate categorization that reveals the length of time a client has been with a firm, the year a matter opened or the type of matter. For example, the designation of "AN/001/89/3" refers to a client named Anderson, whose case was the first one handled by the firm. Services were rendered in 1989 and Anderson's case involved personal injury (code #3).

In Scott's basics, he suggested that proper maintenance of client files is a critical administrative function within a law office. A client file containing work product, client history, and critical correspondence is a valuable item that must be effectively organized and maintained. Numerous malpractice claims have resulted from lost files or misplaced documents. These mistakes were, of course, largely preventable had an organized internal filing system existed. Malpractice prevention aside, organized files are cost effective and efficient, both for the firm and client.

Devising an effective records and file management system requires exploration of the following issues: initial physical file organization, centralized vs. decentralized filing, file documentation, periodic file inventories, file closing, and file retention and destruction.

There have been many changes in recent years regarding digital technology systems, and lawyers have more options than ever when choosing how to create and retain client files. Systems involving scanning paper and storing files electronically are now available at affordable rates. With the right tools and systems in place, a law firm of any size now has the option of saving client files digitally and reducing much of its paper.

Initial file organization sets the standard for effective file maintenance. Right or wrong, competence is associated with organization; and client perception is crucial to malpractice claim avoidance and client retention. If clients must routinely wait on the phone or in attorneys' offices while attorneys and secretaries frantically search through files for documents located either in file cabinets or on computers, competence is questioned.

Every law practice, regardless of size, should establish a uniform file organization system, applicable to both litigation and nonlitigation files. From a risk management perspective, standardized files reduce the chance of lost or misplaced documents. From an operations standpoint, standardized files are very efficient and reduce the amount of time spent searching through other firm members' files for documents, trying to figure out their method of organization.

Guidelines for Implementing Uniform File Organization

The following rules for establishing and maintaining compliance with uniform, initial file organization procedures presuppose that the law practice has at least one support staff person who may assume responsibility for opening and setting up files. Practitioners who handle administrative tasks themselves will have to modify these rules to fit their particular routines. See the appendix for a good example of a File Opening Checklist.

As a part of opening files and client intake, the file should be documented to reflect appropriate contact information on clients. Intake of a new client matter should include questions about the client's preferred mode of communication and whether or not telephone numbers, faxes, and email addresses are accessible by others, be it family members, or employees, or an employer at work. This will then allow the attorney and staff to determine the most appropriate methods of communication based on the nature of this information.

No file number should be assigned for billing purposes until the retainer agreement is signed and the conflicts check has been completed. This is the practice at most larger firms and is recommended in MLM's Law Practice Management's Avoiding Conflicts of Interest booklet.

File Organization Checklist

Centralization of File Opening and Organization Is Optimal

Preferably, one person within a law practice should be responsible for entering new client/matter information into the time/billing system, assigning a new client and/or matter number, and physically organizing the files. Practically speaking, this centralization prevents duplicate client/matter number assignments and promotes uniform file organization.

If file opening responsibilities must be decentralized among individual office units, then they obviously should be responsible for physically setting up and organizing the files.

Standardized Subfile Categories with Corresponding Color Codes

Every law practice should identify, through analysis of practice areas, standard subfile categories. The following is a standard list of categories, although certain areas of law require more specialized subfiles:

> correspondence,
>
> attorney notes and file memoranda,
>
> substantive pleadings,
>
> discovery pleadings,
>
> legal research,
>
> client documents,
>
> drafts,
>
> corporate documents and
>
> demonstrative/documentary evidence.

Color Code Subfiles

In order to readily identify a subfile within a voluminous file, each subfile category should be assigned a different color and the subfiles tabbed accordingly. For example, "correspondence" files will display a blue-framed tab which displays all necessary file information. "Attorney notes and memoranda" will display a red-framed tab.

Every Subfile Displays Case/Matter Name and Attorney Initials

In order to readily identify a subfile within a voluminous file, each subfile category should display case/matter name and attorney initials.

Client and Matter Designations

Every client represented and every matter handled by a law practice must have designation, whether alphabetical, numerical, or alphanumerical, so that time billed can be attributed to the appropriate client/matter and that files can be located quickly and easily.

Many law practices designate their clients and matter either alphabetically, by client last name and matter title, or numerically by sequential number. Although there is certainly nothing wrong with these designation methods, they reveal very little about the client or the matter. Law firms should consider adopting more elaborate designations that reveal the following:

Client's last name

Length of time client has been with the firm

Year matter opened

Type of matter

The legal team makes sure the documents are prepared for filing according to the system selected. The first task is to make sure that the document is physically ready for storage. Classifying a document means deciding what importance the document plays in the life of the law office. Storing the case file (document) is the physical placement of the document. Storage may be either by traditional methods (file cabinets) or electronic.

In a later module, you will be reviewing using computers in a law office and the instructions and processes will be provided in detail.

H. LAW LIBRARIES/REFERENCES

Even the smallest law office maintains some sort of library for legal reference. Most of the attorneys who do not have an expanded law library borrow books from various public-private sources.

Because of the cost both of books and space, many offices only maintain the codes and reporters of the state, or avail themselves of law libraries in the area that grant access to the public or members of the bar. Research materials in all law libraries must be properly maintained, updated, and cataloged for easy reference.

Computers are becoming more prevalent in all law offices and many of the law firms utilize services such as Lexis, and Westlaw. However, these services do charge the user on an hourly basis. Some websites charge membership fees to access research or law library information, and charge transaction fees for downloads, forms, and access time. It is possible now in most states to log into state or federal courts systems and review any case material whether historic and already decided, or currently in process.

You will learn more about law library and Internet legal research in subsequent modules.

QUESTIONS – CHAPTER 5

1. Describe four types of law practices _____

2. The Code of Ethics are written and unwritten rules - T / F

3. It is OK for attorneys to split fees with others T / F

4. The rule relating to the answer of #3 is _____

5. Retainers are fees that are paid in advance T / F

6. A contingency fee means the attorney gets a _____ of the total award

7. It is not important to have a signed fee agreement whatever its nature T / F

8. Could a flat fee be charged for a divorce procedure? Y / N

9. A blended fee includes hourly billing for which entities

_____

10. Pro bono means you discount your service to a lower rate   T / F

11. The ABA encourages attorneys to advertise T / F

12. A rule was established by the ABA just in case marketing gets out of hand. It is noted as

_____

13. If you work as a paralegal on your own, you are not bound by those rules

 T / F

14. If you work for a law office, you should review its written

_____

SPECIAL ASSIGNMENT

Remember the purpose for the special assignments is to research and learn according to the suggested information, which follows. No answers per se are provided.

1. Check your state statute to determine how your jurisdiction regulates attorney's fees. http://www.abanet.org

2. Go online and locate a recent case from your jurisdiction in which the court was presented with a law office billing problem

3. Analyze the next case

After the successful completion of a lawsuit, the law office you are working for presents a bill to a client. A contingency fee agreement with the client specified that the office would receive 30 percent of the award for services rendered, plus costs. The office however, includes in its costs the overhead attributable to the client's representation as well as the cost of your fee (the paralegal) while working on the case. The client refuses to agree to the total, claiming that overhead and paralegal salaries are not "costs," under a contingency fee agreement. Is the client correct? With what you have learned, you know the answer, right?

4. Go online using Martindale-Hubbell, or **www.getareferral.com** locate a law office in your area and note the different designations for the listings.

5. Find an advertisement in your local yellow pages for a law office and analyze its marketing effectiveness as though you were a shopper.

6. Go to online resources and see what kind of software is available for the various business and research applications of a law office.

CHAPTER 6

Interview & Investigation

In this Chapter, we will discuss

      A. Interviewing

      B. Litigation Review

      C. Preparation and Techniques

      D. Investigation

A. INTERVIEW

Interviewing is described for our purposes as "an exchange of information between an interviewer, a witness, a client or other related parties." It is the process utilized to gain the information necessary to proceed, or continue with the resolution process of a legal case. It is, of course, of inestimable importance.

> ### CASE SCENARIOS
>
> *In your office, two new clients, the first of whom is Benjamin Barth, M.D., who has been served by Mary Lamb, a 35-year-old mother of two, for performing a complete hysterectomy during the cesarean-section birth of her second child. She is angry because the surgery, she felt, was not required, and will preclude the chance of having any other children. Dr. Barth has been in practice for over 40 years and has never been sued before. Dr. Barth had a lengthy conversation with your supervising attorney and is quoted as saying; "I felt that I initially made a correct medical judgment," and that he actually did Ms. Lamb a favor by performing the hysterectomy. In his view no one should have more than two children. The procedure was actually of benefit because Ms. Lamb will not have to concern herself with birth control, or menstrual cycles.*
>
> *The second client is Linda Williams who called your firm this morning after the father (Clarence Williams) of her three children, failed to return them to her after a weekend visitation. Ms. Williams is panic-stricken. She does not know where the children are, and is concerned that the father has removed them from the country. As the paralegal, you have been asked to prepare questions and sit in on the initial interview.*

The initial interviews involve various legal principles and applications. Since the bottom line may be litigation, it is important to distinguish between the two in the context of interviewing, and investigation because litigation is an adversarial process resulting in a winner and a loser. Statutes and procedural rules control the process in terms of substance and time. Regardless of how a legal matter begins, it can result in litigation.

Litigation resolves cases through the court system, but individuals frequently resolve issues between them through administrative processes. The practice of administrative law involves procedural and evidentiary rules unlike civil or criminal rules of procedure and evidence.

In this case, Mary Lamb is suing Dr. Barth for medical malpractice. She believes the doctor was at fault for her injuries. Lamb wants to recover some amount of money to compensate her for, among other things, the loss she has suffered—that of not being able to bear another child, and forced early menopause. Although she has tried to settle this matter without going to court, Dr. Barth has refused to compensate her for any of her alleged losses, and in fact has just sent her a substantial bill. Ms. Lamb has the right to try to attempt to prove her allegations and receive some kind of compensation from him. As you know by now, the process of the lawsuit—from beginning to end - is called litigation.

1. Litigation Review

Ms. Lamb, the plaintiff, and has filed a complaint against Dr. Barth, M.D., the defendant. The defendant responds to the complaint by filing an answer in which he admits or denies the statements or allegations made in the complaint. The complaint and the answer are called pleadings.

In some jurisdictions, remember that the aggrieved party must file a demand letter, before beginning a lawsuit. This demand letter informs the defendant that a lawsuit is imminent, thereby providing the parties an opportunity to discuss settlement before a complaint is filed.

After the pleadings are filed, the parties file additional documents to learn the elements of the other side's case. This process, discovery, reveals facts and legal theories relied on by the parties; it also exposes strengths and weaknesses of each party's case. For example, the parties can file written interrogatories, to be answered under oath by the opposing side. At that point, other relevant documents may be requested, and other parties asked questions under oath or deposed.

The discovery process is controlled by a special set of rules written by courts or legislatures. Other rules control the entire litigation process including evidentiary matters. Evidence may include a single piece of information (a paper, contract, receipt, etc.) or a collection of documents, and testimony used at trial to try to prove a case. Evidence from a reliable source is relevant to the case, and is admitted by the judge at trial, proving or disproving a fact in issue.

In the Lamb case, evidence might include bills from the hospital indicating the cost of Ms. Lamb's stay, the cost for the delivery of the baby, and the subsequent removal of the uterus, interrogatory answers from Dr. Barth, deposition testimony from other doctors supporting, or criticizing Dr. Barth's care, or medical decision-making. All of the medical records from both the doctor's office, and the hospital, will become part of the evidence.

A. PROCEDURAL AND SUBSTANTIVE LAW

To review, two sets of laws apply:

PROCEDURAL LAW controls the process and rules relating to time elements, etc. If a party fails to file an answer to the complaint in the required time, usually 20 days, the court can enter a default judgment against that party denying them the opportunity to defend the case, is a good example of procedural law interpretation.

SUBSTANTIVE LAW controls the legal aspects of the case. In the medical malpractice case, if the evidence showed that Ms. Lamb contributed to her own injuries by failing to keep her prenatal appointments, the judge might find her comparatively negligent. That decision is a substantive legal decision because it helps determine the legal rights of the parties.

B. STATUTE OF LIMITATIONS (SOL)

The time period counted from the date of incident determines the amount of time a plaintiff has to bring a lawsuit; this element is procedural in application, but substantive in nature. If the statute requires that a medical malpractice complaint be filed within three years from the date of the injury, and Ms. Lamb waits ten years to sue, the case will then be dismissed by the court because it was not filed within the time the statute required. Even though the filing time is procedural, the substantive legal right the party once had is extinguished. Keep in mind each action depending upon the nature of the given action has its own SOL. SOL does not apply the same way to - for example - a car accident as it does to a contractual issue.

C. CASE FACTS

Case facts address the client's legal concerns in an adversarial context (litigation), as they tend to prove or disprove a theory of law. Proof of a legal theory allows a party to recover damages. In the non-adversarial context (transactional), case facts help form the basis of a transaction or arrangement. For example, in medical malpractice litigation based on the theory of negligence, if the fact that Dr. Barth left Ms. Lamb in the delivery room unattended while he went to the cafeteria to have a cup of coffee was true, it might help establish negligence. In the transactional context, the fact that Ms. Linda Williams is afraid her husband took her children to another geographic area implies the need for immediate attention.

Case facts differ but are critical to each case. They determine which legal theories or legal precedents are suitable and applicable, and which are not.

Whether in the litigation or transactional sense, case facts evolve during the process. As one moves from the interview to the investigation stage of a case, facts are supplemented, clarified, and verified. The factual setting is indeed, primed with information.

D. CLIENT FACTS

Client facts state the client's position or goals. For example, a client who has been convicted of perjury may not make a credible witness in a later case even though the conviction has nothing to do with the current case. The client facts affect his or her position, and may hinder, or render impossible, a realistic attainment of goals. Similarly, a client with limited resources may be unable to take advantage of expensive discovery mechanisms (private investigator for instance).

Citations are used to provide similar cases and make arguments based on them. They are found in The Bluebook: A Uniform System of Citation – you understand how we refer to, or "cite," court rules and other legal materials. Rule 26 of the Federal Rules of Civil Procedure, which regulates discovery, is cited as FED R. CIV. P. 26.

E. APPLICABLE RULES

RULE, 30 DEPOSITIONS UPON ORAL EXAMINATION

In our representation of Dr. Barth, we would seek to depose any physician Ms. Lamb intended to call as an expert witness.

RULE 33, INTERROGATORIES TO PARTIES

We will require in all probability the written questions and answers from Dr. Barth, his office staff, the hospital staff, etc.

RULE 34, PRODUCTION OF DOCUMENTS

We will certainly require documents to review Dr. Barth's and the hospital's medical records.

RULE 35, PHYSICAL AND MENTAL EXAMINATIONS OF PERSONS

In both cases, we need to discover what we can about Dr. Barth's personal feelings perhaps about limiting the size of families, or in Ms. Williams' case, we might seek to have the father examined by an independent psychologist or psychiatrist. In the case of a personal injury suit or disability claim, we would definitely need a full physical and perhaps mental examination performed on the claimant.

RULE 36, REQUESTS FOR ADMISSION

We also have to keep in mind the concept of confidentiality and client-attorney relationship, and how it affects this whole process of interviewing and investigation. The confidential relationship between the attorney (or paralegal), and the client does not extend to a third party. For example, the author's experience as a probation officer for juveniles was many times subpoenaed in child custody hearings pertaining to juvenile clients. The strict confidences disclosed between her clients and their families could jeopardize the clients' claim to privilege. Ethical rules also prevented her from discussing the case with anyone other than the client, the district attorney general, public defender, and the judicial officer in general. As a matter of public policy, the law will not shield information pertaining to attorney-client relationship if there is a broader claim to be addressed. Under this constrict, the communication between an attorney or paralegal and an incompetent or underage person (juvenile client under 18) is privileged.

Remember (as we have discussed before) under Rule 1.6 of the American Bar Association Model of Professional Conduct, any communication, whether oral or written, between the client and the attorney is confidential. In other words, once the attorney-client relationship is established the attorney cannot be made to disclose any information the client has told the lawyer in confidence. Thus, the opposition cannot discover that type of information. The law supports this confidentiality because it guarantees to a client that the information provided to the attorney by the client is in fact secret and privileged, so the client is encouraged to be forthright and truthful with the attorney.

F. EVIDENCE

Evidence is all the information offered by a party, and accepted by the court to prove or disprove some aspect of a case. Information that is discoverable under the Federal Rules of Civil Procedure or state rules will automatically be admitted into evidence at trial. Once discovered, information is judged by a different set of standards—federal or state rules of evidence determine whether the trier of fact (judge or jury) may consider it in making a decision.

The investigation process entails that the investigator be knowledgeable about obtaining evidence and aware of potential evidentiary problems. First, under Rule 401: Federal Rules of Evidence, relevant evidence is concerned with any tendency to make the existence of any fact that is of consequence to the determination of the action more probable or less probable than it would be without the evidence. In other words, evidence is offered to prove or disprove must be material to the claim or defense. In the Bluebook citation for this rule, FED. R. EVID 402, [a]ll relevant evidence is admissible. . . [and evidence] that is not relevant is not admissible."

Review the chart on the next page to fully understand evidence.

DIFFERENTIATION – EVIDENCE

DIRECT EVIDENCE	Does not require the judge and jury to _draw any inferences_ from other facts. Some examples of direct evidence include
Witness testimony that the accused _was observed_ to pull a silver revolver from his pocket and shoot the victim. Witness testifies that s/he _saw_ the plaintiff slip and fall in the icy parking lot.	
CIRCUMSTANTIAL OR INDIRECT EVIDENCE	Requires the judge or jury to _draw a reasonable inference_ from other facts that have been proven. Some examples of circumstantial evidence include (compare to the above statements on direct evidence)
Testimony that the witness <u>observed</u> the accused at the gun store purchasing a silver revolver Testimony that the witness <u>saw</u> the plaintiff leave the store and walk toward the parking lot	
HEARSAY	You have likely read books about or watched enough Court TV to have heard the expression, "evidence is hearsay." This means a statement was made, including oral, written, and demonstrative, out of court, and is offered in court to prove what the statement is saying. Therefore, hearsay is not admissible as reliable evidence because it is not believable. At an interview, you must always be thinking, "how do I prove this"? when the person being interviewed is talking about what "Bob said that Mary said that Harold said," - a mental red flag signals _"credibility problems."_
CHARACTER	Under FED, R. EVID 404, evidence of a person's character is not admissible in proving that the person conformed to that character at the time the cause of action took place. <u>Unless character is an element of the cause of action, evidence of a person's character is generally unimportant at trial</u>. For instance, a libel or slander case where the plaintiff's character has been defamed and "truth" is a defense, evidence of the plaintiff's character is essential to the case. On the other hand, in a criminal case (murder trial) the defendant may present evidence of the deceased victim's violent nature or character if the defendant pleads the murder was committed in self-defense.

IMPEACHMENT	Is the <u>discrediting</u> of a witness at trial. During an interview, you must be alert to the potential of the interviewee's possible impeachment at trial. The Federal Rules of Evidence provide six general justifications for impeachment 1. prior conviction of a crime (FED R. EVID 609); 2. bias (FED R. EVID 607; 3. interest (FED R EVID. 607; 4. prior inconsistent statement (FED R EVID 613; 5. reputation for truthfulness (FED R EVID. 608; and 6. contradiction (FED R EVID. 607). 7.

2. Preparing for the Interview

Interviewing a witness, as well as interviewing a client, plays a very important part of the larger investigation picture. First, good preparation, including an understanding of the law, and your subject, allows for an efficient, focused, productive interview, and will yield a wealth of knowledge about the client or witness you are interviewing. Take for example this case:

> ### SCENARIO - PERSONAL INJURY/AUTOMOBILE ACCIDENT
>
> *Jason Robinson and his daughter were walking down the street in the area of Governor's Square when a late-model luxury car jumped the curb and hit them. The driver of that car did not stop, but continued on its way. This "hit and run driver" injured both Mr. Robinson and his daughter. Apparently, a bystander, Mr. Bob Evans, witnessed it. Mr. Robinson sustained only minor injuries, while his daughter's injuries were more serious. She was hospitalized for more than six weeks, and will require physical therapy for at least six months. There is some question as to the speed of the oncoming car that hit the Robinson's, and whether the driver was drunk.*

Your firm is representing the Robinsons and you have been asked to sit in on the interview. How do you prepare for the interview? What witnesses might there be whom you should interview as well?

A. PURPOSE OF THE INTERVIEW

You are to gather as much information you can from the client or witnesses. Interviews are controlled by various regulations. Remember, a lawyer may delegate to a paralegal any task the lawyer would perform except those requiring a licensed attorney. The attorney remains responsible for the work product, including notes, or internal memoranda drafted in the process.

Preparation for litigation includes interviewing the client and witnesses for all facets of trial work, though also in this category are those conducted for transactions, including non-litigation matters, such as estate planning and contracts. For example, a contract, a will, a patent application, or articles of incorporation are all based on factual information obtained from the client. Procedures in transactions can be lengthy and complicated.

The interview is one of the most critical aspects of litigation. The client or witness may be deposed before trial, or called to testify at trial about case information. Trial preparation often generates further questions that necessitate follow-up interviews in addition to applying the facts to a substantive area of law. An adept interviewer knows what questions to ask because s/he understands the relationship between facts and law.

Although some interviewers have good instincts that can assist in productive interviews, the real skills are usually learned in the process itself. The interview can be time-consuming, and each case presents new personalities, new issues, and a multitude of fact-finding explorations with the outcome an exciting, rewarding, and useful challenge.

B. TECHNIQUES AND SKILLS

The interview process requires that you gain as much insight as you can relate to a client's concern(s). The client and/or witness want to talk about why they are seeking legal recourse. The first thing is to make them feel comfortable in the office environment and with you personally. "Now tell me what brought you here today? Or "how can I help you?" This will allow the client to feel relaxed as s/he tells his/her side of the story. Listen very carefully to what the client is saying, making sure you keep in mind what legal issues are involved. Interruptions of any form are inadvisable because you want as broad a picture as the client will portray. Interruptions break the train of thought (try not to take telephone calls or have much activity around you).

Ask questions which will focus, test, and expand on the initial information available.

C. ASKING THE QUESTIONS

Clients tend to draw their own conclusions. Typical statements are, "She was driving way too fast," or, "He stole my wallet." A skilled interviewer draws out the facts based on how the conclusions were formed, and uses them to support a legal theory or conclusion.

The way questions are asked is key. It will influence both the content and accuracy of the answer.

(1) NONLEADING QUESTIONS do not suggest an answer.

(2) OPEN, CLOSED, DIRECT, AND INDIRECT QUESTIONS

These are types of nonleading questions: "Explain as best you can what the weather was like the day of the accident?" The client will then be able to consider the weather, and what it was like that day. Was it clear, cloudy, dark, light, raining, snowing, sleeting, hailing, windy, to name a few. The question has forced the client to focus on weather without suggesting any particular weather condition.

(3) OPEN QUESTIONS

Open questions invite a broad response with little structure and allow the person more leeway in answering. Open questions give the interviewer insight into the client's ability to articulate, and describe the knowledge of the situation. For example, "Tell me what happened that day?" Or, "Could you describe the accident that day?"

(4) CLOSED QUESTIONS

Closed questions invite a more specific response focusing on a particular subject. On the other hand, closed questions may commit a witness to a particular detail. For example, "Are you positive it was raining hard at the time of the accident?" "Are you sure the car was bright red?" Closed questions can also be used to flesh out a person's response to open questions and focus on the recollection of a situation in demonstrative detail, "You have stated that it was raining hard the day of the accident?" ["yes."]

(5) LEADING QUESTIONS

Leading questions control the flow and content of answers. They can also suggest the answer in the question. "Wasn't it raining hard the day of the accident?" Or, "The car was bright red, wasn't it"?

(6) FOLLOW-UP QUESTIONS

People tend to make snap judgments. "He never was a good doctor-driver-accountant anyway." "She stole her mother's money while she was in the hospital." Because you need objective, accurate information, a statement that concludes, generalizes, judges, or contains hearsay must be followed by a series of probative questions. If, in any way, probing a client's or witness's conclusions elicits hostility or a confrontational response ("Do you think it's a crime to take money from your mother when she's in the hospital?"), an effective interviewer will patiently validate the person's concerns. It is important that the interviewer have all the facts before arriving at conclusions. It is also the interviewer-interrogator's responsibility to make sure that all the elements alleged can be proven. Be as analytical as you possibly can in probing for details. Ask yourself,

Remember the KISS SLOGAN, "Keep it simple, stupid" axiom. Avoid the use of legal language when interviewing. Generally, interviews should be conducted in relatively plain (layman's language), without talking down to a client or a witness. Legal terms sometimes have to be used, but they also have to be explained.

3. Listening

We have said it before and will say it again. "Listening is a critical part of the interview function." Active listening is a method used to encourage a client to become an active participant in the interview process. Empathize without judgment.

(1) PASSIVE LISTENING

Passive listening is similar to active listening wherein a client is encouraged to divulge information without judgment or manipulation. Some techniques in conjunction with passive listening include looking up from your notes from time to time to make eye contact, with the client, or a nod of the head, a smile, a soft "uh huh," or "please go on." Passive listening definitely invites a response.

(2) FOCUS ON THE SUBJECT – CONTROL THE TOPIC AND FLOW

Few clients or witnesses interrupt attorneys or paralegals, but you must be prepared! Control is exercised by keeping the interview orderly and time-effective. In conversational matters, it is typical to digress to other subjects – that's the way the brain works, skipping to another thought that the current one generated. Keep the focus on the topic by politely interrupting and returning to the topic.

(3) TELEPHONE EXCHANGES

Telephone interviews are unavoidable. Considerable time is devoted to clients, witnesses, and other informational sources using the telephone. The disadvantages are that you cannot see the body language, facial expressions, eyes, and hand gestures, all of which are supportive of veracity, and your conclusions. The advantages are that they are sometimes more efficient (time and money), and don't require travel.

If you use a speaker phone to free up your hands for note taking, try to do it in a quiet room where there won't be interruptions or a lot of background noise.

PRECAUTIONARY NOTE: Under no circumstances should a paralegal ever electronically monitor or record a telephone conversation without the explicit knowledge and consent of the supervising attorney. Also, advise the person to whom you are speaking that you are recording the conversation.

(D) TOOLS FOR INFORMATIONAL PURPOSES

With the advent of widespread computer applications, the Internet and other on-line services, a wealth of public information is now quickly available. The national computerized telephone books locate the person you are seeking in the fraction of the time it used to take to find a number, address, etc.

Be very aware of the acts passed by Congress to protect private information the Privacy Act of 1974, and the Freedom of Information Act, are among the most important laws controlling access to records. Disclosures, exchanges of certain kinds of information, medical records, personal information, etc., are governed by state or federal law and often require specific authorization, or signed consent. Working with underage people requires a signed consent for release of confidential information from the parent or guardian of the youth (under the age of 18). 42 C.F.R. §2.13

Medical records such as discharge summaries, psychiatric assessments and treatment records are frequently required for use in a recommendation to the family court judicial officer. Most legal offices have standard forms to accomplish this, which are filled in and signed by the person whose signature is required for official release. Occasionally, institutions or other sources of information require their own form, refusing to accept the standard. Generally, the needed authorizations are obtained from the client at the initial interview.

When the release form is sent, a cover letter explaining the purpose of the request should be sent along with notarized authorization, if your jurisdiction or the entity to whom you are writing, requires the document to be certified.

SAMPLE- RELEASE OF INFORMATION FORMS

RELEASE FORM SAMPLES TO MEET PRIVACY ACT GUIDELINES

A state-agency request (juvenile court) for confidential information looks something like this:

DEPARTMENT OF SERVICES FOR CHILDREN, YOUTH AND THEIR FAMILIES
Division of Child Mental Health

CONSENT FOR THE RELEASE OF CONFIDENTIAL ALCOHOL OR DRUG TREATMENT INFORMATION.

I, _____Client Name_____,
authorize: (Name of person or Organization) _____

to disclose to _____ and to receive
from_____

the following information: [nature of information requested]

_____

The purpose of the disclosure authorized herein is to: _____

I understand that my records are protected under the federal regulations governing confidentiality of Alcohol and Drug Abuse Patient Records 42 C.F.R. Part 2 and cannot be disclosed without my written consent, unless otherwise provided for in the regulations. I also understand that I may revoke this consent at any time except to the extent that action has been taken in reliance on it, and that in any event, this consent expires automatically as follows.

Specification of the date, event, or condition upon which this consent expires

_____

_____

Signature of Parent or Guardian   Print Name   Date

PROHIBITION ON REDISCLOSURE OF INFORMATION CONCERNING CLIENT IN ALCOHOL OR DRUG ABUSE TREATMENT
This notice accompanies a disclosure of information concerning a client in alcohol/drug abuse treatment made to you with consent of such a client. This information has been disclosed to you from records protected by Federal confidentiality rules 42 C.F.R. Part 2. The Federal rules prohibit you from making further disclosure of this information unless further disclosure is expressly permitted by the written consent of the person to whom it pertains or as otherwise permitted by 42 C.F.R. Part 2.

A general authorization for the release of medical or other information is NOT sufficient for this purpose. The Federal rules restrict any use of the information to criminally investigate or prosecute any alcohol or drug abuse patient.

As we told you before, many documents are requested and acquired to adjudicate a case. To keep track of them all and to make sure the requests you made resulted in receipt of information, you should keep a check-list.

INVESTIGATION CHECKLIST FOR DOCUMENTS

CLIENT		INVESTIGATOR		
DOCUMENT	FOR	AUTHORIZATIONS NEEDED	REQUEST DATE	RECEIVEDATE
Police Report	review	no	11/1/14	11/17/14
Physician's Report	review	yes	11/1/14	
Hospital records	review	yes	11/1/14	
Ambulance report	review	yes	11/1/14	
Witness 1 statement	review	No (?) will determine		
Witness 2 statement	review	No (?)		
Court records	review	no	11/1/14	
Corporate business records	review	No – public Yes - company	11/1/14	
Property - real	review	no	11/1/14	11/10/14
Property – personal (auto)	review	no	11/1/14	
Expert needed	med	yes	11/1/14	
Other:				

B. INVESTIGATING

1. Overview

The preliminary investigation is the process by which the paralegal gleans as much information as possible concerning the factual circumstances. Going back to the personal injury automobile incident of the Robinsons, a part of the investigation will include the police report of the accident, medical records, employment data and any eyewitness accounts. If and when the hit and run driver is caught, the paralegal will seek to discover the additional information available.

Case investigation is a real exploration, which is sometimes fun, generally interesting and even exciting, but is also demanding, nerve-wracking and frustrating at times. If you would like to review some summaries of famous criminal cases relating to the investigative process, check website of Court TV. www.courttv.com

Be prepared for the unexpected. For instance, while investigating a breach of contract action or wrongful eviction, you could very well uncover facts to justify a discrimination or tort claim. Investigating a claim for false arrest, you might bring to light the facts supporting a police brutality claim. Be sure to consider all the potential facts and do not be blinded by your own preconceived notions of only what you think the case involves.

2. Informal Investigation

Informal investigation involves factual inquiry and analysis performed outside the scope of formal discovery. The *scope* of the investigation is addressed through answering these types of questions

> How did the incident occur?
>
> How did the incident occur?
>
> When did the incident take place?
>
> Where did the incident happen?
>
> Why do you need this information?

The theory chart and investigation plan are based on the answers to those questions.

3. Investigation Plan

Planning gives insight and allows the paralegal to do a thorough and efficient investigation. For the most part, the plan includes steps necessary to develop and help the eventual outcome of the case. These steps include; interviewing clients and witnesses, gathering of documents, field investigation, and follow-up. A list of the necessary steps:

- preliminary interview

- research applicable law

- prepare theory chart

- organize interview questions for client

- more legal research / additional theory charts

- locate and interview witnesses

- visit site

- obtain documents

- refine legal research based on facts

- follow-up with client (personal/telephone)

- interview new witnesses, experts

- obtain other documents

4. Causation

Causation is the last and most difficult element to investigate. Why? It determines the direct and proximate cause of an incident. Keep after all the possibilities – "It's never over until it's over," a good axiom to follow. Perseverance pays dividends. A reminder, be sure to pay very close attention to what is said, and commit the exchange to writing as soon as possible. Record the conversations-interviews by taking notes, either manually or with a portable dictation machine (the little hand held ones are great).

5. Paralegal as a Witness

Because of the nature of the investigation process, under some circumstances you might become a witness in a case, and be called to testify at trial. Usually this will occur when you have interviewed a witness whose testimony at trial differs from the statement given to you. On the witness stand, the attorney will most likely ask you if you remember talking with the witness, and what exactly was stated. You then recall the situation, and may refer to your notes to support your testimony.

A note on sequestration...in some jurisdictions, there are rules that provide for sequestration (set apart or segregation) of trial witnesses. If an attorney intends to call a witness, that witness cannot be present to hear the testimony of other witnesses, though sometimes with the court's (judge's) permission, witnesses are allowed to remain in the courtroom during other witness testimony. The idea, of course, is to make sure that one witness is not influenced by the testimony of another.

6. Finding People and Other Entities

It is challenging and interesting work to locate people and companies. There are several ways to do this. Be persistent and creative. First, begin with the local telephone directory; it is sometimes all that is needed. Research the registry of vital statistics, cross-reference directories, state department of motor vehicles, tax rolls, and of course, increasingly used, is the Internet.

A chart on the next page for a variety of information sources is provided for your review.

INFORMATION SOURCES	
Court records	Every state and federal government has a court system with two major components, courts of general jurisdiction and courts of specific jurisdiction. In addition, each state has its own court structure and court names. Plaintiff and defendant tables are catalogued under the plaintiff's name and the defendant's name. Criminal records relating to arrest or conviction area available through the judicial information systems used by the state police or other law enforcement agencies. The date of birth and a Social Security number help assist in locating an individual.
Sealed records	Records such as those governing juveniles, adoption, and other miscellaneous records are found in family court jurisdiction. Divorce records are available from the court where a divorce is filed. These records provide a wealth of information, including the individual names, addresses, date and place of marriage, occupation, and often list assets, including bank and stock accounts, real property and any other property in which one or both of the parties hold an interest.
Registry of Deeds	The office where deeds are kept contains information on every piece of real estate in the county, including names of the grantor (seller) and grantee (buyer) under the Grantor/Grantee Index. These records are also found in the county recorder's office.
Registry of Vital Statistics	This bureau has information pertaining to where an individual was born, married, divorced, or dies. The information is available in various state offices (usually the bureau of vital statistics) and can often be electronically downloaded. Birth records are also available from the hospital where the individual was born. As a paralegal you can obtain a copy of the record "Certificate of Live Birth." The information listed on the certificate is usually that of the mother. Social Security numbers are not routinely given to children at birth. The mother usually has to apply to the Social Security office. Birth records of alien children adopted by U.S. citizens can be obtained from the Immigration and Naturalization Service (INS).
Death certificates	They provide the deceased's name, address, date and place of birth, Social Security number, marital status, race, education, occupation, parents' names, date, time, place, cause of death and physician who signed the death certificate.

Miscellaneous	Various and sundry other research sources are tax rolls, voter lists, census, religious records/cemetery records, military/Department of Defense Records, VFW and Veterans Organizations, United States Postal Services, and State Offices, to name a few. On the net are also found people locators – "find anybody ads" – are now quite common. Here are a few sites to check out:
Online Search engines	http://cornell.edu/ (Search for Law Library, and explore Resources and Databases) Google http://google.com Yahoo http://www.yahoo.com Findlaw http://www.findlaw.com Webcrawler http://www.webcrawler.com Excite http://www.excite.com Medical http://www.nlm.nih.gov National Library of Medicine

7. Interoffice Assignments/Communications

A. PARALEGAL-ATTORNEY RELATIONSHIP

Rules controlling the relationship between the legal assistant and the attorney are found in the ABA Model Guidelines for Legal Assistant Services website:

> http://www.paralegals.org and http://www.nala.org
> - the National Association of Legal Assistants.

The paralegal must strive to develop and maintain a good working relationship with the attorney with whom s/he works. Clarity is definitely needed in understanding the tasks assigned, with the general features of the assignments to be in writing. This allows both the paralegal and the attorney the capability to focus accurately on the task at hand.

The paralegal should check with the attorney on a regular basis to discuss and update assignments.

Make sure a copy is kept of all cases assignments, including name of attorney, date assigned, date due, date completed, time estimated, and time spent. This will help the paralegal learn to manage time and to document the nature of the work.

On a regular basis, the paralegal should request an evaluation by the supervising attorney

Elements of an assignment sheet or organizational chart materials might include an assignment log, a legal theory chart, or a contract action process, samples of which follow. Such logs make checking where you are at in the process an easier task – at a glance type records – which can be put on your computer using a word processing system, and tied to your client record.

SAMPLE - ASSIGNMENT LOG

DATE ASSIGNED		DATE DUE	
CLIENT		ATTORNEY	
ASSIGNMENT	HOURS ESTIMATED	HOURS SPENT	DATE COMPLETED
Government/City Immunity Application to law enforcement	50	75	11/1/2014

SAMPLE – LEGAL THEORY CHART

Legal theory, for our purposes, is described as legal principles that establish the rights and responsibilities of individuals. Breach of contract, negligence, assault, defamation, and trespass are examples of topics, which would fall under legal theory. The theory chart is a visual way of observing the elements of the law at issue and the facts of a case.

THEORY CHART		
Negligence action		
Client		
Date		
Incidence Date		
Statute of Limitations		
Elements	Source of Fact/Law	Evidence
Duty Breach of duty Cause Damages		

CASE SCENARIO

The Town of Georgetown, represented by town counsel, Mr. Walker, is coming to your office for an initial interview. Apparently, the town had a contract with a hot dog vendor, "Red Dog," to provide hot dogs for the town's festivities, which were held at the Georgetown Youth's T-ball Team, Main Street, Georgetown. This event was held on Labor Day and the vendor's driver failed to deliver the dogs on time. The town was in total uproar with no hot dogs to eat. Georgetown was to get a share of the profits, and wishes to pursue the company, which defaulted.

What does your client, Walker, have to prove to show a violation of the contract? First, locate relevant law in your version of state law under contract, and that entry will refer you to the law and cases addressing contract issues. Also look in the state digest to find the law, and then note what you found on the chart.

SAMPLE - CONTRACT ACTION

Client: Town of Georgetown

Date of Interview: 11/1/2014

Date of Incident :   Labor Day

Statute of Limitations:

Assumption: Contract with "Red Dog." is legally binding.

Contract Provision(s)	Req'd Company To	Violation	So What?	Any Defenses?
Delivery of goods	Deliver to client	Breach occurred Not as scheduled	Damages Lost revenue/mad public	

By examining the organization chart you can make sure that the relationship between the elements of the "breach of contract," and the "facts," support each element.

If you had not done research on the law and noted what facts your client needed to show a breach, your questioning of the client may have been less focused. Without the preparation you may have eventually determined the issues, but it would have been less efficient.

Now let's go back to our personal injury client, Jason Robinson. One of the theories of relief is negligence. Each element of the tort will generate numerous questions, all of which must be addressed in detail. As mentioned, the elements of the tort of negligence are

- duty to adhere to a standard of conduct

- failure to conform to the duty

- actual damages resulting from the failure to conform

- proximate (legal) cause

Therefore, you need to establish

- the obligation on the part of the driver not to hit a pedestrian

- driver hit the pedestrian(s)

- injuries occurred

    o the "hitting" and the injury(-ies) were definitely connected

- whether any defenses, such as contributory or comparative negligence, might apply

Similar charts may also be used for assault, battery, infliction of emotional distress, and any other applicable tort theories along with potential defenses.

Well, now you know all about the way a law office works, how to interview clients, the investigation process, building and preparing your case, and are prepared to go to trial (or settle), right (smile)?? Let's see what you can do with these questions and assignments.

QUESTIONS CHAPTER 6

1. Ms. Lamb is the _____ in the lawsuit contemplated

2. Dr. Barth is the _____

3. Sometimes if a person has a complaint, they have to first write a
_____

4. Is the discovery process controlled in any way Y / N - if yes, describe by whom
_____

5. What are the two sets of law _____

6. What is a statute of limitation _____

7. What are case facts _____

8. What are client facts _____

9. Categorize the following into "case facts," or "client facts"

    a. Your client, McMann informs you he wants to sue the trucking company that owned the truck that struck his 10-year-old daughter
_____

    b. Your client, Ms. Jasper would like to keep her attorney's fees as low as possible
_____

    c. Your client, Watts informs you that the person who rear-ended him has insurance
_____

    d. Your client, Porsche informs you that the car that hit him ran the light
_____

10. What is the book called which gives access to a uniform citation system
_____

11. Under the Federal Rules of Civil Procedure, which Rule governs Production of Documents_____

12. The attorney-client privilege allows the attorney to testify in a trial Y / N

13. The ABA has a rule about attorney/client relationships – it is
_____

14. Evidence only includes the information the client relates   T / F

15. All evidence available is admissible at the trial   T / F

16. Direct evidence does not draw inferences from other facts   T / F

17. When interviewing a client, your first priority is to
_____

18. Give an example from the chapter of a nonleading question
_____

19. Closed questions focus in on particular _____

20. KISS stands for what _____

21. Always record you telephone conversations   T / F

22. The Privacy Act of (a) _____ and the (b) _____are critical when accessing records

23. Medical records can be obtained by calling the doctor or hospital and requesting that copies be sent to your office   T / F

24. Causation is described as _____

25. SOL stands for what?: _____

26. Statutes of Limitation are the same in all cases regardless of their nature.

   T / F

SPECIAL ASSIGNMENT

MAKE A TABLE OF ALL THE DIFFERENT STATUTES OF LIMITATIONS AND AS YOU STUDY THEM IN THE NEXT SEVERAL MODULES, INSERT THE APPROPRIATE SOL FOR EACH TYPE OF CASE.

AND MORE SPECIAL ASSIGNMENTS

(no answers)

1. Determine whether your state trial court has *rules of civil procedure* involving "discovery," and whether they are similar to the Federal Rules of Civil Procedure.
http://www.law.cornell.edu/

Federal Rules of Evidence   www.law.cornell.edu/rules/fre

Federal Rules of Civil Procedure: www.law.cornell.edu/rules/frcp

2. Research the law of evidence in your state to answer the following questions

website: **www.findlaw.com** Click on "your state," Click on "law of evidence."

3. What form of government does your town/city/county have? Are there by-laws? Ordinances? Charters?

4. Dr. Casey performed abdominal surgery on your client, Mork Ork. - several weeks following the surgery, Ork was readmitted to the hospital complaining of severe abdominal pain. An examination showed that a small surgical clamp remained in Ork's abdominal cavity, which was removed by emergency surgery. Because of complications of the emergency surgery (wound infection), he was in the hospital for additional three weeks. Ork wants to sue Dr. Casey.

List the elements of negligence on one side of a piece of paper. Across from each element, write what fact could support the element.

Find your jurisdiction's definition of "negligence," on the Internet. **www.findlaw.com**
Click on state (choose your state), type in "negligence," and click on search.

5. Morten and Lisa Downey hired "Tim, the Toolman," who is a television handyman, plus in real life, he is a small-scale improvement contractor. Part of the contract was for Tim to enclose their side porch before their daughter's late summer wedding. Tim had done great work for one of their closest friend the year before. The Downey's gave Toolman a $5,000.00 down payment on a total contract price of $10,000.00. There was nothing in writing verifying the contract amount. The porch however, was to be completed in six weeks in time for the wedding. When Toolman did not start the first week as promised, the Downey's tried to contact him but were unsuccessful. Sometime later, Morten Downey ran into Tim by accident. When he confronted Toolman about the work, Toolman informed Mr. Downey, he was just too busy for the job. Tim immediately shouted to Downey to "get lost; go get a lawyer," and "see you in court."

In the meantime, Mr. Downey hired another contractor to complete the job that Toolman never finished. The Downey's were recommended to your firm by a neighbor. All that the Downey's request want is that Toolman return their $5,000.00.

How should you structure the interview of the Downey's?

What legal issues are involved?

What personal issues do the Downey's have?

6. Raymond Stone, a steelworker operating a crane for a construction company in North Jersey was injured in a fall from the Delaware Memorial Bridge. Apparently his safety harness broke and he fell 40 feet into the Delaware River. Two of his fellow workers jumped in after him and pulled him to safety. Stone was taken to Christiana Care (a Delaware hospital) where he was treated for a broken collarbone and a compound fracture of his left leg. State safety inspectors have been alerted in the investigation

Draw up an investigation plan (graphic) with the following categories (BLANK PAGE FOLLOWS THIS PAGE TO USE AS A WORK SHEET)

INVESTIGATION PLAN

Client: Raymond Stone,   Occupation: steelworker, crane operator

Interview client

Issues:

> Negligence
> Liability
> Infliction of emotional distress
> Construction supervisor.
> Develop a theory chart.
> List of witnesses
> Questioning area of concern for each witness
> Interview witnesses
> Construction co-workers
> State regulations pertaining to bridge construction.
> Registration and permit information
> Ambulance reports
> Hospital reports
> Possible experts
> Medical doctors
> OSHA safety authorities
> Construction management
> Actuarial

7. Go to your local DMV and ask to see any information that has been compiled on you (make sure you don't have any outstanding tickets – or any warrants - smile)

8. Make a chart of your state court system, listing every court, it location, and the kinds of cases it handles.

9. Do the same for the federal courts in your state.

10. Choose a piece of real property in your area (if you own a home, use the property description on your deed), go to the registry of deeds, or county recorder's office and determine who the last three owners were.

11. Find out what agency has a local voter's list. Ask if it can be inspected.

12. Call or make a trip to your local US Post Office. If a return address is a box number, what information can the postal service supply? What information will they not divulge?

13. Use an on-line yellow page or white page service to see who and what you can find.

NOW WASN'T THAT FUN?

CHAPTER 7

Legal Writing

In this Chapter, we will discuss

ENGLISH GRAMMAR 101

Grammatical errors in legal information are common. A brief overview of English will be undertaken to point out correct usage as a first step. We will review spelling, usage and grammar generally. Then you will do self-evaluation exercises to test your understanding of the concepts covered.

You might not believe that you need help with English, but it's a virtual guarantee that you do. In our experience, we have come across no one, not one person, who had a good command of the language even though they thought they did. If you decide to skip this chapter, instead go to the exercises and give them a try. Then you will be able to determine what your command of English is.

Note the heading uses a parenthetical phrase saying "AMERICAN, THAT IS." This is because American English and the purer English used by Britain, and every colony she has lost, differs in many respects, mostly spelling. Only a small example is necessary because we'll be dealing only with American English.

American: harbor / British: harbour
American: color / British: colour

It is not our intention to provide a complete and exhaustive review of English with all of its strange and inexplicable rules. Instead, we will discuss English as it applies to the most common errors in dictation. Working in the legal field, you are expected to use, and if presented incorrectly, to fix such errors. In addition, the appropriate usage of English is an integral part of the paralegal's job on the completed reports.

A. Nouns

The world is full of people, places and things. A noun is a word that names a person, place or thing. A singular noun is a noun that names one person, place or thing. A plural noun is a noun that names more than one person, place or thing. To make most singular nouns plural, an *s* is added. "Books and magazines" are examples of plural nouns. If a singular noun ends with *s, ss, x, ch, sh* an *es* is added to write the plural:

gas=gases, boss=bosses, box=boxes, branch=branches, wish=wishes

If a singular noun ends with a consonant and a *y* (remember consonants are all the letters remaining after vowels, *a, e, i, o and u*, are eliminated) change the *y* to *i* and add *es* to form the plural:

library=libraries, story=stories

Some nouns become plural in a more confusing way:

child=children, man=men, woman=women, ox=oxen,
foot=feet, tooth=teeth, goose=geese, mouse=mice

A few nouns remain the same whether they are singular or plural:

sheep=sheep, deer=deer, fish=fish, moose=moose

Common and proper nouns name any person, place or thing; for example, "girl, state, country." A proper noun is a noun that names a special person, place, or thing, and is almost always capitalized:

Jenny Shung (the name of a person)

The United States of America
Uintah Basin Medical Center
ABC Clinic
Personal Edge Legal Transcription Training Course

B. Possessive Nouns

A noun that shows ownership is a possessive noun and can be either singular or plural, having more than one owner. An apostrophe (') and an *s* is added to show the ownership. If the word already ends in an *s*, the *s* after the apostrophe is optional. It can be added if it doesn't make pronouncing the word more difficult.

student's books - or more than one student - students' books
assistant's techniques or assistants' techniques

However, when using the word "it" with possessives, the rules change. *It's* actually is the shortened version of "it is." So, the possessive form for "it is" is "its," with no apostrophe:

It's a beautiful day
It's not its main problem

C. Abbreviations

Abbreviations are intentionally "shortened words." "Mr." is an abbreviation for Mister and "Dr." for Doctor. Never write out the long word for these titles. Always use a period since that mark tells the reader that it is an abbreviation. Addresses with roads, street names and avenues may be abbreviated, however, remember to capitalize them.

D. Verbs

Verbs are used to describe an action. The *tense* of a verb may describe a past, present or future action.

> **Present**: (See Verb and Subject Agreement in the next section to learn how and when to add *s* or *es*).
>
> A scientist develops new ideas.
>
> **Past**: Scientists *developed* new ideas.

Add *ed* to most verbs to form the past tense. If a verb ends in *e*, drop the *e* and add *ed*:

> Leonardo da Vinci *painted* many famous portraits and frescoes. He *lived* in Italy.

Sometimes the last letter of a verb is doubled before you add the *ed*. The rule is this that if a one syllable verb ends with a consonant, double the last consonant:

> Leonardo *planned* many buildings (plan=planned).
> He *stepped* back to look at the plans (step=stepped).

Remember too that some verbs change the last letter when *ed* is added:

> Leonardo *studied* art and science (study=studied).
> The paint *dried* quickly (dry=dried).

Future= The words will, may, and shall precede the verb to show that the tense denotes future action.

> Future: Scientists *shall* develop new ideas.

E. Verb and Subject Agreement

The rules with how and what letters you add to the verb are: 1) add an *s* to verbs in the present tense when the simple subject is singular (one person, one thing); 2) if the verb already ends in *s*, *x*, *z*, *zz*, *ch*, or *sh* - add *es*.

Verbs work with the main subject (what the sentence is about), so the subject and verb must agree. In the following example, when the subject is singular the verb assumes an *s*, and when the subject is plural the verb has no *s*.

Verb ends with an s	Verb doesn't end with *s*
The boy walks home.	The children practice.
A woman rushes by.	The violinists play loudly.

It's worth briefly covering here how possessives and plurals work with the above letters and letter combinations. For this we'll just give examples:

All of these quizzes are driving me crazy!
This quiz's summary is outdated!
All of these quizzes' summaries are outdated!

Note the possessive of quiz/quizzes. The one with the apostrophe outside the *s* is plural usage. Something similar goes for other words, and in the following case for proper noun:

Those Davises are bizarre people.
The Davis' home went up in smoke.
The Davis's home went up in smoke.

Note two versions of the same possessive regarding the home being torched - both are correct (See "Possessive Nouns").

If a verb ends in a consonant and a *y*, change the *y* to *i* and add *es*:

Study=studies, fry=fries, marry=marries

Compound subjects must match compound verbs:

The <u>patient and her husband</u> were observed chatting in the hospital room.

You cannot use *was* since the subject involves more than one person (or thing). However, there is a tricky sort of sentence that requires your attention at this juncture. From time to time the actual subject of a sentence can be confusing. Examples:

The photography of Fred, Wilma and that *Dino* dog were quite grainy.
The photography of that crazy couple and that dog were quite grainy.

You guessed it (or perhaps not!), in both cases the verb *were*, is incorrect. In both cases the subject is *photography*, which is singular.

The photographs of Fred, Wilma and that *Dino* dog were quite grainy.
The photographs of that crazy couple and that dog were quite grainy.

In both cases, of course, the word photographs is plural and is the subject.

A good way to learn to make the determination is to drop some words from the sentence to find out if the subject agrees with the verb.

Tomography of the lungs and kidneys _____ normal.

What words do you drop out? First determine what the subject is. In this case it's tomography. Then drop off the lungs and kidneys and what you have is: Tomography _____ normal. You undoubtedly now know which verb belongs in the blank. Right? Tomography is the singular noun, but the choice of verb-was or is--will depend on the tense-past or present. Yet the plot thickens.

Though this is covered in greater detail later, we'll touch on it here. In legal terminology we're often dealing with Latin, which has some rigid and ancient rules regarding plurals:

The addenda to that document was completely irrelevant!
The addendum to that document were completely irrelevant!

As you've probably determined, they're both wrong! If you transpose the verbs, putting *were* with *addenda* and *was* with *addendum*, you'd have it. The word *addenda* is the plural of addendum.

F. Contractions

English uses contractions as shortcuts to get from place to place in less time. A contraction is a word made up of two words. The words are joined together by leaving out one or more letters and adding an apostrophe (') which shows the reader that one or more letters are missing.

I am=I'm, you are=you're (never your as a short cut for you are),
he is=he's, she is=she's, it is=it's, we are=we're, they are=they're

G. Homonyms or Confusing Words

Some words in English sound just like other words. These words are called "homonyms." Homonyms sound alike but have entirely different spellings and meanings. Examples are:

their, there

The players got their first goal. Put the ball there.

two, too, to

Two players ran to the ball. The coach ran too.

its, it's

It's a close game. Brazil sent its best team.

whether, weather

I wonder whether it will rain. The weather is fine.

you're, your

You're coming to the game. Here is your ticket.

who's, whose

Who's coming with us? Whose tickets are these?

knew, new

We knew you were coming. Is your jacket new?

whole, hole

My ticket has a hole in it. Your ticket is whole.

peace, piece

We all want world peace. I want a piece of pie.

peace, piece.

We all want world peace. I want a piece of pie.

You will find more homonyms in the next chapter related directly to legal words.

H. Punctuation

A sentence must always start with a capital letter. Use a period at the end of a sentence (or a question mark [?] if the sentence is a question, or an exclamation point [!] if special emphasis is needed).

COMMAS

Commas also have certain rules. Use a comma to set off the name of a person who is spoken to directly in a sentence:

Ginny, have you ever visited the San Diego Zoo?

Use a comma to set off introductory words such as *yes, no,* and *well* when they <u>begin</u> a sentence.

Yes, I visited the San Diego Zoo last year.

Use a comma to separate the name of a city and state:

I live in Salt Lake City, Utah.

Use a comma to separate the date from the year:

Today is June 8, 2014.

It is my daughter, Jodi's, birthday.

Use a comma to set off parenthetical phrases:

When I'm like this, although I try not to be as often as possible,
I get terrible cramps in my ears!

The parenthetical phrase, of course, is "...although I try not to be as often as possible...."

Note the use of the periods, which are known as an "ellipsis" (or the plural as "ellipses"), and also note that there are four periods at the end. They're used with the omission of one or more words from a quoted passage, and the fourth period at the end serves to end the sentence. An explanation for more detailed use of ellipses, may be found in any good dictionary.

Use a comma to separate a series of three or more words in a sentence. The comma after the last item, and before and, or, or is preferred, but may be omitted if there is no possibility of misreading.

We saw giraffes, zebras, bears, and lions in outdoor cages.

Use a comma before the word "and" in a compound sentence.

We watched the animals, and mom took pictures.

Use a comma after a greeting and/or closing of a letter unless it is a business letter in which case, after the greeting, "Dear so and so," you use a colon [:].

Dear Dr. Smith:

Thank you for your kind referral of Mr. Flintstone. He presented today with...

Sincerely,

Dear Grandma,

We will be home soon.

Love,

Here are a few other examples of proper usage that are often misunderstood:

"Well, I'm never wrong but, if you think about it, neither is anybody else."

Alternatively, depending on where the stress lies:

"Well, I'm never wrong, but if you think about it neither is anybody else."

If you really get confused about commas (except for the above guidelines), one further rule usually works – if in doubt, leave it out.

APOSTROPHES

Let's look at apostrophes. We'll review how they're used in possessives and contractions.

Yes, I'm telling you, Jodi's here! No. I'm going to tell
you only one more time, she's not here!

Note the exact same usage as with possessives, but this time the apostrophe - *'s* - is used in place of *is*. You recall the example with "it's," in its "it is" context? Some immortal power, however, decided that we could no longer use it's as a possessive form, even though we can do so with virtually every other word.

Your not supposed to be here. (Wrong.)
You're not supposed to be here! (Right.)

Another example: Three different usages of the same-sounding word, the last being a possessive.

"They're not supposed to be there!" their captain shouted.

Another often used apostrophe is:

It was in the 60's that he wrote that immortal line! (Wrong.)
It was in the '60s that he wrote that immortal line! (Right.)

The apostrophe takes the place of *19*, and because this is not a possessive, you don't use *'s*. However, it's appropriate to use an apostrophe to form plurals if used following single digits or letters:

Always use *e's* before *i's* in spelling when following *c's*.

QUOTATION MARKS

Always enclose quoted material in quotation marks:

Well, Betty, she said, "You take that grumpy, saber-toothed-tiger-skin-wearing
husband of yours and tell him he's lucky to be living in Bedrock!"

Sometimes quotation marks, first double, then single, have to set the dialogue of two different speakers apart:

> The witness was clearly distraught when she proclaimed, "That beefy faced heathen had the nerve to say, 'Dear, I'm only going to the bank.'" She paused for a moment, wiping away her tears, then with a trembling voice, whispered, "Then he said, 'Ta-ta, my Sweet,' and then vanished from the face of the earth with all our savings!" she finished with a burst.

Note how the ending exclamation mark, in this usage, doesn't denote the end of a sentence, as it is most often used.

As a general rule, enclose titles of poems, short stories, articles, lectures, chapters of books, short musical compositions, and radio and TV programs in quotation marks:

> I'm referring to Dean Willoughby's seminal article on bipolar botany, entitled, "The Dream Life of Moss."

> Did you see the TV show, "Gasping for Wind"?

Slang, special usage, newly coined terms, or words or phrases borrowed from somebody else are always enclosed in quotation marks:

Slang:

> Oh, the crazy little criminal was "popped" for using "crank," and now he has to face "the man in the black robe" with that crazy "wooden hamma'."

Special usage:

> "But what if he 'comes in from the cold'?" asked the rather dim-witted spy in terms he thought were esoteric.

Newly coined terms (well, a few years old, coined by VP Al Gore):

> I envision an "Information Superhighway" connecting every corner of the globe by the year two-thousand.

This could also be written:

> "I envision an 'Information Superhighway' connecting every corner of the globe by the year two-thousand."

Borrowed:

> No, she wrote that "Bugseye" was a "very strange character."

Let's go on to the use of question/exclamation and quotation marks, and see how they work together.

When Fred said that, did he say "The gravy is too cold"?

Note the quote is inside the question mark. This is because the quoted statement is not the question. Also, you don't always have to use a comma at the end of a clause or phrase before going into quoted material if it is not a direct quote, as shown in the last example. Alternatively:

After a look of bewilderment, Fred's question went like this: "Is the gravy too cold?"

Now the quote is outside the question mark. This is because the quoted statement is in fact the question. Now for an exclamation mark example:

I was as angry as a saber-toothed badger when Fred asked, "Is the gravy too cold?"! Just answer the question, "yes" or "no," did or did not the accused exclaim in an unkind tone "The gravy is too cold!"?

QUOTATION MARKS / QUESTION MARKS / EXCLAMATION POINTS

Examples:

I didn't know how to respond when he said, "I don't think I want to do this anymore": sometimes he changes his mind, however.

I figured out how to respond, however, when he said, "But I always change my mind for all the wrong reasons"; well, I thought, that's not quite true.

Commas and periods with quotation marks: In American written English, quotation marks are always outside the comma or period.

The dude was dead crazy when he babbled, "Crime pays all right when you're starting from the bottom," but in an oblique sort of way, it made sense. After all, operating a dinosaur day in and day out isn't exactly what he had in mind when he struck out all full of plans.

PARENTHESES

We touched on parenthetical phrases previously. Let's see what "Webster's" has to say about it: "...an amplifying or explanatory word, phrase, or sentence inserted in a passage from which it is usually set off by punctuation...." So a parenthetical phrase can be set off by commas, dashes, etc. But when the "...interruption is more than that indicated by commas..." use parentheses. Parenthesis is the singular, and would be spoken or written, for example, "...left parenthesis...open parenthesis...close parenthesis...." Or, plurally, as "...and please enclose that last phrase in parentheses...."

Open parenthesis refers to the first, or left, parenthesis. Close parenthesis refers to the second, or right, parenthesis:

> That Mr. Flintstone is one cool customer (he had a fellow with him In dictation, this would have been spoken like this:
>
> "That Mr. Flintstone is one cool customer - open parenthesis - he had a fellow with him named Barney that seemed to be a bit of a "sidekick" - close parenthesis, period."

Use brackets to enclose something already within parentheses:

> (Most of that equipment [all now unoperational] will be recycled.)

Alternatively:

> (Most of that equipment will be recycled [it's now all unoperational].)

Common misusage:

> Quite some time back I read somewhere that if, (where did I read that?) and or when a person was ready, the teacher would come.

The correct version:

> Quite some time back I read somewhere that if (where did I read that?), and/or [or and, or] when a person was ready, the teacher would come.

The comma, semicolon, colon, exclamation mark and question mark *always* follow the closing parenthesis, unless the parenthetical phrase is a complete sentence and can stand on its own as information that must be included but interrupts the flow of the present passage, in which case it would be handled this way:

> It was Betty's contention that things weren't always what they seemed to be at home - she may have been Wilma's only confidante. (Fred was often late coming home from work, his feet sore from propelling that idiotic car of his, and his best friend Barney - Betty's husband - never alleviated the edgy circumstances because he always seemed to be standing in one of their open-air windows at the wrong time.) Indeed, she was adamant that they were constantly "putting on airs."

Alternatively:

> It was Betty's contention that things weren't always what they seemed to be at home - she may have been Wilma's only confidante (For example, Fred was often late coming home from work, his feet sore from propelling that idiotic car of his, and his best friend Barney - Betty's husband - never alleviated the circumstances because he always seemed to be standing in

one of their open-air windows at the wrong time.). Indeed, she was adamant that they were constantly "putting on airs."

The parenthetical information is a complete sentence and can be ended with any sentence ending punctuation mark, but the sentence from which it was being set off also must have a sentence ending punctuation mark. It can, and often is, written or read this way.

ITALICS

The first rule of italicization is to italicize titles of books, magazines, newspapers, plays, movies, works of art, and long musical compositions. Now distinguishing between using quotation marks or italics to set apart titles can be confusing, and here in America we're not sticklers when it comes to the elements of style, but a good rule of thumb is if you're not sure which usage is proper for a given title, italicize it.

Trevanian's *Shibumi* was frequently a scathing editorial on the myriad absurdities that exist in today's Western society.

The *Saturday Evening Post* ran an excellent expose on the hypocritical habits of the Ultraconservatives.

The *New York Times* is un*questionably* an excellent Web resource for learning tools for families.

Cats was absolutely astonishing!

The *Mona Lisa* will *always* be considered a masterpiece, not just for that enigmatic smile (and style!), but also because of its geometrical themes.

Also the names of spacecraft, aircraft and ships are italicized:

The *USS Sinbad* went down off Cape Horn after the gigantic amphibious cyclops known as the "Cracken" tore it asunder.

Oh, joy. *Atlantis* blasted off today for another mission in space. And for our next story....

Also, words, letters and numbers, when *referred* to as words, letters and numbers are italicized.

You see, you take the letter *d* and you add it to *Fre* and what you come up with is *Fred*.

In that report, throughout the entire thing, the numbers *3* and *6* can't be read without some effort.

Any word, or portion of a word, you wish to emphasize could be italicized (or underlined), as you have seen throughout the preceding examples.

All foreign words, and Latin scientific terms, are italicized (except in the legal field where their common use has obviated the need for that).

> "*Merci*," mewed the adorable *mademoiselle*.

> Humans, human beings, *Homo sapiens*, one should think, would be too clever to completely destroy the host upon which it as a virus thrives, but alas this is not the case. Neanderthal man (*Homo sapiens neanderthalensis*), who lived close to the land and worshipped it as a giver-of-life, was *infinitely* more advanced than we are today.

Case titles in legal citations are italicized or underlined:

> *Davis v. The Establishment*, a landmark case in which the author of a legal transcription training program was sentenced to a lifetime of subhuman subservience just for being an intelligent woman.

NUMBERS

We will briefly address rules about how numbers are handled in most typewritten documentation. When quoting someone, or at least rendering into written form anything spoken that includes numbers, when there are two or fewer words needed to express a number you spell them out. When there are three or more words needed to express a number, use the numerical form.

> "I believe that was in sixty-eight."

> "I believe that was in 1968."

However, in legal documents you would rarely write anything out; years would be expressed as their numeric form, and if foreshortened, e.g., 68 would be properly written as '68. More about number rules will be provided subsequently in this course.

Often you will see numbers written incorrectly:

> The figure was actually one-hundred and twenty-eight dollars.

Correctly, when spoken:

> The figure was actually one-hundred twenty-eight dollars.

> The figure was actually one-hundred twenty-eight dollars and forty-two cents.

In spoken or written English, the "and" serves as the decimal point. Every day, people use it correctly when writing out checks, but seldom in other forms of writing or with speech. Naturally, if you were transcribing the last example sentence, you would type:

The figure was actually $128.42.

Why? Review the first rules.

EXERCISE – CHAPTER 7-A

Since answers to the exercises often appear on the same page immediately following the exercise, please **do not read the answer** before you work with the questions.

1. Circle the letter corresponding to the correct sentence
a. The client's complaint, and subsequent brief was prepared by Attorney Smith.
b. The client's complaint and subsequent brief, was prepared by Attorney Smith.
c. The client's complaint and subsequent brief were prepared by Attorney Smith.

ANSWER 1 - c

2. Spell the following. If correctly spelled, write "correct" in the blank	
a. adbomen	
b. independent	
c. asscertain	
d. labratorie	
e. satelite	
f. surgeon	
g. stomack	
h. compatable	
i. clinikal	
j. taged	

k. aggresive	
l. pateint	
m. psichology	
n. resistence	
o. diarhea	
p. collecter	

ANSWER – 2

a. abdomen   p. collector

b. correct

c. ascertain

d. laboratory

e. satellite

f. correct

g. stomach

h. compatible

i. clinical

j. tagged

k. aggressive

l. patient

m. psychology

n. resistance

o. diarrhea

	3. Check the following sentences for grammar and punctuation and circle the most correct choice.
a	We will see how this medication affects the patient's seizures
b	We will see how this medication effects the patient's seizures
c	We will check the affect of this regimen in one week.
d	We will check the effect of this regimen in one week.
e	We saw Mr. Smith, and the patient's blood pressure was normal.
f	We saw Mr. Smith, and the patients' blood pressure was normal.
g	The patient was kept in ICU, with frequent monitoring of his status.
h	The patient was kept in ICU with frequent monitoring of his status.
i	The patient's height, weight, and blood pressure were checked.
j	The patient's height, weight and blood pressure was checked.
k	The child was awake alert and playful and eating well and ready to be discharged.
l	The child was awake, alert, and playful, eating well, and ready to be discharged.
m	Following administration of general anesthesia, the patient was placed on the operating room table.
n	Following administration of general anesthesia. The patient was placed on the operating room table.

o	One of the medications is an antibiotic.
p	One of the medications are an antibiotic.
q	Your sure you want to go visit your mother-in-law.
r	You're sure you want to go visit your mother-in-law?

ANSWERS – 3 – a, d, e, g, i, l, m, o, r

4. Insert the correct punctuation in the following sentences:	
a	John and his sister Mary and his brother Fred all suffer the same condition.
b	The patient stated my stomach hurts.
c	The nurse Mrs. Daniels was called to the bedside.
d	Dr. Twitch a neurosurgeon was consulted.

ANSWERS - 4

a. John and his sister, Mary, and his brother, Fred, all suffer from the same condition.

b. The patient stated, "my stomach hurts."

c. The nurse, Mrs. Daniels, was called to the bedside.

d. Dr. Twitch, a neurosurgeon, was consulted.

5. If a word is misspelled, spell it correctly; if spelled correctly, write "correct."	
a	accommodate

b	garantee
c	specified
d	debter
e	receipt
f	installation
g	columes
h	humanitarian
i	precision
j	requirment
k	parallel
l	immaterial
m	nullafy
n	abbreviate
o	believe
p	delivery
q	litagation
r	plead
s	manuever
t	equaliser
u	authoratative
v	idiom
w	acknowledge

x	suppliment
y	defecet
z	pronounciation

ANSWERS - 5

a. correct

b. guaranty or guarantee

c. correct

d. debtor

e. correct

f. correct

g. columns

h. correct

i. correct

j. requirement

k. correct

l. correct

m. nullify

n. correct

o. correct

p. correct

q. litigation

r. correct

s. maneuver

t. equalizer

u. authoritative

v. correct

w. correct

x. supplement

y. deficit

z. pronunciation

6. Make plural nouns of the following words:	
a. child	

b. tooth	
c. fish	

ANSWERS – 6

a. children

b. teeth

c. fish

7. Use capital letters, abbreviations, commas and periods in the following sentences:	
a	james watson attorney at law 401 cross river rd des moines ia
b	ms gilbert ramirez 1582 windy hill ave los altos ca
c	capt susan a ralston 888 rodeo hwy el paso tx
d	prof a j arnold 11 hilltop ave nashville tn
e	jari davis president meditech, inc. a utah company providing medical courses
f	president barack obama was elected as the president of the us

g	dr albert schweitzer, chief, department of surgery, millennial medical center

ANSWERS – 7

a. James Watson, Attorney at Law, 401 Cross River Road, Des Moines, IA

b. Ms. Gilbert Ramirez, 1582 Windy Hill Ave., Los Altos, CA

c. Capt. Susan A. Ralston, 888 Rodeo Highway, El Paso, TX

d. Prof. A. J. Arnold, 11 Hilltop Ave., Nashville, TN

e. Jari Davis, President, Meditech, Inc., a Utah company providing medical courses

f. President Barack Obama was elected as the president of the U.S.

g. Dr. Albert Schweitzer, Chief, Department of Surgery, Millennial Medical Center **8. Add an apostrophe to show possession (belongs to) in the following:**	
a	child	
b	children	
c	worker (one)	
d	assistants (more than one)	
e	people	
f	patients rooms	
g	patients room	

ANSWERS - 8

a. child's

b. children's

c. worker's

d. assistants'

e. people's

f. patients' rooms

g. patient's room

	9. The following are true or false answers – check off which – the statements may be related to any of the information relating to English usage, including punctuation	T	F
a	The people got there wish by electing President Clinton.		
b	I ran to close to the road and nearly got hit by a car.		
c	The whether outside is chilly, and it may rain.		
d	Your coming with us to the party, right?		
e	My hole wardrobe is outdated.		
f	I new all the time that it was a trick.		
g	The boy and his dog walks down the street.		
h	Both of them is going to the store.		
i	The patient receive his medication at noon.		
j	We're studying the text for legal terminology.		

k	Mary Lou studys for an exam.		
l	The patients' nose was noted to be red and swollen.		
m	The oxes are slow movers.		
n	We're in Bangkok, Thailand.		
o	It's a city with a rich history.		
p	She's watching the famous Thai Dancers.		
q	They're graceful and beautiful.		
r	He's interested in music and dance.		
s	Soccer began in China too thousand years ago.		
t	Modern soccer got it's start in England.		
u	Pele is you're favorite soccer player.		
v	Soccer has spread two many countries.		
w	Well we saw many different animals from Africa.		
x	Amy, Martha, Paul and me went fishing in Perth Australia.		
y	The patient's arm, wrist, and hand was prepared and draped for surgery.		
z	I said, "What are you going to do with that scalpel, doctor?"		
*	He said, "better to cut you with my dear."		

ANSWERS - 9

a. F – their

b. F – too

c. F – weather

d. F – You're

e. F – whole

f. F – knew

g. F – walk

h. F – are

i. F – either receives or received

j. T

k. F – studies

l. F – patient's

m. F – oxen

n. T

o. T

p. T

q. T

r. T

s. F – two

t. F – its

u. F – your

v. F – to

w. F – Well,

x. F – I, (not me) and Perth, Australia

y. F - were

z. T

* F – "Better to cut you with, my dear."

10. Write each proper noun correctly.	
a	september	
b	john newbury	
c	la paz mexico	
d	university of utah medical clinic	
e	Department of obstetrics	
f	United states congress	
g	oklahoma city, oklahoma	

h	Today is tuesday, june 10th	
i	St. Louis' center for the arts	
j	emergency room	
k	emergency room at ABC Hospital	
l	susie is a proper noun	

ANSWERS – 10

a. September
b. John Newbury
c. La Paz, Mexico
d. University of Utah Medical Clinic
e. Department of Obstetrics
f. United States Congress
g. Oklahoma City, Oklahoma
h. Tuesday, June
i. Center for the Arts (note small words are not capitalized)
j. emergency room
k. Emergency Room
l. Susie

KIND OF FUN, WASN'T IT?

I. LATIN

LANGUAGE ORIGINS AND ADAPTATIONS - ETYMOLOGY

WHERE DID LEGAL WORDS COME FROM...or the *"ETYMOLOGY"*

(eh-tih-mol-ogy) of words?

1. Etymology

Let's start with the word *etymology*. It means the "origin and historical development of a word." The study of languages is called *linguistics*. A branch of this discipline studies the origin and history of words. Let's start with English. If you look up *English* in the dictionary, you will find that one definition is: "The Germanic language of the people of the United States and Britain." Does that mean that those who speak English are in reality speaking German? No, not precisely. The English language is a composite mixture of the Germanic language, which includes those spoken in Scandinavian countries, and all of them have elements that evolved from Latin and Greek.

If you researched further the English language evolution, you would find the Vikings wandering up and down the Rhine and Rhone Rivers, raiding, conquering and remaining in the vanquished countries, taking the existing language of communication and integrating it into their own. Likewise, the Romans conquered Greece and adopted and adapted lots of Greek words into Latin. In the countries they vanquished, Latin and other (Etruscan, etc.) existing languages were also combined. When the Vikings arrived, they borrowed Latin and Greek (and their predecessors') into their language. English then is derived from a mix of languages including Latin. If you look up an English word in the dictionary, you will find the "roots" of the word and what the roots mean. Let's take the word, *school*: it is derived from a Greek word, *skhole*. Does it look like it would be pronounced as we do the word school? Well, it had to be adapted to fit the Germanic English, so the letters were changed to match the Germanic alphabetic sounds ending up in English as "school."

Language then is a dynamic process growing and evolving as communication requirements change. Greeks began changing their language thousands of years ago, and the process continues today, even with our language, English. Law has its own vocabulary, and anyone entering a legal career must learn this language.

Greek and Latin form the basis of almost all of the law. The Latin alphabet is a modification of the Greek, and is similar to English, except that some letters are pronounced differently and most words are accented – stressed – on the next-to-the-last syllable, like "introduction."

As you can see English has been strongly influenced by other languages, notably those mentioned, plus Celtic, Saxon, German, and French, among others. The fact that legal terms are based on Greek and Latin makes them logical, more difficult to complicate. Here in the U.S., we have Anglicized some of the Latin/Greek words as you will clearly see in the Latin dictionary, which follows.

Reading, hearing and learning the words in a meaningful context provides an enjoyable way of learning to pronounce, spell and define legal terms in an environment where the learner may see how the words are formed, and how they are used in context with actual legal reports. It helps to have good English skills, be a good speller, and have a good memory.

PRONUNCIATION KEY

The primary stress mark ['] is placed after the syllable bearing the heavier stress of accent. The secondary stress mark ['] follows a syllable having a somewhat lighter stress, as in re com men da tion (re' kom en da' shen).

LETTERS AND SOUNDS

A ADD, MAP	m move, seem	u up, done
a ace, rate	n nice, tin	ur urn, term
air care, air	ng ring, song	yoo use, few
a palm, father	o odd, hot	v vein, eve
b bat, rub	o open, so	w win, away
ch check, catch	o order, jaw	y yet, yearn
d dog, rod	oi oil, boy	z zest, muse
e end, pet	ou out, now	zh vision, pleasure

e even, tree	oo pool, food	e the schwa, (looks like a backwards "e" - an unstressed vowel representing the sound spelled "a" – in above, "e" in sicken, "i" in clarity, "o" in melon, "u" in focus
f fit, half	oo took, full	
g go, log	p pit, stop	
h hope, hate	r run, poor	
i it give	s see, pass	
i ice, write	sh sure, rush	
j joy, ledge	t talk, sit	
k cool, take	th thin, both	
l look, rule	th this, bathe	

2. Latin Words and Phrases

One nice thing about Latin is that the words are pronounced pretty much like they appear. Let's try a few...

Take the first one in the list, "a fortiori;" it is pronounced, "ah for-she-or-ee." The second is a "mensa et thoro," pronounced "ah-men-suh-ett-thore-oh." "Ad hoc" is "odd–hock," "ad infinitum" is "odd-in-fin-eye-tum" - see where the English word "infinite" came from? And infinity? Look at "alii," which is "ail-ee-eye." Pretty fun, huh? How about some ponderous-sounding ones... "capias ad satisfaciendum," "cap-ee-oss, odd, sought-iss-foss-ee-end-uhm." Sounds really impressive doesn't it? Lots more interesting than its English counterpart, "arrest to satisfy?" Anyway, as you read through the words, try to pronounce a few. Also look at the meanings and note how many of the words are used as standard English words.

In more modern times, Latin words and phrases have become less common with every day utilization, however, you will still see them used from time to time, and you will now know where the English words commonly used in law came from.

LATIN WORDS AND PHRASES	
a fortiori	with strong reason; much more
a mensa et thoro	from bed and board
a priori	from what goes before; from the cause to the effect
ab initio	from the beginning
actions in personam	personal actions
ad faciendum	to do
ad hoc	for this; (for this special purpose)
ad infinitum	indefinitely, forever
ad litem	for the suit; for the litigation; guardian ad litem is a person appointed to prosecute or defend a suit for a person incapacitated by infancy or incompetency
ad quod damnum	to what damage; what injury
ad valorem	according to value
alias dictus	otherwise called
alii	others
aliunde	from another place, from without
alius	another
alter ego	the other self
alumnus	a foster child
amicus curiae	friend of the court
animo	with intention, disposition, design, will
animus	mind, intention
animus furandi	the intention to steal
animus revertendi	intention to return
animus revocandi	intention to revoke

animus testandi	an intention to make a testament or will
anno Domini (a.d.)	In the year of the Lord
ante	before
ante litem motam	before suit brought
arguendo	in the course of the argument
bona fide	in good faith
bona vacantia	vacant goods - personal property no one claims which escheats (returns) to the state
capias	take, arrest
capias ad satisfaciendum	arrest to satisfy
causa mortis	by reason of death
caveat	let him beware, a warning
caveat emptor	let the buyer beware
certiorari	to be informed of, made certain in regard to
cestui	beneficiaries
consortium	a union of lots or chances, (a lawful marriage)
contra	against
corpus	body
corpus delecti	the body of the offense, the essence of the crime
corpus juris	a body of law
cum testamento annexo	with the will annexed
damnum absque injuria	damage without injury
datum	a thing given, a date
de bonis non administratis	of the goods not administered
de bono et malo	for good and ill
de facto	in fact, in deed, actually

de jure	of right, lawful
de minimis non curat lex	the law does not concern itself with trifles
de novo	anew, afresh
de son tort	of his own wrong
dies non	not a day
donatio mortis causa	a gift by reason of death
duces tecum	you bring with you
durante minore aetate	during minority
durante viduitate	during widowhood
eo converso	conversely, on the other hand
eo instanti	upon the instant
erratum (plural is errata)	error
et alii (et al)	and others
et alius (et al)	and another
et cetera (etc)	and other things
ex cathedra	from the chair
ex contractu	arising from the contract
ex delicto	arising from a tort
ex gratia	as a matter of favor
ex necessitate legis	from legal necessity
ex officio	from office, by virtue of his office
ex parte	on one side only, by or for one party
ex post facto	after the fact
et uxor (et ux)	and wife
et vir	and husband
fiat	let it be done

fieri	to make up, to become
fieri facias	cause to be made up – to become
flagrante delicto	in the very act of committing a crime
habeas corpus	you have the body
in esse	in being, existence
in extremis	in extremity, last illness
in fraudem legis	in circumvention of law
in loco parentis	in the place of a parent
in pari delicto	in equal fault
in personam	a remedy where the proceedings are against the person as distinguished from against a specific thing
in re	in the matter
in rem	a remedy where the proceedings are against the thing as distinguished from those against the person
in rerum natura	in nature, in life, in existence
in specie	in the same, or like, form
in statu quo	in the condition in which it was (status quo)
in toto	in the whole, completely
in transitu	in transit, in course of transfer
indicia	marks, signs
innuendo	meaning
inter	among, between
inter vivos	between the living
interim	in the meantime
intra	within, inside
ipse dixit	he himself said it

ipso facto	by the fact itself
ita est	it is
jura personarum	rights of persons
jura rerum	rights of things
jure divino	by divine right
jure uxoris	in the wife's right
jus (plural jura)	law, laws collectively
jus ad rem	a right to a thing
jus civile	civil law
jus commune	common law, common right
jus gentium	law of nations, international law
jus habendi	right to have a thing
jus priprietatis	right of property
levari facias	cause to be levied, writ of execution
lex loci	law of the place
lex loci rei sitae	the law of the place where a thing is situated
lex mercatoria	the law merchants
lis pendens	litigation pending, pending suit
locus delecti	the place of the crime or tort
locus in quo	the place in which
locus sigilii	the place of the seal
mala fides	bad faith
mala in se	wrongs in themselves
mala praxis	malpractice
malo animo	with evil intent
malum in se	evil itself

mandamus	we command
manu forti	with a strong hand (forcible entry)
mens rea	guilty mind
nolo contendere	I will not contest it
non compos mentis	not of sound mind
non est factum	it is not his deed
non prosequitur (non pros)	he does not follow up or pursue
nudum pactum	nude pact, without consideration
nul tort	no wrong done
nulla bona	no goods
onus probandi	the burden of proof
opus	work, labor
ore tenus	orally, by word of mouth
pari delicto	in equal guilt
particeps criminis	an accomplice in crime
pater familias	head (father) of a family
peculium	private property
pendente lite	pending the suit (during litigation)
per annum	by the year
per autre vie	for another's lifetime
per capita	by the head
per centum	per cent
per contra	in opposition
per curiam	by the court
per diem	by the day
per se	by itself

per stirpes	by stems or root (estate distribution)
post-mortem	after death
post-obit	to take effect after death
praecipe or precipe	command, written order to the clerk of the course to issue a writ
prima facie	at first site, on the face of it
pro	for
pro confesso	as confessed
pro forma	as a matter of form
pro hoc vice	for this occasion
pro rata	according to the rate or proportion
pro tanto	for so much, to that extent
pro tempore	for the time being, temporarily
procheim ami	next friend
publici juris	of public right
pur autre view	for or during the life of another
quare	query, question - wherefore
quantum	how much, amount
quantum meruit	as much as he deserved
quantum valebant	as much as they were worth
quare	wherefore
quare clausum fregit	wherefore he broke the close (trespass)
quasi	as if, as it were
quid pro quo	what for what, something for something
quo warranto	by what right or authority
quoad hoc	as to this

reductio ad absurdum	reduced to the absurd
res	a thing, an object, the subject matter
res gestae	things done, transactions
res ipsa liquitur	the thing speaks for itself
res judicata	a matter adjudicated
scienter	knowingly
scilicet ss. or ss.	to wit: that is to say
scintilla	a spark, the least particle
scire facias	cause to know, give notice
se defendendo	self defense
semper	always
seriatim	severally, separately
sigillum	a seal
simplex obligato	a simple obligation
sine die	without day (specified day)
situs	situation, location
stare decisis	to abide by decided cases
status quo	state in which
sub judice	under consideration
sub modo	under a qualification, in a qualified way
sub nom	under the name
sui juris	of his own right
supersedeas	that you supersede, a writ commanding a stay of proceedings
supra	above
terminus a quo	the starting point

tort	a civil wrong
ultra vires	without power
venire facias	cause to come – a kind of summons
verba fortius accipiuntur contra proferentem	words to be taken most strongly against the one using them
versus (vs., v.)	against
vi et armis	by force and arms
via	a road, a right of way, by way of
vice versa	on the contrary, on opposite sides
videlicet (viz) (contraction of videre and licet)	it is easy to see, that is to say, namely
virtute officii	by virtue of his office
viva voce	by the living voice, by word of mouth
voir dire	to speak the truth

NOLO CONTENDERE, YOUR HONOR,

DE MINIMIS NON CURAT LEX...

QUIZ:

WHAT DOES THAT STATEMENT MEAN?_____

Please drop over to this site:

www.abanet.org/publiced/glossary.html

Key in four or five of the words from the above list to see how the lookup works. It's a very good resource when you need to find legal words.

Here's another good site to find legal words and phrases.

www.answers.com/library/Law%20Dictionary

J. Writing

Writing is essentially teaching. The writer must convey to the reader certain information sufficient to educate the reader so s/he will know about the topic. Similarly, when lawyers or paralegals write legal documents they are educating. It is important to take the thoughts of the writer and translate them into a format, which is understandable to the reader. One of the keys used for that communication is a logical, comprehensible format, which makes it much easier to understand the information. The format as a consistent tool also simplifies the process.

In legal writing, the paralegal, as well as the supervising attorney, learn to master the mechanics of writing. This is especially true when writing case briefs, court documents, etc. The reader must understand all the pleadings, arguments, and claims that you are trying to make. Be sure to focus on making what you write in an effective manner, using a simple form of communication. All that legal jargon known as "legalese" is an analytical, informative style of persuasive communication between law professionals. Legal writing has a definite style of its own and is intended for the legal audience. In most cases legal writing reflects the cornerstone of the legal profession. Communication however, has a way to also obfuscate information, and confuse the reader. This is not a noteworthy goal.

Writing reflects believability by convincing the opposition, an attorney, or a judge, or others who may use the information, of the facts relating to the client. No matter which style is chosen, we should be aware that we might influence the outcome by our choice of words. Words our most essential writing tools. To gain effective writing ability, we must become close friends with nouns and verbs that form the English language. Utilization of a dictionary and a thesaurus are integral major tools for writing. A legal writer needs a close relationship with words to feel comfortable using legal research books, words to translate what is found, and presented to others for review.

Although a paralegal does not always appear in court, s/he often spends a lot of time preparing written documents. Effective legal writing is critical to success as a paralegal. However, the paralegal needs to be aware that no matter what or how we write, we must follow the simple rules of English composition. You may even surprise yourself, and learn that grammar is not all that boring. By using interesting illustrations to impact your ideas, you make stronger cases.

First, ask yourself these two questions: "What is the purpose of this document?" "What are you trying to relay to the reader in order to set the stage or tone?" There is no point using persuasive language when your mission is to notify a client that a will is ready to be executed. Secondly, adopt a neutral and purely informative style. By reminding yourself of the purpose of your writing, you will be able to maintain the appropriate tone and style of the message.

As a reminder, focus on the intended recipient—a client, a supervising attorney, adverse counsel, or a judge. Take for instance, the word "interrogatory" may be commonplace to you, but is puzzling to a newcomer to litigation. A client may be a sophisticated real estate broker and a complex discussion of prepayment penalty clauses in mortgage notes may be easily understood. Use a straightforward style for a layperson. Clients will not be impressed by your use of Latin phrases, and may well become frustrated by overuse. Clients expect to be informed, not confused or mystified, by legal writing.

One of the most difficult tasks can be writing for your supervising attorney who has not thought through the way he wants to express his views. For the most part, your job as a paralegal is to structure the approach that will meet reasonable expectations.

Case in point: The supervising attorney has access to certain facts and information that you do not, and your writing may be criticized for being incomplete.

Writing for judges presupposes a certain level of expertise; you need not give definitions or long-winded explanations for commonly known terms or phrases. Keep in mind, most judges rely heavily on law clerks to read briefs, who, in turn, give an initial opinion to the judge. Most judges are usually overwhelmed with heavy caseloads and do not appreciate an overly long message that resorts to jargon and legalese. More and more courts are adopting a more concise writing style by establishing page limits for documents submitted.

Case in point: we already did this once - "KISS" — "keep it simple stupid." Be brief and to the point.

Precision is another important characteristic of legal writing. Judges, administrators, and others will assume the information provided to them is correct. Therefore, being right is fundamental to effective legal writing. No judge will render a decision in a client's favor if the conclusions you have reached are faulty and incorrect.

Be accurate pertaining to "big" issues such as legal conclusions and arguments. Just as spelling errors cast doubt on your ability, so does accuracy, so errors have a negative impact on the reader. In recent years the legal profession has become a more adversarial process, and even clients are quick to point out an error. Because your audience is highly critical, you must be as accurate and precise as possible.

Case in point: proofread carefully to ensure the ideas and the language that represents them is appropriate.

Improper word selection or the use of vague words causes imprecision in writing. Use of qualifying language or words can cause unintended meanings. For example, hearing, "Your firm is not immediately in danger of going bankrupt," as a statement, would certainly not comfort a client. The use of the qualifier "immediately," implies that a danger exists. Descriptive words lend strength and vitality to your writing.

In addition, the use of "will," "may," or "shall," causes ambiguity and inaccuracy. Use "may," for optional action, "will," for future action ("I will appear in court on Thursday"), and "shall," or "must," for obligatory action.

When selecting a word, consider its connotation, or suggested meaning. Take for instance the word "cheap," comes across as shoddy or low, while "affordable," conveys a neutral or desirable meaning. Keep in mind, certain words carry hostile undertones and will immediately make the reader defensive or angry.

Clarity ensures the reader that what you are saying projects an understanding of what was being said. Therefore, your writing style should be invisible. Legal writing is a function that makes your point clear. Three primary legal writing flaws that obscure clarity are

- ELEGANT VARIATION

You can, of course, learn to substitute one word for another commonly used word, avoiding repetition, which we are calling elegant variation, though useful at times, consider this sentence in order to get a clear view of the downside of that type of use.

"Three of the defendant's witnesses were women while all of the plaintiff's witnesses were ladies."

What does this sentence infer? Is it that the defendant's witnesses differ from women, and ladies in some way? Did the writer just try to substitute another word for women?

- OVERUSE OF NEGATIVES

Do not overuse negatives, they can be confusing to the reader. For instance, if you read, and interpret statutes; they are often written in a negative fashion by describing what is prohibited, using more than two negative words in a sentence, forcing the reader to stop and think what is really being said. For example, the phrase, "not unlikely" should be converted to simply "unlikely," or even "probable."

- IMPROPER WORD ORDER

The third flaw, "word order," is a common problem. The most common sentence structure in the English language is the placement of the subject first, the verb second, and the object third such as, "The defendant attacked the victim." It could also be expressed as, "The victim was attacked by the defendant." The reader anticipates that sentences will follow the expected pattern of subject, verb, and object.

Case in point: A benefit of using "normal" sentence structure is that you will be compelled to phrase your thoughts in the active voice. A weakened point created by a passive voice may differ from the anticipated order of the sentence.

Most legal writing is often complex, and rather boring at times, however, you need to create your document in a way that the reader will be able to understand unfamiliar legal topics. To enhance readability you must first use an active voice that focuses attention on the subject. The passive voice focuses the reader's attention on the object of action by placing it first.

Because legal writing is somewhat formal, adopt an emotionless tone in writing. By using vivid and forceful words, you will not only keep your readers interested, but at the same time aid in converting them to your viewpoint. Use of a thesaurus or dictionary will come in handy when selecting words that are vivid and forceful, and finding those that are not so repetitious.

A pure example of the finest form of writing is in the "The Gettysburg Address," which contains only 286 words but remains one of the most powerful speeches ever written. It represents a most compelling and well-known presentation of ideas that are brief, and to the point. Thus, the length of a document does not necessarily translate into quality, but brevity certainly does.

Case in point: Judges complain that lawyers' inability to write succinct briefs is a problem. Keep in mind, the reader's time is of the essence, and you cannot afford to frustrate her/him with redundancy.

Brainstorming ideas is a good way to start. Then outlining starts the logical ball rolling. Divide into headings and subheadings. Headings serve as signals to readers to alert them to the topics to be discussed and to indicate a change in topics. Use effective paragraphs to break up a discussion into units that are easy to read. Avoid paragraphs that are too long. The mind craves a break from a long discussion, as is also true of the eye. Also, avoid short paragraphs (rule of thumb is a paragraph must have more than one sentence).

The use of the computer has certainly brought more interest, adaptability and speed to the drudgery of writing. It makes the job easier, faster, and allows for far easier correction and editing, to say nothing of the forms, formats, and macros stored for immediate access, and adaptation to a current case. In fact, most law offices have purchased software specialized, and written specifically for the elements of documentation in the practice of law. Office supply stores sell CDs with legal forms of every variety, plus, the sources on the Internet have dozens of websites where forms can be downloaded, some free of charge. You can well imagine the time involved with the use of a typewriter in comparison to a word processor. Dictation is probably the fastest method of translating the early elements (outline) right up to when the entire document is done, if you are using legal transcriptionists to type your work. If you do your own work, you will probably prefer a word processing system, though hand held dictation units are certainly handy for lots of the functions leading to the final documentation process.

Legal writing extensively uses technical terminology that may be categorized into four categories:

1. Specialized words and phrases unique to law, e.g., *tort, fee simple*, and *novation*.

2. Quotidian words having different meanings in law, e.g., *action* (lawsuit), *consideration* (support for a promise), *execute* (to sign to effect), and *party* (a principal in a lawsuit).

3. Archaic vocabulary: legal writing employs many old words and phrases that were formerly quotidian language, but today exist mostly or only in law, dating from the 1500s; English examples are *herein, hereto, hereby, heretofore, herewith, whereby,* and *wherefore* (pronominal adverbs) ; *said* and *such* (as adjectives).

4. Loan words and phrases from other languages: For instance, in English, this includes terms derived from the French language, *estoppel, laches,* and *voir dire,* and Latin, *certiorari, habeas corpus, prima facie, inter alia, mens rea, sub judice,* and are not italicized as English legal language, as would be foreign words in mainstream English writing.

These features tend to make legal writing formal. This formality can take the form of long sentences, complex constructions, archaic and hyper-formal vocabulary, and a focus on content to the exclusion of reader needs. Some of this formality in legal writing is necessary and desirable, given the importance of some legal documents and the seriousness of the circumstances in which some legal documents are used. Yet not all formality in legal writing is justified. To the extent that formality produces opacity and imprecision, it is undesirable. To the extent that formality hinders reader comprehension, it is less desirable. In particular, when legal content must be conveyed to nonlawyers, formality should give way to clear communication.

What is crucial in setting the level of formality in any legal document is assessing the needs and expectations of the audience. For example, an appellate brief to the highest court in a jurisdiction calls for a formal style - this shows proper respect for the court and for the legal matter at issue. An interoffice legal memorandum to a supervisor can probably be less formal because it is an in-house decision-making tool, not a court document. And an email message to a friend and client, updating the status of a legal matter, is appropriately informal. However, the office email has many rules. We will present those in a law office module in this course, *Legally Large.*

Transaction documents - legal drafting - fall on a similar continuum. A 150-page merger agreement between two large corporations, in which both sides are represented by counsel, will be highly formal. It should also be accurate, precise, and airtight (features not always compatible with high formality). A commercial lease for a small company using a small office space will likely be much shorter and will require less complexity, but may still be somewhat formal. A proxy statement allowing the members of a neighborhood association to designate their voting preferences for the next board meeting ought to be as plain as can be. If informality aids that goal, it is justified.

Many U.S. law schools teach legal writing in a way that acknowledges the technical complexity inherent in law and the justified formality that complexity often requires, but with an emphasis on clarity, simplicity, and directness. Yet many practicing lawyers, busy as they are with deadlines and heavy workloads, often resort to a template-based, outdated, hyperformal writing style in both analytical and transactional documents. This is understandable, but it sometimes unfortunately perpetuates an unnecessarily formal legal writing style.

Historically, legal writing contained some of the most flowery, and creative use of the English language of virtually any profession except creative writing itself. We have referred you to the Gettysburg address and have reviewed much of the Constitution and the Bill of Rights language earlier in this course.

A wonderful model of the creative use of writing we found in an actual case in 1934 in a Texas court where the plaintiff (Hattie Beatty) sued the defendant, Missouri, Kansas, Texas Railroad for damage sustained to her person when she had solicited sex from a railroad employee (Dockery) while he was working. They had undertaken the process in a switchroom tower belonging to the railroad company. She alleged she was "injured" by a lever and some electric shock in the switchroom tower in that process, and sought damages. The whole case was fraught with rather touchy subject matter, with masterful written command of language to make the case of the defendant. Here is the railroad 's answer:

HATTIE BEATTY VS THE RAILROAD

ANSWER (to complaint)

NOW COMES DEFENDANT RAILROAD, and "Defendant demurs generally to the allegations in the plaintiff's petition contained and says the same are not sufficient in law to constitute a cause of action against the defendant, and of this, prays judgment of the Court.

For further answer, it necessary, this defendant denies all and singular, the allegations in said petition contained, and demands strict proof thereof.

Answering further, if need be, this defendant Railroad Company would reveal to the Court that in truth and in fact, the plaintiff, Ms. Hattie Beatty, for several nights prior to the occasion of which she now complains, had strolled by the signal tower in question, and on each occasion, persistently propositioned this defendant's employee at said tower, one Dockery, to engage with her in the ancient and popular pastime. That the said Dockery is an old and trusted employee, a man of over 60 winters, with snow in his hair, but with summer in his heart; that the faint odor of perfume touched his delicate nostrils, and the full red painted lips of this modern Aphrodite brought back youthful dreams to his aging head. And, although the season was fall time, the sap began to rise in his erotic soul as in romantic springtime of yore. It was on the unlucky night of Friday, the 13th of September, A.D. 1934, that said Dockery finally succumbed to the plaintiff's feminine allurements, the price being one dollar paid in advance.

That in all truthfulness, the only mechanical contrivance, or unique lever about the said tower in which the plaintiff expressed any interest whatsoever, was that which was hung on the person of said Dockery.

That this defendant Railroad Company had not equipped its said tower for such passionate purposes, and had in fact instructed its said employee to admit no visitors thereto, but that unbeknown to this Defendant, the said Dockery permitted the plaintiff to come into the crowded quarters of said tower switchroom to indulge with him in an indoor session of Spanish athletics; that while she reclined upon a cushioned chair and unfolded her female charms to his approach, her bare knees did touch an open electric switch upon the wall of said tower, thereby creating an electrical contact quite different from the one for which she was prepared; that either from shocked surprise at the seemingly amative powers of the said Dockery or for other reasons unknown to this defendant, the said plaintiff sank to the floor of said tower in an apparent swoon, leaving the said Dockery unrewarded and bewildered, raiment disarranged and struggling desperately to operate his signals for a fast train which he discovered at the moment approaching unexpectedly upon the defendant's tracks.

That as to this defendant, the transaction was ultra vires and completely outside the scope of employment of said Dockery, and clearly without benefit to this corporation except for the publicity that might possibly attend as proof to the world of the exemplary manner in which the Railroad cares for and preserves the virility of its aging employees.

That it should be held, however, that the said Dockery was on the occasion in question for this defendant railroad, which is, as the court has often heard plaintiff's counsel charge, a heartless and bloodless corporation, a poor creature without pride of ancestry or hope of posterity and physically incapable of becoming enraptured in ethereal paroxysms of love, then, and in that event only, this defendant pleads that the plaintiff was guilty or contributorily negligent in the following manner:

That the said Dockery urged the plaintiff to remove herself from the cushioned chair to the floor of the tower in order that his engagement might be fulfilled in the good old fashioned way, but that the plaintiff proclaimed her efficiency, and maintained her ability to handle the entire situation from her position in the chair, and that she remained in said chair contrary to Dockery's urgent solicitations, and entreaties, and received the electric shock as a direct and proximate result of her insistence upon departure of well-recognized precedent; that the plaintiff was negligent in failing to pursue her activities horizontally from the floor, and that her failure so to do proximately contributed to cause her injury, if any.

And now, becoming actor herein only in the event the Court should hold that the said Dockery represented this defendant corporation in question, which will never be admitted, this defendant shows as against the plaintiff one devalued dollar of United States currency, and that it received no value therefore as agreed by plaintiff, and the said dollar has never been returned to its owner, and that under all facts hereinabove alleged, it is entitled to recover said sum of money.

PRAYER FOR RELIEF

WHEREFORE, this defendant Railroad Company prays that the plaintiff take nothing in this suit as did the said Dockery take nothing from the plaintiff, and that in the alternative alleged, it recover from the plaintiff the sum of one dollar and all costs herein, and that the virtue of the Railroad Company be in all things vindicated, and that it be further relieved of all possible insinuations against its chastity that may arise as the result of this lawsuit, and for such other relief as it may merit."

Needless to say, the railroad company won the case and got the $1.00 refunded to Dockery. Needless to say, Hattie had that one really blow up on her and it was mostly likely due to the language and portrayal noted.

- Legal writing places heavy reliance on authority. In most legal writing, the writer must back up assertions and statements with citations to authority. Citations will be covered in the training to follow.

- Legal writing values precedent, as distinct from authority. Precedent means *the way things have been done before*. For example, a lawyer who must prepare a contract and who has prepared a similar contract before will often re-use, with limited changes, the old contract for the new occasion. Or a lawyer who has filed a successful motion to dismiss a lawsuit may use the same or a very similar form of motion again in another case, and so on. Many lawyers use and re-use written documents in this way and call these re-usable documents *templates* or, less commonly, *forms*.

MAIN LEGAL WRITING CATEGORIES

Legal writing has of two broad categories:

1. Predictive Analysis

2. Persuasive Analysis

In the United States, in most law schools students must learn legal writing; the courses focus on:

(1) predictive analysis, i.e., an outcome-predicting memorandum (positive or negative) of a given action for the attorney's client; and

(2) persuasive analysis, e.g., motions and briefs. Although not as widely taught in law schools, legal drafting courses exist; other types of legal writing concentrate upon writing appeals or on interdisciplinary aspects of persuasion.

PREDICTIVE ANALYSIS

The legal memorandum is the most common type of predictive legal analysis; it may include the client letter or legal opinion. The legal memorandum predicts the outcome of a legal question by analyzing the authorities governing the question and the relevant facts that gave rise to the legal question. It explains and applies the authorities in predicting an outcome, and ends with advice and recommendations. The legal memorandum also serves as record of the research done for a given legal question. Traditionally, and to meet the legal reader's expectations, it is formally organized and written.

PERSUASIVE ANALYSIS

The persuasive document, a motion or a brief, attempts to persuade a deciding authority to favorably decide the dispute for the author's client. Motions and briefs are usually submitted to judges, but also to mediators, arbitrators, and others. In addition, a persuasive letter may attempt to persuade the dispute's opposing party.

Persuasive writing is the most rhetorically stylized. Although a brief states the legal issues, describes authorities, and applies authorities to the question, as does a memorandum, a brief's application portion is framed as an argument. The author argues for one approach to resolve the legal matter and does not present a neutral analysis.

LEGAL DRAFTING

Legal drafting creates binding, legal text. It includes enacted law like statutes, rules, and regulations; contracts (private and public); personal legal documents like wills and trusts; and public legal documents like notices and instructions. Legal drafting requires no legal authority citation, and generally is written without a stylized voice.

PLAGIARISM

In writing an objective analysis or a persuasive document, lawyers write under the same plagiarism rules applicable to most writers. Legal memoranda and briefs must properly attribute quotations and source authorities; yet, within a law office, a lawyer might borrow from other lawyers' texts without attribution, in using a well-phrased, successful argument made in a previous brief.

Plagiarism is strictly prohibited in academic work, especially in law review articles, seminar papers, and similar writings intended to reflect the author's original thoughts.

Legal drafting is different; unlike other legal writing categories, plagiarism is accepted, because of the high value of precedent. As noted, lawyers extensively use formats (contracts, wills, etc.) in drafting documents; so borrowing from previous documents is common. A good lawyer may frequently copy, verbatim, well-written clauses from a contract, a will, or a statute to serve his or her client's legal interests.

LEGALESE

Legalese is an English term first used in 1914 for legal writing that is designed to be difficult for laymen to read and understand, the implication being that this abstruseness is deliberate for excluding the legally untrained and to justify high fees. It is characterized by long sentences, many modifying clauses, complex vocabulary, high abstraction, and insensitivity to the layman's need to understand the document's gist. Legalese arises most commonly in legal drafting, yet appears in both types of legal analysis. Today, the Plain Language Movement in legal writing is progressing and experts are busy trying to demystify legalese. The *Hattie and the Railroad* case is a good example.

K. Effective Brief Writing

RULES FOR EFFECTIVE BRIEF WRITING

- Know the rules of the court to which the brief will be submitted (trial or appellate)
- Use the appropriate format for the court
- Carefully consider the client's perspective, omitting references to you, as the writer, e.g.,
- "we believe," or "we argue." Use the third person
- Avoid a routine method of writing, variety enhances readability and credibility
- Make sure the citations (sources) are used correctly; avoid string citing
- Avoid sarcasm, humor or irony
- Avoid the overuse of quotations
- Focus on your argument
- Do not distort or overstate your position
- Emphasize strongest arguments by prominent placement in the document

- Weaker portions of the argument are to be placed in the middle of the brief

- Tailor your writing for the primary reason that the reader will comprehend what you have written, and at the same time, be immediately informed or persuaded as to whether your writing achieves its purpose.

REMEMBER!

- Legal writing is a "process"

- Legal writing is for the "legal audience"

- Clarity ensures the reader's understanding

- Enhancing readability underpins more beneficial use by reader

- Practice makes "perfect"

QUESTIONS CHAPTER 7-I-K

Instructions: select the correct word in the following

1. The realtor will have the property *appraised/apprised* before the house

   is sold _____

2. All who were present in the courtroom were greatly *affected/effected* by

   her testimony. _____

3. The *principle/principal* purpose of the hearing was to resolve all

   pretrial matters _____

4. The case *Brown v. The Board of Education* is different *from/than* the present case

   _____

5. The plaintiff was unwilling to *accept/except* the settlement offer

   _____

6. The preponderance of the *memorandum/memoranda* addressed the issue of fraud

   _____

7. Ms. Dale provided the terms of the contract to me *verbally/orally* in our recent telephone

   conversation _____

8. The defendant was found *liable/guilty* for breach of contract

   _____

9. The plaintiff is charged with making serious misstatements which are considered

   libel/liable _____

10. The court issued a gag order, *prescribing/proscribing* all parties from commenting on the

    proceedings _____

11. The parties agreed that a neutral, and *disinterested/uninterested* arbitrator should hear

    the dispute _____

12. The arbiter *listens to/hears* a dispute _____

Rewrite the following sentences for more precision or better clarity

13. The plaintiff must state a cause of action; moreover, the complainant

    must seek actual damages

    _____

14. The ruling of the court was that there had been jury misconduct

    _____

15. The court issued a decision that the contract had been rescinded

    _____

16. The judge ruled on this matter holding the lease had been terminated

    _____

Use the "active voice" to make the sentence more forceful (focus on the subject)

17. A decision to hold a pretrial settlement conference was agreed to by all parties

    _____

18. The exhibits were reviewed by the jurors

    _____

19. The lease was terminated by the landlord

    _____

20. A decision was made by the court that the defendant's statements were actionable

    _____

Eliminating the legal jargon, rewrite the following sentences so they are understood by a layperson

21. After perusing the above-mentioned exhibits, he opined that they were irrelevant

    _____

22. Pursuant to our telephonic communication of June 8, and notwithstanding our discussion, this letter will set forth the settlement proposed in the above-described matter

    _____

23. A cause of action must be initiated by a petitioner within the limitations period prescribed by the relevant statutory authorities

    _____

24. Enclosed herewith please find the aforementioned documents which we discussed in our previous written correspondence

    _____

25. Notwithstanding anything to the contrary herein, all rent payments must be made by the first of each month

    _____

Omitting needless words, and redundancies, rewrite the following sentences to achieve "brevity."

26. The plaintiff, who had earlier filed the complaint, and who was viewed as a vexatious litigant, refused and failed to appear for his hearing

    _____

27. The defendant's reckless, willful, and intentional actions, and conduct resulted in the injuries, and damages to the plaintiff

    _____

28. Although the agreement was signed by the parties, the exhibits were not attached, and this failure to attach the exhibits was the reason the agreement needed to be re-signed and re-dated.

    _____

29. The defendant's contentions, and assertions were directed to, and focused on plaintiff's failure, and refusal to wear, and use her seat belt at the time the accident occurred.

    _____
    _____

30. The jurors, although they attempted to reconcile testimony given at trial, reviewed jury instructions, and examined exhibits, and still were unable to reach a consensus

----

L. Dictation, Word Processing and WP File Organization

Material generated in the law office, of course, has certain characteristics peculiar to the legal field.

Common practice requires that legal documents conform to the requirements of the court when they are to be filed in a court, and certainly, attorneys prefer specific styles relating to correspondence, and non-court documents.

It's a good idea to put together for your use the examples of various types of documents in this section, then add your own as you build expertise in the field. Software is readily available and is used by most law offices that have many of the formats and macros already in place. You may already be familiar with those, if you are working in a law office, or you will certainly be learning when you go to work either in an office, or for yourself. Arrange them in some order that makes sense to you, either alphabetically according to the name or type of the instrument, or, if you prefer, break them down into litigation, and nonlitigation types.

Many phrases, clauses, and short paragraphs are used over, and over again in legal work. The dictator's familiarity with them either causes him or her to dictate at a higher rate of speed, or just refer you to the standard format. Often, the entire clause or paragraph will not be dictated, but just a reference to "use our standard format on that." It is a good practice to develop your own macros as you learn so that you can recall them instantly when you need to integrate them into your current document.

You learn to macro headings for all the courts your office employs for its cases, standard formats for most of the documents employed in the cases wherein you simply fill in the necessary words, plaintiff, defendant, case number, judge, etc. Most law offices also have available software specifically designed for law.

1. Wordy Sentences

The importance of understanding dictated material can't be emphasized enough. A well-trained legal secretary should be able to listen to, and transcribe dictation accurately. The dictated material is rarely monotonous, and is usually quite interesting. Sometimes the material dictated can be very lengthy due to the nature of fairly long briefs, trusts, testimony, depositions, etc.

Most lawyers are pretty good dictators; they think clearly and express themselves well due to the nature of the logic of legal ideology. However, sometimes sentences in the works are long and involved, and the best dictators sometimes make errors in grammar, and sentence structure. Responsibility for the English grammar, then, is mostly yours. You should be able to catch and repair obvious errors. One of the main errors is the omission of a main verb or a conjunction when a parenthetic clause intervenes. To detect inaccuracy in sentence structure, read the independent clause in the sentence without the intervening subordinate clauses or parenthetic material. If you are following the dictator's thought, you will realize something is wrong with the sentence.

As an example, let's analyze the following dictated paragraph:

> "The courts below have decided, [although this plaintiff failed to bring her action within the time limit because an alternative remedy, which as against the employer was exclusive, was apparently granted to her by a statute] yet the courts are powerless to afford her any relief, if under the express terms of the statute the action is now barred."

The words in brackets are parenthetic. During dictation, the transcriptionist places a comma after decided and mentally awaits the objective clause that should follow. Without the intervening parenthetic clause, the sentence reads:

> "The courts below have decided, yet the courts are powerless, etc. In this instance, the dictator evidently intended to follow the material in brackets with the conjunction that; but, intent on the point s/he was making, lost sight of the sentence structure. The transcriptionist immediately realizes the sentence is incomplete, but s/he cannot supply the word because the dictator might have intended to say "...decided ... against the plaintiff, yet the court ...."instead of simple " .... Decided that ...." Call the omission to the lawyer's attention.

Another common error, and one you can easily detect and correct, is the repetition of the conjunction that in introducing a single clause when a phrase or clause intervenes between that and the clause it introduces. For example, in the sentence cited above, the dictator might easily have preceded and followed the bracketed material with that instead of omitting it altogether.

Another slip on the part of the dictator that you must guard against is when s/he calls the plaintiff the defendant and vice versa. You will likely easily detect this slip when transcribing.

2. Legal Homonyms

As we discussed in the English Chapter, many words used frequently in legal work sound alike. Some of them have similar but not exact meanings, and it may be difficult to judge from the sense in which the word may have been used, which is the correct word. Be sure you know and understand the difference in the meaning of each sound alike word. A list of pairs of words that are confusing follows. It is limited to words used frequently in legal work, and does not include typical English words, such as "affect" and "effect." Also, spellcheckers will not find these words since they are, for technological purposes, correct. Only careful proofreading will find them.

Study them, and differentiate the meanings.

Check the web for other references to homonyms, homophones, homographs, synonyms, polysemes, etc.

LEGAL HOMONYMS	
abjure	adjure
act	action
adverse	averse
apperception	perception
arraign	arrange
atonement	attornment
avoid	void
avoidable	voidable
case	cause
casual	causal
casualty	causality
cite	site
collision	collusion
comity	committee
cost	costs
corporal	corporeal
descent	dissent
defer	differ
depository	depositary
devisable	divisible
devisor	devisee
disburse	disperse
dower	dowry
drawer	drawee
estop	stop
in re	in rem
interpellate	interpolate

judicial	judicious
jura	jurat
malfeasance	Misfeasance (and nonfeasance)
mandatory	mandatary
payor	payee
persecute	prosecute
precedence	precedents
prescribe	proscribe
presence	presents
situate	situated
status quo	statu quo
thereon	therein
therefore	therefore
transferor	transferee

M. TYPING RULES

1. Spacing

With the advent of word processing software which has its own intelligence (that's arguable and a matter of opinion), you are occasionally pointed to correct something, sentence structure, spacing, commas, etc. Let's start with the actual typing standard:

ITEM	SPACING
after a comma	1 space
after a semi-colon	1 space
after every sentence	2 spaces
after a colon	2 spaces
before or after a dash (two hyphens)	no space
between quotation marks and the matter enclosed	no space
between any word and the punctuation following it	no space
after an exclamation mark used in the body of a sentence	1 space

after a period following a figure or letter at the beginning of a line or in a list of items	2 spaces
after period following an abbreviation or an initial	1 space
after a period following a figure or letter at the beginning of a line in a list of items	2 spaces
between dots to show an ellipsis	no space
between asterisks to show an ellipsis	1 space
before and after an x (meaning times) as in 3 x 5 card	1 space
before or after an apostrophe in the body of a word	no space
between the initials that make a single abbreviation, for example, c.o.d.	no space
fill in spaces, June , 2014 this _____ day of June, 2014	3 spaces 6 spaces

2. Underscoring

Underscoring or underlining in typed material is equivalent to italics in printed material, but is used less freely. For example, the title of a book is italicized in print but preferably is enclosed in quotations in typed material. The underlining is continuous, and not broken at the spacing between words. The following use of underscoring is not typical in legal work, and is not recommended.

- Underscoring for emphasis

- Underscoring material that is in italics

- Underscoring to indicate Latin words and phrases, or abbreviations of them. Words of other foreign languages may be underlined, but Latin is not since it is used most frequently in legal work.

3. Quotes, Indents, Italics, Ellipses

The left margin of quotations and other indented material is typically five spaces to the right of the left margin.

A. Line spacing

Quotations are usually single-spaced, but this does not apply to all indented material. Triple spacing is sometimes used before and after the quotation or other indented material, particularly if the document is already in a double spaced motif. Double spacing is always done between paragraphs of single spaced material.

B. Quotation marks

Place double quotation marks at the beginning, and end of the quotation, and at the beginning of each new paragraph within the quoted material. Change double quotation marks in material quoted to single quotation marks, thus conforming to the rule that quotations within quotations should be enclosed in single quotation marks.

C. Italics

If words in the original document, or quote are in italics, underscore them. If words that are not in italics in the original are underscored at the direction of the dictator, the words, "Italics ours," in parentheses are added at the end of the quotation. It frequently happens that part of a quoted passage is italicized, and that the dictator wishes to emphasize another part of it. In that case, "italics theirs" is placed in parentheses immediately following the italicized matter, and the words, "emphasis ours," in parentheses at the end of the quotation.

D. Omissions-ellipses

Omissions of part of quotation are indicated by the use of ellipses. They may be periods (dots) or asterisks, (stars) and are usually placed in groups of three. Preferably, there is a space between asterisks, but not points. Remember too, that if you are using points, they take the place of words, so place them accordingly. If a quote begins in the middle of a sentence, there is no space between the quotation mark, and the first ellipsis, but there is a space between the final ellipsis, and the following word.

For example:

The pertinent part of the opinion rendered by the Copyright Office at our request reads as follows:

> "The Copyright Office does not undertake to pass upon his [the author's] rights, leaving the question to the courts in case of dispute. It simply records (italics theirs) his claims, and by this recording, gives him certain rights provided his claims can be substantiated."

> "...this [copyright] is taken out in the name of the publisher rather than of the author, as the contract itself is really a license to sell from the publisher to the author [sic]. It is also the duty of the publisher to take all necessary steps to effect renewals ... ."
>
> "An author should be 'guided' by his publisher in all questions of copyright." (Emphasis ours.)

E. Ditto Marks

Ditto marks are not permissible in a legal document. They are used in exhibits and schedules, but not in the document to which the exhibits and schedules are annexed.

N. Electronic Files

As a legal specialist, it is imperative that you become familiar with files you use in your own as well as any law office computer system. By creating, naming, saving, retrieving, and producing legal documents, these files names should be indicative of the information contained in them sufficient to assist you to find them quickly.

The attorney's signature line, followed by the attorney's state bar number, mailing address, telephone and FAX number (as well as e-mail address if applicable) will be used repeatedly.

Create directories and subdirectories by client name, case number, forms, correspondence, or area of law. In this way, you will be able to identify files needed to process daily tasks in a timely manner. Some examples of extensions for your word processing files are in the following table.

IDEAS FOR NAMING FILES

ACK	acknowledgment	MOT	motion
ADD	addendum	NOT	notice
AFF	affidavit	OAT	oath
AGR	agreement	OFR	offer
AMD	amendment	OPN	opinion
ANS	answer	ORD	order
ART	article(s)	OUT	outline
BRF	brief	PET	petition
BYL	bylaws	PLN	plan
CERT	certificate	PLD	pleading
CR	court	P & A	points & authorities
COD	codicil	PRO	procedure(s)
CPL	complaint	PR	promissory note
CO	consent	POS	proof of service
XAN	cross-answer	PXY	proxy
XCM	cross-complaint	QST	questionnaire
DEC	declaration	REJ	rejection
DEE	deed	REL	release
DOT	deed of trust	RPY	reply
DMD	demand	RPT	report
DMR	demurrer	REQ	request
DSC	disclosure	RES	resolution
DIS	dismissal	RSP	response
DFT	draft	SAT	satisfaction
DPA	durable power of attorney	SCH	schedule

ESC	escrow	STL	settlement
EXH	exhibit	SMT	statement
FAX	facsimile	STP	stipulation
FRM	form	SUB	subpoena
GRT	grant	SDT	subpoena duces tecum
NDX	index	SUM	summary
INS	insert	SUP	supplement
INT	interrogatories	TBL	table
JI	jury instructions	TOA	table of authorities
LBL	label(s)	TOC	table of contents
LSE	lease	TRN	transcript
LTR	letter	VER	verification
LIC	license	WIL	will
LST	list	RIT	writ
MIN	minutes	GOV	government
SUPR CT	superior court	FAMCT	family court
CSE MGR	case manager	PO	probation officer
REHAB	rehabilitation	ADJ	adjudication
JUV	juvenile	DYRS	division of youth rehabilitative services
MIT	mitigating	AGGR	aggravating
MST	multi-systemic therapy	PS	personal service
JAR	juvenile assessment rpt	DS	discharge summary
VOP	violation of probation	NARR	narrative
DFS	Division of Family Services	CMH	child mental health
DJ	department of justice	AG	attorney general

DAG	district attorney general	PD	public defender
CSE	child support enforcement section	CRIM	criminal
BOT	back-on-track	DP	due process
AFT	aftercare/parole	INC	incarceration
SS	suspended sentence	CS	community services
DISPO	disposition	LEV I	administrative probation
LEV II	moderate intensity probation program	LEV III	intensive probation
LEV IV	staff secure care	LEV V	locked secure care
IM	internal memorandum	IA	internal affairs

Formatting for the captions varies from state to state, as well as from jurisdiction to jurisdiction within a state. Many of the captions and formats are now available online. Otherwise, the legal specialist will check with the clerk of the appropriate court to be absolutely sure in choosing the correct jurisdiction and format.

By creating a separate file for the caption of each case, you can retrieve the caption at the beginning of each new document, and not have to re-enter the information into the database. Take for instance, a file name such as SAMAUS.CAP or JASBROWN.CAP, allows easy identification and retrieval of an appropriate caption.

QUESTIONS CHAPTER 7-L-N

TRUE OR FALSE

	STATEMENT	T	F
1	You should make sure that everything you write or transcribe is grammatically perfect even if you have to rewrite a paragraph		
2	When typing, you always put 2 spaces after a comma		
3	After quotation marks are used, at the beginning of the quoted material, you leave no spaces		
4	After a period following an initial, always put 2 spaces		
5	Legal work uses lots of underscoring		
6	Always double space in quoted material		
7	Ellipses are dots or commas placed in groups of three		
8	Jurisdictional formats are always the same in every state		
9	Quotes within quotes are signified by an ' (apostrophe)		

CHAPTER 8
Research and Citation

In this Chapter, we will discuss

A. Research

B. Citations

C. Purpose and Type

D. Shepardizing

A. RESEARCH

In our social world, things happen that irritate, hurt, rile and aggravate people. Those with a grievance sometimes resort to a lawsuit to address and solve the problem. With government, they enact laws to cover just about every part of life and living, whether it is how far you're your property line you can build a house or how fast you can drive down the street. The laws they enact are defined by codes.

In common law countries, court opinions are legally binding under the rule of stare decisis. That rule requires a court to apply a legal principle that was set forth earlier by a court of the same jurisdiction dealing with a similar set of facts. Thus, the regular publication of such opinions is important so that everyone—lawyers, judges, and laymen can all find out what the law is, as declared by judges.

What are Codes?

Codes are sets of laws adopted by a state or nation. A code is a type of legislation designed to exhaustively cover a complete system of laws or a particular area of law as it existed at the time the code was enacted. Codifications are similar in common law and civil law systems. There are civil, criminal, and municipal codes (you have likely seen common references to the IRS Codes). In your research, you will encounter federal, state and local codes as the statutory sources for a variety of case information. In a criminal case, the appropriate criminal code will be selected to best describe what the individual being prosecuted allegedly did.

Please visit this website: www.amlegal.com

American Legal website lists codes by state. Scroll down and click on Code Library. You may click on the list of states provided, or click on "View Google Map of Online Clients" to look at the map then select your state and the next screen will list the cities. You can then click on the city in which you live and a list of all the codes will be displayed. Pick two or three and read them.

Gavel2Gavel is a site you may locate state laws, codes and statutes, visit their website at https://www.ncsc.org/consulting-and-research/areas-of-expertise/court-leadership/gavel-to-gavel.

The codes are part of the citation listing. In a case we are going to review shortly,

Roe v. Wade, 410 U.S. 113, U.S. stands for "United States Code." The numbers tell us where the particular codes cited are located, like a book with the chapter, sometimes a page number, and even a verse. The parties in the lawsuit are Roe and Wade.

Researching a case is much like writing a term paper. You are provided or assigned the subject, but then you have to find all the sources that will support whatever idea or Chapter you are trying to put forth in your paper on the subject matter. You must list those resources within the paper itself, super and subscripts, footnotes or in your bibliography. That provides the proof to the reviewer that you did the research and found rationale or arguments that support your idea. If you make a good presentation, you may influence what someone might think about the subject matter. So, imagine that your case is the term paper and the reviewer is the judge. Your "authorities" and argument are what win or lose cases.

Legal research generally involves tasks such as:

1) Finding primary sources of law, or primary authority, in a given jurisdiction (cases, statutes, regulations, etc.);

2) Searching secondary authority (for example, law reviews, legal dictionaries, legal treatises, and legal encyclopedias such as American Jurisprudence and Corpus Juris Secundum), for background information about a legal topic;

3) Searching non-legal sources for investigative or supporting information.

Legal research is performed by anyone with a need for such information, including lawyers, law librarians, legal assistants, and paralegals. Sources of legal information range from printed books, to free legal research websites and information portals to fee database vendors such as LexisNexis and Westlaw. Law libraries around the world provide research services to help patrons find the legal information they need whether it is a law school, a law firm or other research environments. Many law libraries and institutions provide free online access to legal subscription websites.

One of the most challenging aspects of legal research is reading, and understanding an opinion. An opinion may span dozens of pages, but the relevant information for your research may not exceed a sentence or two from that. We will examine how opinions are structured and how to properly read, and analyze a case.

In contrast to statutes and regulations, case decisions do not strictly follow a particular format. On the contrary, like ordinary people, judges are individuals, and decide cases differently. Those differences are reflected in their opinions. Some judges write long, detailed opinions, whereas others write short, tersely worded ones. In essence, they summarize the whole story as told by the parties and their representatives. You will occasionally encounter opinions in which all the paragraphs are numbered; others may have subheadings. Whatever the format, the applicability and effect of judge-made precedent remain the same. As a paralegal assisting attorneys in researching legal issues, your responsibility is to piece together whatever form the opinion may be to determine its relevance, and applicability to your client's case.

RESEARCH SOURCES

Law Libraries

Law libraries are designed to assist law students, attorneys, judges, paralegals and even the public itself in finding the legal resources necessary to correctly determine the state of the law. Law schools have libraries and some courthouses do as well. The United States Supreme Court building houses one of the most extensive in the world, rivaled by the Law Library of Congress. Some larger law firms maintain a private library for their own attorneys. In some U.S. states all counties are required by state law to maintain a public law library for the benefit of the general public.

Large libraries may contain many additional materials covering topics like legal education, research, and writing; the history of the American legal system and profession; the history behind certain high-profile cases; techniques of oral argument; and the legislative history of important federal and state statutes. In contrast, a small law library, at a minimum, may contain only one unofficial Supreme Court reporter, selected West national reporters and digests specific to the state in which the library is located, the United States Code, a few state-specific reporters and statutory compilations (if they exist for a particular state), and several state-specific treatises and practice guides.

A typical law library will include in its collection a large number of works including the various *code* references:

Online Research

In recent years, the advent of online legal research outlets such as Findlaw, Westlaw, LexisNexis, HeinOnline has reduced the need for some types of printed compilations. A number of law libraries have therefore reduced the availability of printed works that can easily be found on the Internet, and have increased their own Internet availability.

Many law librarians and academics have commented on the changing system of legal information delivery - brought about by the rapid growth of the Internet as a legal resource. A law professor recently wrote that the "primacy of the old paper sets [printed law reports] is fading, and a vortex of conflicting claims and products is spinning into place."

You have already learned the Internet is a vast resource for your online reference library. Hopefully, you have bookmarked or made notes on the sites you found interesting and useful. Findlaw, Westlaw, LexisNexis, Hein Online are the largest and best known of the online research systems. Large law firms carry both systems, plus many colleges have them. Most colleges, law libraries and law offices use them. They are not all free services though students are usually given a discount or you may visit a law library to access their online services. You will find some guest or free options on many of the subscriber sites

Cornell Law School Legal Information Institute publishes a vast amount of state and federal legal materials. We will be using Cornell's citation section as we explore that subject.

www.law.cornell.edu/

Government Printing Office (GPO) provides access to the Federal Register, Code of Federal Regulations, and the Congressional Record. Massachusetts (links to federal, state, SEC, GPO) can be found on

www.sociallaw.com

California	**https://www.courts.ca.gov/**
General sources	www.law.cornell.edu/
State statutes	www.findlaw.com/ (scroll down to State Laws under US map)
Federal Opinions	www.georgetown.edu (search for Bluebook Guide for Citing Cases and Opinions)

Reporters and Reports

State laws and constitutions are found in volumes known as "general laws." If one of these laws is challenged in court, the decision of the judge interpreting the law is reported in a series of books called "reporters."

Official law reports or reporters contain publications to provide authoritative, consistent, and authentic statements of a jurisdiction's primary law. Official case law publishing may be carried out by a government agency, or by a commercial entity. Unofficial law reports are not officially sanctioned and are published as a commercial enterprise.

For the publishers of unofficial reports to maintain a competitive advantage over the official ones, usually provide helpful research aids (e.g., summaries, indexes), like the editorial enhancements used in the West American Digest System. Some commercial publishers also provide court opinions in searchable online databases that are part of larger fee-based, online legal research systems, such as Westlaw and Lexis-Nexis.

Unofficially published court opinions are also often published before the official opinions, so lawyers and law journals must cite the unofficial report until the case comes out in the official version. When a court opinion is officially published, case citation rules usually require a citation (citing a report for a case in progress) from the official reports.

1. Case Opinions (Case Law)

In law, an *opinion* (also known as a *consilia*) is usually a written explanation by a judge or group of judges that accompanies an order or ruling in a case, laying out the rationale and legal principles for the ruling.

Opinions are usually published at the direction of the court, and to the extent they contain pronouncements about what the law is and how it should be interpreted, they reinforce, change, establish, or overturn legal precedent. If a court decides that an opinion should be published, the opinion is included in a volume from a series of books called *law reports* as just discussed. Published opinions of courts are also collectively referred to as *case law*, which is one of the major sources of law in common law legal systems.

In the United Kingdom and other common law countries, a legal opinion also refers to written legal advice on a point of law issued by either a barrister (often referred to as "counsel's opinion") or occasionally a senior government law officer, such as an attorney general. The latter form of opinion is sometimes made available to the public either because of public pressure or because a general clarification of the law is called for. In the United States, several state attorneys general issue attorney general's opinions.

Several areas of commercial practice call for formal legal opinions of counsel. The Legal Aid scheme in the United Kingdom requires a legal opinion showing reasonable prospects for success before the Legal Aid board will fund any claim. Insurance policies for professional negligence will frequently require an opinion of counsel before the insurer is required to pay out on any putative claim (sometimes called a QC [Queen's Counsel] clause, when it must be an opinion of leading counsel).

Not every case decided by a higher court results in the publication of an opinion; in fact most cases do not, since an opinion is usually only published when the law is being interpreted in a novel way, or the case is a high-profile matter of general public interest and the court wishes to make the details of its ruling public.

In the majority of American cases, the judge issues what is called a *memorandum decision* that explains how state or federal law applies to the case and affirms or reverses the decision of the lower court. A memorandum decision *does not* establish legal precedent or re-interpret the law, and cannot be invoked in subsequent cases to justify a ruling. Opinions, on the other hand, *always* establish a particular legal interpretation.

We will review two case opinions, Case Number 1, is rather well known, Roe *v. Wade*.

Roe v. Wade, 410 U.S. 113 (1973) was a landmark decision by the United States Supreme Court on the issue of abortion. The Court held that the constitutional right to privacy extends to a woman's decision to have an abortion, but that right must be balanced against the state's two legitimate interests for regulating abortions: protecting prenatal life and protecting the mother's health. Noting that these state interests become stronger over the course of a pregnancy, the Court resolved this balancing test by tying state regulation of abortion to the mother's current trimester of pregnancy:

- In the first trimester, the state's two interests in regulating abortions are at their weakest, and so the state cannot restrict a woman's right to an abortion in any way.

- In the second trimester, there is an increase in the risks that an abortion poses to maternal health, and so the state may regulate the abortion procedure only "in ways that are reasonably related to maternal health" (defined in the companion case of *Doe v. Bolton*).

- In the third trimester, there is an increase in viability rates and a corresponding greater state interest in prenatal life, and so the state can choose to restrict or proscribe abortion as it sees fit ("except where it is necessary, in appropriate medical judgment, for the preservation of the life or health of the mother").

Here is how the citation appears:

Full case: *Jane Roe, et al. v. Henry Wade*, District Attorney of Dallas County.

Citations: 410 U.S. 113 (more), 93 S. Ct. 705;35 L. Ed. 2d 147; 1973 U.S. LEXIS 159

Prior History: *Judgment for plaintiffs, injunction denied*; 314 F. Supp. 1217 (N.D. Tex. 1970); *probable jurisdiction noted*, 402 U.S. 941, (1971); *set for reargument* 408 U.S. 919 (1972)

Subsequent: *Rehearing denied*, 419 U.S. 959 (1973)

Argument: Oral argument

Holding: Texas law making it a crime to assist a woman to get an abortion violated her due process rights. U.S. district Court for the Northern District of Texas affirmed in part, reversed in part.

Chief Justice: Warren E. Burger, Associate Justices: William O. Douglas, William J. Brennan, Jr., Potter Stewart, Byron White, Thurgood Marshall, Harry Blackmun, Lewis F. Powell, Jr., William Rehnquist.

Majority: Blackmun, joined by Burger, Douglas, Brennan, Stewart, Marshall, Powell. Concurrence: Burger, Douglas, Stewart.

Dissent: White, joined by Rehnquist, Rehnquist

Laws Applied: US. Const. Amend. XIV; Tex. Code Crim. Proc. arts. 1191-94, 1196

CASE HISTORY

In September 1969, Norma L. McCorvey discovered she was pregnant. She returned to Dallas, where friends advised her to assert falsely that she had been raped, because then she could obtain a legal abortion (with the understanding that Texas' anti-abortion laws allowed abortion in the cases of rape and incest). This attempt failed, as there was no police report documenting alleged rape. She then attempted to obtain an illegal abortion, but was unable to do so. Eventually, she was referred to attorneys Linda Coffee and Sarah Weddington.

In 1970, her attorneys filed suit in a U.S. District Court in Texas. At the time, McCorvey was no longer claiming her pregnancy was the result of rape, and she later acknowledged she had lied earlier about having been raped. The defendant in the case was Dallas County District Attorney, Henry Wade, representing the State of Texas.

You now see why the case is referred to as *Roe v. Wade*.

The district court ruled in McCorvey's favor on the merits, but declined to grant an injunction (an injunction is an equitable remedy in the form of a court order, whereby a party is required to do, or to refrain from doing, certain acts) against the enforcement of the laws barring abortion. The district court's decision was based upon the Ninth Amendment, and the court also relied upon a concurring opinion by Justice Arthur Goldberg in the 1965 Supreme Court case of *Griswold v. Connecticut*, regarding a right to use contraceptives. Note: This is a good example of reviewing and citing precedent). Few state laws proscribed contraceptives in 1965 when the Griswold case was decided, whereas abortion was widely proscribed by state laws in the early 1970s.

Roe v. Wade ultimately reached the U.S. Supreme Court on appeal. Following a first round of arguments, Justice Harry Blackmun drafted a preliminary opinion that emphasized what he saw as the Texas law's vagueness. Justices William Rehnquist and Lewis F. Powell, Jr. joined the Supreme Court too late to hear the first round of arguments. Therefore, Chief Justice Warren Burger proposed that the case be reargued; this took place on October 11, 1972. Weddington continued to represent Roe, and Texas Assistant Attorney General Robert C. Flowers stepped in to replace Wade. Justice William O. Douglas threatened to write a dissent from the reargument order, but was coaxed out of the action by his colleagues, and his dissent was merely mentioned in the reargument order without further statement or opinion.

The court issued its decision on January 22, 1973, with a 7 to 2 majority vote in favor of McCorvey. Burger and Douglas' concurring opinion and White's dissenting opinion were issued separately, in the companion case of *Doe v. Bolton*.

The rationale and legal principles for the decision and the opinion include:

The Roe Court deemed abortion a fundamental right under the United States Constitution, thereby subjecting all laws attempting to restrict it to the standard of strict scrutiny. The opinion of the Roe Court, written by Justice Harry Blackmun, declined to adopt the district court's Ninth Amendment rationale, and instead asserted that the "right of privacy, whether it be founded in the Fourteenth Amendment's concept of personal liberty and restrictions upon state action, as we feel it is, or, as the District Court determined, in the Ninth Amendment's reservation of rights to the people, is broad enough to encompass a woman's decision whether or not to terminate her pregnancy." Stewart in his concurring opinion from the companion case *Doe v. Bolton*, stated more emphatically that, "The Ninth Amendment obviously does not create federally enforceable rights." Thus, the Roe majority rested its opinion squarely on the Constitution's due process clause (*due process* is the principle that the government must respect all of the legal rights that are owed to a person according to the law. Due process holds the government subservient to the law of the land, protecting individual persons from the state).

As you read through the case history and the deliberation process, you can see how the judges arrived at their decision.

The next Case for review is *Doe v. Kohn*

The heading on the legal documents in the case appear as follows:

862 F.Supp. 1310

John DOE, Esquire (Pseudonym for an attorney)

And

Equal Employment Opportunity Commission,

Plaintiff-Intervenor

v.

KOHN, NAST & GRAF, P.C. d/b/a Kohn Klein

Nast & Graf, P.C. and Kohn Savett

Klein Graf, P.C., Harold E. Kohn, and Steven, Asher, Defendants

Civ. A. No: 93-4510

United States District Court, E.D. Pennsylvania. Aug. 4, 1994

As Amended Sept. 2, 1994

CASE SCENARIO

An attorney infected with Human Immunodeficiency Virus (HIV), filed action against his former employer claiming that he was terminated because of the infection. On the employer's motion for summary judgment, the District Court, Gawthrop, J., held:

- fact remains as to whether attorney was terminated in retaliation for engaging in protected activity in violation of Americans with Disabilities Act (ADA) precluding summary judgment on ADA retaliatory discharge claims;

- fact as to whether termination of attorney constituted violation of ADA as discriminatory discharge precluding summary judgment;

- fact that attorney had physical or mental impairment that substantially limited one of his major life activities, and thus had disability within the meaning of ADA;

- fact remains that attorney was regarded as having impairment within the meaning of ADA precluded summary judgment on ADA discrimination claim;

- fact remains that attorney was terminated in order to deprive attorney of participation in law firm's disability program precluding summary judgment on attorney's Employee Retirement Income Security Act (ERISA) claim; and firing of attorney did not constitute intentional infliction of emotional distress.

Defendant's motion for summary judgment, involves a lawyer infected with the HIV who claims that his law firm fired him because of his infection.

Plaintiff's First Amended Complaint alleges that the defendants violated a number of federal and state statutes;

Title 1 of the Americans with Disabilities Act, 42 U.S.C. § 12101, et seq. [ADA], as amended by the Civil Rights Act of 1991;

42 U.S.C. § 1981a; section 510 of the Employee Retirement Income § 1314 Security Act of 1974, 29 U.S.C. § 1140 [ERISA]; the Pennsylvania Human Relations Act, 43 Pa.S. § 955 [PHRA];

the Pennsylvania Wage Payment and Collection Law, 43 P.S. § 260.5, Act of July 14, 1961, P.L. § 5.

The complaint also alleged a cause of action for breach of contract, breach of the implied covenant of good faith and fair dealing, invasion of privacy, defamation, intentional infliction of emotional distress, and civil conspiracy.

Defendants sought summary judgment on all claims. Under Federal Rule of Civil Procedure 56(c), summary judgment is proper if "there is no genuine issue as to any material fact and ... the moving party is entitled to judgment as a matter of law." The inquiry for the court is "whether the evidence presents a sufficient disagreement to require submission to a jury or whether it is so one-sided that one party must prevail as a matter of law."

The relationship between the plaintiff and the defendants began in July 1991, when plaintiff was hired under contract to work for the Kohn firm. He spent most of his time working for Steven Asher, Esquire. Things seemed to be working out well. Mr. Asher gave the plaintiff a lot of responsibility, and often praised his work. Six months after he arrived, the shareholders voted the plaintiff a $3,500 bonus, $1000 more than he was expecting. Apparently, the year 1992 went well also. In order to terminate the plaintiff's contract, the firm was required to give him ninety days written notice by October 1; it did not do so.

Plaintiff alleged that the situation began to change after the Fall of 1992, when he learned that he was HIV-infected. He had a high fever, lost weight, and developed a dry, scaly skin condition. He contacted several physicians. Some members of the firm's support staff wondered aloud whether he had acquired AIDS.

On November 25, 1992, plaintiff received a letter from one of the physicians he had contacted, John Bartlett, M.D. The letter was written on stationery, the letterhead of which contained the words "Infectious Diseases" and "AIDS Services." This letter must have sparked the controversy among the staff at Kohn, Nast & Graf, feeling one of their staff members, had the AIDS virus.

The plaintiff contends that just days after he received this letter, defendant Asher stopped assigning him work, stopped speaking with him, and avoided physical contact with DOE.

The next year, the Kohn firm did not give the plaintiff a pay raise. On January 13, 1993, Mr. Asher told the plaintiff that he had not met expectations, and that the firm had decided not to renew his contract for 1994. The Kohn firm disputed the accuracy of the discussion with plaintiff regarding his employment status. In addition, Mr. Asher informed Doe that after working with him for roughly 18 months, he came to the conclusion that Doe's work was substantially below the acceptable level of work required by the firm.

Plaintiff also alleges that at this juncture the defendants tried to nudge him out by assigning him work that was beneath his abilities, reassigning his secretary to another attorney, taking away his computer, and conducting meetings without including him, among other minor and not-so-minor indignities. Plaintiff says he tried to bring his concerns to the attention of the firm management, but they did nothing. Finally, plaintiff contacted an attorney and, on March 8, 1993, sent a box of materials from Kohn, Nast & Graf in Philadelphia to his then-lawyer's office in Washington, D.C. The Kohn firm's administrator asked about the contents of the box, Plaintiff says he avoided a direct answer by jokingly stating "what do you think a bomb or something?" Shortly thereafter, the administrator warned the plaintiff that if he sued the firm, Harold Kohn, and Dianne Nast would "blackball" him in Philadelphia.

On March 11, 1993, the plaintiff traveled to Washington, D.C. Upon his return to the firm the next day, he found the contents of his office boxed up, and the locks on his office changed. The firm administrator, and Harold Kohn demanded that he return his key, and office pass. Plaintiff says he was fired; the defendants say he left on his own accord. On August 19, 1993, plaintiff sued both the firm, and Steven Asher.

CAUSE FOR COMPLAINT: Intentional Infliction of Emotional Distress

The claim for intentional infliction of emotional distress was against defendant Steven Asher, only. Under Pennsylvania law, a claim for intentional infliction of emotional distress is viable only if premised on conduct to be "so outrageous in character and so extreme in degree, as to go beyond all possible bounds of decency, and to be regarded as atrocious, and utterly intolerable in a civilized community."

Plaintiff suggests that defendant Steven Asher acted in an outrageous manner by failing to renew Doe's contract for 1994 because he believed him to be HIV-positive, and that he did so in various ways: By disseminating false, and defamatory information to conceal his discriminatory purpose; by taking steps to force DOE to voluntarily leave the firm; and then, by retaliating against him by abruptly terminating DOE on March 12, 1993, and threatening to forcibly remove him from the premises of Kohn, Nast & Graf. Even if the jury were to find all this to be the case, it would establish only that the defendant's role in the plaintiff's firing stemmed from an "improper motive" which is not sufficient to support a claim of intentional infliction of emotional distress.

See also *Doe v. William Shapiro, Esquire, P.C.* 852 F. Supp. 1246 (E.D. Pa 1994).

PUNITIVE DAMAGES

Plaintiff requested punitive damages as part of the "relief." Defendants contested plaintiff's claim that he was entitled to punitive damages under the ADA, the PHRA, the invasion of privacy, the defamation, the civil conspiracy, the breach of contract, and the breach of the duty of good faith, and fair dealing counts. With respect to the contract claims, plaintiff had conceded that punitives do not lie as to contracts. Tr. of July 11, 1994 at 106-107. Defendants' quarrel over punitives for remaining counts is that their behavior was not sufficiently egregious. That was an issue of fact for the jury to decide.

In the above case, here is the citation.

CASE CITATION:

Doe v. Hohn, Nast & Graf, 862 F. Supp. 1310 (E.D. Pa. 1994)

PROCEDURAL FACTS

Defendant-employer's motion for summary judgment
granted-in-part and denied-in-part

SUBSTANTIVE FACTS

Plaintiff, Doe, was hired under contract as an associate attorney with the defendant law firm in July 1991. After six months, Mr. Doe was given substantial responsibilities, and received praise, including a bonus, for his work. Mr. Doe alleged that after learning that he was HIV–positive, his work environment deteriorated. Physically, he began showing signs of illness, including weight loss and dry, scaly skin. On November 25, 1992, Mr. Doe received a letter from his doctor (presumably at Mr. Doe's place of employment) on stationery with a letterhead containing the words "Infectious Diseases," and "AIDS services."

In January 1993, Mr. Doe did not receive a raise, and was told that his work was not meeting the firm's expectations. Finally, he was advised that his contract would not be renewed. At this time, Mr. Doe claimed that the firm gave him simple work, reassigned his secretary, took away his computer, and did not include him in firm meetings.

Mr. Doe then contacted an attorney to prosecute a disability discrimination case against the firm, sending him materials from the office. The mailing was discovered, and the contents examined by the firm's administrator. Mr. Doe was fired on March 11, 1993, after returning from a trip to his then-lawyer's office in Washington, DC.

ISSUES

Did Mr. Doe present evidence regarding the alleged retaliation by the firm for his engaging in protected activity under the Americans With Disabilities Act?

Is HIV–positive status protected under the Americans With Disabilities Act?

Was a firm partner liable for intentional infliction of emotional distress because Mr. Doe's contract was not renewed upon the grounds that he was HIV–positive?

HOLDINGS – AS TO ABOVE THREE ISSUES

Yes

REASONING

Pursuant to 42 U.S.C. § 12203, no person shall discriminate against any individual because that individual has made a charge of discrimination. Making such a charge is therefore "protected activity," and to be discriminated against for doing so, raises a claim of retaliation by the employer. In this case however, the judge explained that to establish a *prima facie* (on the face of it) case of retaliation, a plaintiff must show that (1) s/he engaged in "protected activity; (2) s/he was discharged after, or near the time of the activity; and (3) a link exists between the activity, and the discharge, i.e., the employee was fired because of engaging in the protected activity.

Here, the judge concluded that contacting an attorney for advice, and representation was protected activity under the statute. The judge then found sufficient evidence to support a conclusion that Mr. Doe was fired because of his contacts with his attorney. In particular, the judge pointed to the firm administrator's comment that if he sued the firm, he would be "blackballed," and that the firm, after learning of Mr. Doe's contacts, decided to ask him to leave.

The judge discussed whether HIV–status qualified as a disability under The ADA. Under the ADA, a plaintiff must demonstrate that (1) the Disability was protected; (2) he was qualified for the job; and, (3) that he was terminated. Here the judge noted that Mr. Doe was qualified for the job, and that he was discharged due to his condition. The key inquiry, however, was whether the HIV–infected status constituted a condition covered by the ADA. Applying the definition of "disability" contained in the statute, 42 U.S.C. § 12102(2), found that having HIV, at least as it had manifested in Mr. Doe, was covered.

First, Mr. Doe's high fever, and skin disorder were considered as "physical impairments" under the statute, and its implementing regulations. Second, the condition impaired a "major life activity" because HIV affected Mr. Doe's ability to procreate, which was within the plain meaning of the statute's definition of "disability." Accordingly, HIV–positive status constituted a "physical impairment" under the statute, and regulations.

SUMMATION

Mr. Doe failed to state a claim for damages under the tort (any wrongful act that does not involve a breach of contract, and for which a civil suit can be brought) of intentional infliction of emotional distress. Under Pennsylvania law, a claim for intentional infliction of emotional distress can succeed only if the complained-of conduct is "so outrageous in character, and so extreme in degree, as to go beyond all possible bounds of decency, and to be regarded as atrocious, and utterly intolerable ..." *Cox v. Keystone Carbon Luzerne County Community College*, 861 F, 2d 390 (3rd Cir. 1988). In this case, the judge concluded that the partner dismissing Mr. Doe, even though he may have done so for an improper motive, did not engage in "outrageous conduct;" even with threats to forcibly remove Mr.

Doe from his office, thus did not rise to the level of intentional infliction of emotional distress.

Please enter *Doe v. Shapiro* into a search engine. See what references you can find related to this similar case.

Read through that case or any that you are able to find that relate to our case and note the citations to other cases that are supportive in the arguments. For example:

> (5) The importance of the precluded evidence in light of the failure to comply." *Id.* (citation omitted). The trial court can impose no more "severe sanction" than dismissing the lawsuit. *Croydon Plastics, Inc. v. Lower Bucks Cooling & Heating*, 698 A.2d 625, 629 (Pa. Super. 1997). [*8] Therefore, dismissal is only appropriate where after "balancing the equities," the court concludes that "the violation [of the discovery rules] is willful and the opposing party has been prejudiced." *Estate of Ghaner v. Bindi*, 2001 PA Super 195, 779 A.2d 585, 589 (Pa. Super. 2001).

LAW AND LEGAL REASONING

Remember that in U.S. society, the "ideal" reflects a set of values called the "rule of law." As a matter of principle, Americans tend to believe that the coercive powers of government should be limited by law (and relating back to the Constitution, where "no person shall ... be deprived of life, liberty, or property, without due process of law."). Much of what the government does, of course, deprives people of life, liberty, or property. For example, a court's judgment may require one person to pay money, or transfer property to someone else, may incarcerate a person, or otherwise restrict her/his freedom, and, harsh as it may sound, even exact the death penalty. In any instance, the rule of law requires coercion to be used by state, or federal officials only when, and as authorized by the standards of law.

Consequently, people want to know by what right someone sitting behind a bench or standing behind a badge uses the state's power to deprive them of life, liberty, and pursuit of happiness. In most instances, we may confront a legal problem with conflicting instincts. On the other hand, we may try to solve it as required by the formalistic version of the *rule of law*. At the same time, we may rely on whatever intuitions and former experience we have mustered regarding nonlegal causes of legal decisions. Sometimes, it is confusing to determine how a judge has decided.

In the "scales of justice," law provides competing reasons that must be weighed. A criminal law case, for example, contains the *charge* with the components of *mitigating and aggravating*, circumstances. The court must decide under what sanctions, the *perpetrator* will be sentenced.

The chief feature of legal reasoning is that it is used in the process of anticipating or settling disputes of every nature. Every society develops methods for settling persistent disputes among its members. Therefore, different methods are employed by different societies in different times and places. Sometimes disputes in developed societies can be settled, if need be, by appealing to judges to apply the law. Generally, this method is better than the alternatives as disputes should be settled with finality in peaceful and justifiable ways. Dispute settlement by law is more peaceful than duels or feuds after all. Adjudication is however, more public, accountable and revisable in cases of error. It becomes obvious that law, and legal reasoning enable judges to reach final, peaceful, and justifiable dispute settlements.

We have discussed precedents: "what happened in a given case, and how that process and result affects the current case under review." In law, the doctrine of precedent gives a special status as established points to law cases decided in the past by the highest court in the relevant jurisdiction. The U.S. legal system includes a federal jurisdiction in which federal courts are primarily responsible for matters of national interest. The U.S. Supreme Court is the highest court for these matters. It also includes fifty state jurisdictions in which state courts carry primary responsibility for most other matters. Remember that the cases decided in the past by the highest court of appeals or Supreme Court are the most authoritative precedents for deciding future cases within their respective jurisdictions.

Deductive legal reasoning, however, is most closely associated with reasoning from enacted law (usually consists of general rules). These rules are found in a variety of official legal documents, such as constitutions, statutes, codes, regulations, and executive orders.

Deductive legal reasoning differs from analogical legal reasoning in a number of ways. First, reasoning starts from a rule, not a case. Rules are enacted before cases governed by the rule have materialized. Second, the principle of legislative supremacy generally requires judges to play a subordinate role to the more democratic branches of government. Courts however, have no authority to reformulate enacted rules as the case law interpreting the rules unfolds. Third, the static statement of enacted rules leads legal reasoning from such rules to focus heavily on problems of rule interpretation.

Casting legal arguments in the deductive form serves a number of valuable functions. Legal rules establish the framework of law within a legal system, setting up an elaborate classification scheme that specifies the conclusions that judges might reach in determining decisions. Reasoning from settled rules makes law manageable, simply by transforming vague questions of what is "just" into more concrete questions that are often less controversial.

On the other hand, deductive legal reasoning can be highly misleading; it may seem that the rules dictate the result in a case when this is not so. Both analogical legal reasoning and deductive reasoning do not avoid the need to judge importance.

APPLYING CASE LAW

Google (or use your preferred search engine) for *Mohr v Williams*. The citation is:

Mohr v. Williams, 95 Minn. 261, 104 N.W. 12 (1905)

Here is a summary of the facts in the case:

www.lawnix.com/cases/mohr-williams.html

See what you are able to locate on the reasoning and conclusions of that case.

Now try this one: *Coblyn v. Kennedy's Inc.*, 359 Mass. 319, 268 N.E. 2d 860 (1971). Google Scholar (a nifty subsearch tool) will provide you several sites for review. It deals with charges of false imprisonment and emotional distress.

Note the citations used to shore up the case.

The pivotal question before us as in most cases of this character is whether the evidence shows that there were reasonable grounds for the detention. At common law in an action for false imprisonment, the defense of probable cause, as measured by the prudent and cautious man standard, was available to a merchant.

Standish v. Narragansett S.S. Co. 111 Mass. 512, 517

Jacques v. Childs Dining Hall Co. 244 Mass. 438, 439

Muniz v. Mehlman, 327 Mass. 353, 358

In enacting G.L.c. 231, § 94B, the Legislature inserted the words, "reasonable grounds." Historically, the words "reasonable grounds" and "probable 324*324 cause" have been given the same meaning by the courts. In the case of *United States v. Walker*, 246 F.2d 519, 526 (7th Cir.) it was said: "Probable cause' and 'reasonable grounds' are concepts having virtually the same meaning."

The following cases have expressly stated that the words may be used interchangeably and without distinction. *Draper v. United States*, 358 U.S. 307, 310. *United States v. Vasquez*, 183 F. Supp. 190, 193 (E.D.N.Y.). *Smallwood v. Commonwealth*, 305 Ky. 520, 524. *McKeon v. National Cas. Co.* 216 Mo. App. 507, 524. *Adams v. State*, 137 Tex. Cr. 43, 46. *Stelloh v. Liban*, 21 Wis.2d 119, 125.

In the case of *Lukas v. J.C. Penney Co., supra*, at p. 361, the Oregon Supreme Court construed the meaning of the words "reasonable grounds" in its "shoplifting statute" as having the same meaning as they have in a statute authorizing arrest without a warrant and applied the probable cause standard to the facts before it.

Now assume that you've done the research and briefed the two sample cases noted above. Your task now is to apply the law you've learned from those cases to the actual controversy that prompted the legal research.

The Doe versus Hohn decision may be relevant to persons suffering from long-term illnesses who are terminated from employment because of their condition. The illness does not necessarily have to be AIDS-related of course. For example, an employee with multiple sclerosis (MS) may argue, in a case where s/he was terminated from employment, that the AIDS-related fact pattern in Doe's case is similar, or analogous, enough to be applicable to the claim of wrongful dismissal.

Here are two other case scenarios using the sample case(s) mentioned above.

FIRST SCENARIO

Mr. Goble has made an appointment and comes to your office. He plans to sue his physician, Dr. Marvel, for the tort of battery, the "intentional offensive touching of one's person." Mr. Goble reports that he underwent surgery to have his nose made somewhat less prominent. While Mr. Goble was under anesthesia, Dr. Marvel noted that Mr. Goble's ears stuck out a little too far and performed a procedure to correct that defect. The surgery was successful. However, after Mr. Goble had his bandages removed, he was horrified at the change in his ears since he believed that others considered his "Clark Gable ears" to be distinguished. He then threatened to sue for "battery." In response to the threat to sue for battery, the doctor noted that Mr. Goble stated just before the operation, he "wanted to be made handsome," and, therefore, had granted permission for the ear procedure. Permission, or "informed consent," Dr. Marvel rightly noted, is a defense to battery.

SECOND SCENARIO

Ms. Bopp arrives in your office and makes arrangements to sue "Babes-R-Us." According to Ms. Bopp, while shopping at Babes-R-Us, she placed a toy bear that was for sale in her pocketbook. Apparently, store security observed her actions. She returned the bear a little later, but had a similar one in her pocketbook. After paying for other purchases, Ms. Bopp stopped before leaving the store, entering a small room beside the cash register. As she attempted to leave, the security guard restrained her. The guard opened her pocketbook, and discovered the bear. He then accused Ms. Bopp of shoplifting. She denied the charge and was able to show the guard a receipt for the bear.

Ms. Bopp wants to sue Babes-R-Us for false arrest.

Review the cases we abstracted and think about how you would use the research and the information we have already discovered so that you can decide how those citations might work in your cases with Goble and Bopp. Now you would begin to make your notes and commence with your reasoning and citation.

CASE BRIEFING

As we have earlier noted opinions may be quite lengthy or may discuss issues not relevant to your research. Most often your supervising attorney will ask that you brief these opinions to allow for their efficient review or to have a permanent condensed record of the case.

Case briefing can best be described as "idiosyncratic," meaning "a distinctive ability" to which every attorney, as well as every paralegal utilizes her/his own method and style. All case briefs should contain certain information to ensure their utility for the attorney. In essence, remember that the purpose of a brief is just that – to *briefly summarize* the important points of a case. A case brief is rarely more than two pages in length. If by chance, a brief rambles longer, it may be easier for the attorney just to read the opinion itself.

Case briefs should both alert an attorney to relevant law that should be reviewed, and refresh the memory of both the attorney, and/or the legal assistant regarding an opinion. Generally, all case briefs should contain the following elements:

case citation

facts—procedural history

facts—substantive

issues

holdings or results

QUESTIONS CHAPTER 8A-1

True/False

1. A code is a type of legislation designed to cover a system of laws or a particular area of law as it existed at the time the code was enacted. T/F

2. Legal research is performed only by attorneys. T/F

3. Findlaw, Westlaw, LexisNexis, HeinOnline are library research books. T/F

4. The decision of a judge interpreting the law is reported in a series of books called "reporters." T/F

5. Official case law publishing may be carried out by a government agency, or by a commercial entity. T/F

6. an *opinion* is usually a written explanation by a judge relating to a ruling in a case.

7. All cases decided by a higher court are published in a recorder. T/F

8. A *memorandum decision* always reverses the decision of the lower court. T/F

9. Opinions *always* establish a particular legal interpretation. T/F

10. Rose v. Wade was a famous New York District Court Case. T/F

11. 410 U.S. 113 (more), 93 S. Ct. 705;35 L. Ed. 2d 147; 1973 U.S. LEXIS 159 is a citation. T/F

12. Henry Wade was Roe's attorney. T/F

13. In Roe v. Wade, the Court deemed abortion a fundamental right under the United States Constitution. T/F

14. *Due process* is the principle that the government must respect all of the legal rights that are owed to a person according to the law. T/F

15. Due process holds the government subservient to the law of the land, protecting individual persons from the state. T/F

Select the Correct Answer

16. Doe v. Kahn was a case alleging:
    a. Breach of contract
    b. Discrimination
    c. Invasion of privacy
    d. All of the above

17. The chief feature of legal reasoning is that it is used to:

a. Weigh the scales of justice

b. Deprive criminals of their freedom

c. Settle disputes

d. Establish precedents

18. The most authoritative precedents come from:

a. State superior courts

b. Supreme Court

c. Justice Court

d. Circuit Court

19. Law incorporated from usage and custom is called

a. administrative

b. statutory

c. civil

d. common

20. Case briefing entails:

a. Summarizing legal opinions

b. Briefly summarize the important points of a case

c. Detailing law to prove the case

d. Preparing a brief

21. Case briefs should contain:

a. Facts

b. Issues

c. Holdings

d. All of the above

2. Citators

The literal meaning of citator would be "one who citates." A more common word is "cite." In legal research, a *citator* is a citation index of legal resources, one of the best-known of which in the United States is Shepard's Citations. Given a reference of a legal decision, a citator allows a researcher to find newer documents which cite the original document and thus to reconstruct the judicial history of cases and statutes. Using a citator in this way is colloquially referred to as "Shepardizing."

There are two types of citations: proprietary and public domain citations. There are many citation guides; the most commonly acknowledged is called the Bluebook, published by student-run law reviews at several eminent law schools, namely *Columbia Law Review*, *Harvard Law Review*, *University of Pennsylvania Law Review* and *Yale Law Journal*. Public domain citations are those which refer to the official reporters, rather than a publication service such as Westlaw, LexisNexis, particular legal journals, or specialization-specific reporters.

Many court decisions are published by more than one reporter. A citation to two or more reporters for a given court decision is called a "parallel citation." For U.S. Supreme Court decisions, there are several unofficial reporters, including the Supreme Court Reporter (S. Ct.) and United States Supreme Court Reports, Lawyers' Edition (commonly known simply as Lawyer's Edition) (L. Ed.), which are printed by private companies and provide further annotations to the opinions of the Court. Although a citation to the latter two is not required, some attorneys and legal writers prefer to cite all three case reporters at once:

Griswold v. Connecticut, 381 U.S. 479, 85 S. Ct. 1678, 14 L. Ed. 2d 510 (1965)

The "2d" after the L. Ed. signifies the second series of the Lawyers' Edition. United States case reporters are sequentially numbered, but the volume number is never higher than 999. When the 1,000th volume is reached (the threshold in earlier years was lower), the volume number is reset to 1 and a "2d" is appended after the reporter's abbreviation. Some case reporters are in their third series, and a few are approaching their fourth.

Some very old Supreme Court cases have odd-looking citations, such as *Marbury v. Madison*, 5 U.S. (1 Cranch) 137 (1803). The "(1 Cranch)" refers to the fact that, before there was a reporter series known as the United States Reports compiled by the Supreme Court's Reporter of Decisions, cases were gathered, bound together, and sold privately by the Court's Reporter of Decisions. In this example, Marbury was first reported in an edition by William Cranch, who was responsible for publishing Supreme Court reports from 1801 to 1815. Such reports, named for the individual who gathered them and hence called "nominative reports," existed from 1790 to 1874.

In 1874, the U.S. government created the United States Reports, and at the same time simultaneously numbered the volumes previously published privately as part of a single series and began numbering sequentially from that point.

When a case has been decided, but not yet published in the case reporter, the citation may note the volume but leave blank the page of the case reporter until it is determined. For example, *Bowles v. Russell*, 551 U.S. ___ (2007).

Lower Federal Courts

United States *court of appeals* cases are published in the Federal Reporter (F., F.2d, or F.3d).

United States *district court cases* and cases from some specialized courts are published in the Federal Supplement (F. Supp. or F. Supp. 2d). Both are published by Thomson West; they are technically unofficial reporters, but have become widely accepted as the de facto "official" reporters of the lower federal courts because of the absence of a true official reporter. Only one court, the D.C. Circuit, has an official reporter, United States Court of Appeals Reports, and even that one is rarely used today.

State Courts Citators

State court decisions are published in several places. Many states have their own official state reporters, which publish decisions of one or more of that state's courts. Reporters that publish decisions of a state's highest court are abbreviated the same as the state's name (note: this is the traditional abbreviation, not the postal abbreviation), regardless of what the actual title of the reporter is. Thus, the official reporter of decisions of the California Supreme Court (titled California Reports) is abbreviated "Cal." (or for subsequent series, "Cal. 2d," "Cal. 3d" or "Cal. 4th").

> *Palsgraf v. Long Island R.R. Co.*, 248 N.Y. 339 (1928) - a case in the New York Court of Appeals, reported in New York Reports. (Note that the New York Court of Appeals is actually the highest court in New York.)

> *Green v. Chi. Tribune Co.*, 286 Ill. App. 3d 1 (App. Ct. 1996) - a case in the Illinois Appellate Court, reported in Illinois Appellate Court Reports. Note that, in contrast to New York, the Illinois Appellate Court is only the intermediate court of appeals in Illinois; decisions of the Illinois Supreme Court are reported in Illinois Reports, abbreviated "Ill." (or "Ill. 2d").

In addition to the official reporters, Thomson West publishes several series of "regional reporters" which cover several states. They are the North Eastern Reporter, Atlantic Reporter, South Eastern Reporter, Southern Reporter, South Western Reporter, North Western Reporter, and Pacific Reporter. California, Illinois, and New York also each have their own line of Thomson West reporters, because of the large volume of cases generated in those states (titled, respectively, *West's California Reporter*, *Illinois Decisions*, and *West's New York Supplement*). Some smaller states (like South Dakota) have stopped publishing their own official reporters, and instead have certified the appropriate West regional reporter as their "official" reporter.

When a case appears in both an official reporter and a regional reporter, either citation can be used. Generally, citing to the regional reporter is preferred, since nonresident (out-of-state) attorneys are more likely to have access to these. Many lawyers include both citations.

Like the United States Supreme Court, some very old state case citations include an abbreviation of the name of either the private publisher or the reporter of decisions, a state-appointed officer who originally collected and published the cases. For example, in *Hall v. Bell*, 47 Mass. (6 Met.) 431 (1843), the citation is to volume 47 of Massachusetts Reports, which, like United States Reports, was started in the latter half of the 19th century and incorporated a number of prior editions originally published privately into the series, and began numbering from that point; "6 Met." refers to the 6th volume that had originally been published privately by Theron Metcalf.

An example of a case cited to a reporter that has not been subsequently incorporated into an officially-published series is Pierson v. Post, 3 Cai. 175 (N.Y. Sup. Ct. 1804), reported in volume 3 of Caines' Reports, page 175, named for George Caines, who had been appointed to report New York cases; the case was before the New York Supreme Court of Judicature (now defunct). Most states gave up this practice in the mid- to late-1800s.

QUESTIONS – CHAPTER 8A-2

TRUE/FALSE

1. A *citator* is a citation index of legal resources.

2. Shephardizing is designed to review the entire case from the original document to the most recent.

3. The Bluebook is an example of a proprietary citator.

4. Court decisions are published by only one reporter.

5. Lawyers Edition is an unofficial reporter but is prohibited from reporting Supreme Court Decisions.

6. In the case *Marbury v. Madison*, 5 U.S. (1 Cranch) 137 (1803), Cranch refers to the district in which the case was heard.

7. When a case has been decided, but not yet published in the case reporter, the citation may note the volume but leave blank the page of the case reporter.

8. State court citators abbreviate the name of the stat, e.g., Cal. for California.

9. *Green v. Chi. Tribune Co.*, 286 Ill. App. 3d 1 (App. Ct. 1996 was a case heard in the Ohio State Court.

Choose OR insert the correct answer

10. North Eastern Reporter, Atlantic Reporter, South Eastern Reporter, Southern Reporter, South Western Reporter, are _____ reporters.
    a. Regional
    b. Public
    c. Private
    d. All of the above

11. State reporters contain
    (a) federal statutes
    (b) regional cases
    (c) federal cases
    (d) state statutes

12. Regional reporters contain:
    (a) county cases
    (b) federal cases)

    (c) federal statutes

    (d) state statutes

13. The United States Code (USC) contains

    (a) state statutes

    (b) federal statutes

    (c) county statutes

    (d) all of the above

14. The Code of Federal Regulations (CFR) has

    (a) state statutes

    (b) administrative laws

    (c) federal cases

    (d) federal statutes

15. Public domain citations refer to _____ reporters.

16. A citation to two or more reporters is termed a _____ citation.

17. In the case, *Griswold v. Connecticut*, 381 U.S. 479, 85 S. Ct. 1678, 14 L. Ed. 2d 510 (1965), the L. Ed. Is an abbreviation for _____.

B. CITATION

1. Overview

Case citation is the system used in many countries to identify the decisions in past court cases, either in special series of books called *reporters*, or in a *neutral form* which will identify a decision wherever it was reported. Although case citations are formatted differently in different jurisdictions, they generally contain the same key information.

Where cases are published in paper form the citation will usually contain:

- the title of the reports

- the volume number

- page number

- year of decision

Citation employs the use of a standard language that allows legal professionals to refer to legal authorities with sufficient precision that other lawyers or judges can follow the process. Secondly, it is a language, which uses abbreviations, and special terms. In the cases we have reviewed, you saw how the reasoning and logic followed with the facts and supportive case law citation. As you become an experienced reader of written law, you will learn to follow a line of argument through the use of citations.

When the legal research process is complete, citation follows. As one begins to research, notes are made to capture all the information needed, and citations are encountered which are either closely or loosely related to the research. The purpose of a citation is to provide a reference tool specifically pointing to the case under study. The citation contains various words, abbreviations, and numbers presented in a specific format allowing the reader to locate the cited material. Typical information in a citation includes the author, the name of the authority or source, and information about where it can be found. Subsequent users of that information should be able to discern the type, and degree of support provided by the citation for a particular set of circumstances. Citations establish that the research is well supported.

The purposes for the citation process are to identify a document(s) to which the author is referring, provide the reader with sufficient information to locate a document in sources to read where available, and furnish important additional information about the referenced materials in connection with the writer's philosophy and argument. The reader must then decide whether or not to pursue the particular related material and whether it relates to the case at hand.

Most decisions of courts are not published in printed law reports. The expense of typesetting and publishing them has limited the printed law reports to significant cases. Internet publishing of court decisions resulted in a flood of information. The result was that a medium-neutral citation system had to be adopted. This usually contains the following information:

- year of decision

- the abbreviated title of the court

- the decision number (not the court file number)

Rather than utilizing page numbers for *pin-point* references, (pointing to specific reporters) which would depend upon particular printers and browsers, pin-point quotes refer to paragraph numbers.

A growing number of court decisions are not published in case reporters. For example, only seven percent (7%) of the opinions of the California intermediate courts (the Courts of Appeal) are published each year. This is primarily because judges certify only significant decisions for publication, due to the massive number of frivolous appeals flowing through the courts and the importance of avoiding information overload. We might add that it is also in part because in many states, [especially California], the legislature has failed to expand the judiciary to keep up with population growth (political and fiscal reasons). To deal with their crushing caseloads, many judges prefer to write shorter-than-normal opinions that dispose of minor issues in a case using just a sentence or two. They avoid publishing these abbreviated opinions to avoid the risk of creating bad precedents.

Unpublished Decisions:

Attorneys have several options in citing "unpublished" decisions. For cases that have not been published or put into an electronic database, a citation to the case's docket number before the court that decided it is required. Example:

> *Groucho Marx Prods. v. Playboy Enters.*, No. 77 Civ. 1782 (S.D.N.Y. Dec. 30, 1977) - a decision of the U.S. District Court for the Southern District of New York; the docket number and specific date allow a researcher to track down the printed copy maintained by the court if needed (legal citation forms strongly prefer citations to traditional printed resources).

Cases which are intentionally left *officially unpublished* are still often "published" on computer services, such as LexisNexis and Westlaw. These services have their own citation formats based on the year of the case, an abbreviation indicating the computer service (or a specific database of that computer service), and a serial number (issued sequentially from 1 as documents are added to the database each year). Citations to online databases also usually include the case's docket number and the specific date on which it was decided (due to the preference for citation to traditional printed resources). Examples include:

> *Fuqua Homes, Inc. v. Beattie*, No. 03-3587, 2004 WL 2495842 (8th Cir. Nov. 8, 2004) - a case found on the Westlaw electronic database, decided by the U.S. Court of Appeals for the Eighth Circuit; the citation includes the case's original docket number (No. 03-3587), and a citation to the electronic database that indicates the year of decision, the database (WL for Westlaw) and a unique serial number in that database (2495842).

> *Chavez v. Metro*. Dist. Comm'n, No. 3:02CV458(MRK), 2004 U.S. Dist. LEXIS 11266 (D. Conn. June 1, 2004) - a case decided by the U.S. District Court for the District of Connecticut; the citation includes the case's original docket number (No. 3:02CV458(MRK)), the year of decision, the database (U.S. Dist. LEXIS, indicating the LexisNexis database for U.S. District Court cases), and a unique serial number in that database (11266).

Some court systems—such as the California state court system and the federal Court of Appeals for the Second, Seventh, and Ninth Circuits—forbid attorneys to cite unpublished cases as precedent. Other systems allow citation of unpublished cases only under specific circumstances. For example, in Kentucky, unpublished cases from that state's courts can only be cited if the case was decided after January 1, 2003 and "there is no published opinion that would adequately address the issue before the court." From 2004 to 2006, federal judges debated whether the Federal Rules of Appellate Procedure (FRAP) should be amended so that unpublished cases in all circuits could be cited as precedent. In 2006, the Supreme Court, over the objection of several hundred judges and lawyers, adopted a new Rule 32.1 of FRAP requiring that federal courts allow citation of unpublished cases. The rule took effect on January 1, 2007.

With the rise of the web, many courts placed new cases on various websites. Some were published while others never lost their "unpublished" status. Unfortunately, officially published sites from some vendors noted a copyright interest. As a result, the U.S. Supreme Court in *Feist Publications v. Rural Telephone Service* found that the mere alphabetical listing of telephone subscribers was an inadequate amount of effort to be sufficiently valid to claim a copyright on page numbering of court decisions. Thus, the copyright is probably not valid.)

This resulted in a *vendor-neutral citation movement* which led to provisions being made for citations to web-based cases and other legal materials. A few courts modified their rules to specifically take into account cases "published" on the web. An example of a vendor-neutral citation:

Equal. Found. of Greater Cincinnati, Inc. v. City of Cincinnati, 1997 FED App. 0318P (6th Cir.) - a 1997 case decided by the U.S. Court of Appeals for the Sixth Circuit; the citation to the numbering system adopted by the court ("1997 FED App. 0318P") eliminates the need to cite to a specific vendor's product, in this case Thomson West's Federal Reporter (i.e., 128 F.3d 289).

Pinpoint Citations

In practice, most lawyers go one step farther, once they have developed the correct citation for a case using the rules discussed above. Most court opinions contain holdings on multiple issues, so lawyers need to cite to the page that contains the *specific holding* they wish to invoke to support their own case. Such citations are known as pinpoint citations, "pin cites," or "jump cites."

For example, in Roe v. Wade, the U.S. Supreme Court held that the word "person" as used in the Fourteenth Amendment does not include the unborn. That particular holding appears on page 158 of the volume in which the Roe decision was published. A full pin cite to Roe for that holding would be as follows:

Roe v. Wade, 410 U.S. 113, 158 (1973).

And a parallel cite to all three U.S. Supreme Court reporters, combined with pin cites for all three, would produce:

Roe v. Wade, 410 U.S. 113, 158, 93 S. Ct. 705, 729, 35 L. Ed. 2d 147, 180 (1973).

But in its opinions, the Court usually provides a direct pin cite only to the official reporter. The two unofficial reporters, when they reprint the Court's opinions, add on parallel cites to each other, but do not add pin cites. Therefore, a citation to Roe v. Wade in a later Supreme Court decision as viewed on Lexis or Westlaw would appear as follows:

<u>Roe v. Wade</u>, 410 U.S. 113, 158, 93 S. Ct. 705, 35 L. Ed. 2d 147 (1973).

Even then, such citations are still quite lengthy, and obviously look quite mysterious and may even be a little intimidating to people when they try to read court opinions. Since the 1980s, there has been an ongoing debate among American judges as to whether they should relegate such lengthy citations to footnotes to improve the readability of their opinions, as strongly urged by Bryan Garner, one of the leading authors on legal writing style issues. Most judges do relegate some citations to footnotes (though some jurists have refused to use footnotes in their opinions.

Remember too that states may have their own unique style for court documents and case opinions and they publish their own style guides which include information on their citation rules.

Many rules are employed to master legal citation

- full address

- minimum content rules which require inclusion in a citation of additional information beyond a retrieval address

- compaction rules that reduce the space taken up by the information so use standard abbreviations "United States Code" becomes "U.S.C."

- format relates to punctuation, underlining, and the order of the items within a citation

QUESTIONS CHAPTER 8B-1

TRUE/FALSE

1. Case citation is typically used to identify decisions in past court cases. T/F
2. Citations establish that research is well supported. T/F
3. Most decisions are published in printed law reports. T/F
4. Cases which are officially unpublished still often end up published on Internet services. T/F
5. In 2006, the Supreme Court, over the objection of several hundred judges and lawyers, adopted a new Rule 32.1 of FRAP requiring that federal courts allow citation of unpublished cases. T/F
6. The *vendor-neutral citation movement* led to provisions to prevent private vendors from copyrighting citation information. T/F
7. States use the same style for court documents and case opinions as does the Federal Court(s).
8. United States Code is abbreviated as "U.S." T/F
9. U.S. Dist. LEXIS, in a citation tells you it is from the LexisNexis database for U.S. District Court cases. T/F

CHOOSE THE CORRECT ANSWER OR INSERT THE CORRECT WORD(S)

10. Lawyers citing the page that contains the *specific holding* they wish to invoke to support their own case are using _____ citations.
11. In *Fuqua Homes, Inc. v. Beattie*, No. 03-3587, 2004 WL 2495842, the *WL* stands for

    _____.
12. Published cases usually contain
    a. Report titles
    b. Page number
    c. Decision year
    d. All of the above

13. A primary source for citation is
        (a) case law
        (b) law review articles
        (c) legal encyclopedia
        (d) restatements
14. In *Roe v. Wade*, 410 U.S. 113, 158 (1973), 158 represents the_____.

2. Rules And Formats

Parties to a Lawsuit – Case Names:

Formerly, reference to a case had rules about whether to underline or italicize depending on how it was referenced, e.g., within a sentence or standing alone. If within a sentence, it was italicized and otherwise, it was underlined. The most recent rules are:

The following citation elements should be italicized:

- case names (including procedural phrases)

- book titles

- titles of journal articles

- introductory signals used in citation sentences or clauses

- prior or subsequent history explanatory phrases

- words or phrases attributing one cited authority to another source

- the cross reference words: "id.," "supra," and "infra"

  In the case of *Lukas v. J.C. Penney Co., supra,* at p. 361, the Oregon Supreme Court construed the meaning of the words "reasonable grounds" in its "shoplifting statute" as having the same meaning as they have in a statute authorizing arrest without a warrant and applied the probable cause standard to the facts before it.

Having originated much of the material in this text over several years, you may occasionally see cases with underlined names, so please remember the rule.

When referring to one of the parties but not to the case itself, use regular type. In the above case, if you were referring to Lukas himself, you would write it:

Lukas in his lawsuit alleged that...

Abbreviations

Commonly used procedural phrases include words, or pieces of words like "In re," which means "regarding." This is the usual method of labeling a proceeding with no adversarial parties, but some "res," such as a bankrupt's estate or a proposed public project. Additionally, *In re* is used to replace phrases such as "in the matter of," "petition of," and "application of."

"Ex parte" means "from, or on behalf of only one side to a lawsuit." It is the usual method of labeling an action made by, for, or on behalf of one party, often without notice to, or contest by the other side. For instance, an ex parte divorce hearing is one in which only one spouse participates and the other does not appear. Ex parte motions are often used where the counsel for either party approaches the court (judge) to sign an order without benefit of first notifying the other party of that process.

"Ex rel." is the abbreviation for "ex relatione" which means "upon relation or information." It is the usual method of labeling an action instituted by one person on behalf of another. In citations, "ex rel." is used to replace phrases such as "on the relation of," for the use of," and "on behalf of."

"In sum" is the abbreviation for "in summary."

"Writ of Certiorari," is a "writ cer" (a written order) a word encountered in, and used by courts of last resort, specifically the United States Supreme Court. This court has discretion over selecting cases they want to hear. If the party who lost in a lower court seeks review in a court with discretion to hear the appeal, that party files a "Petition for Writ of Certiorari." If the court grants the petition, it will hear the appeal; conversely, if the court denies the petition, it will not hear the appeal.

Denials of certiorari—abbreviated "cert, denied" in citations—carry no precedential value, and do not indicate that the higher court agreed with the lower court's decision. Accordingly, denials of certiorari typically should not be included as subsequent history. Moreover, denials inform readers that the lower court's decision has become final, therefore information should be included if the cited lower-court decision is two years old or less. Two years was selected mainly because that is the time within which most cases are resolved on appeal.

A denial of certiorari is important if the case is the focus of the discussion. It also is important when the higher court issues an opinion explaining why a petition for certiorari was denied, or when a judge issues a dissenting opinion concerning the denial of certiorari.

If you see other abbreviations and you are not sure what they mean, visit any of the legal terminology websites we have provided, or others you may have found on your own.

CASE CITATION

The standard case citation format in the United States looks like this:

Roe v. Wade, 410 U.S. 113 (1973)

- *Roe v. Wade* is the *abbreviated* name of the case. Generally, the first name, Roe, is the surname of the plaintiff, the party who filed the suit in the original case, or the appellant, the party appealing in a case being appealed from a lower court, or the petitioner when litigating in the high court of a jurisdiction; and, Wade, is the surname of the defendant, the party responding to the suit, or the appellee, the party responding to the appeal, or the respondent, when defending in the high court of the jurisdiction.

There are exceptions. For example, under the Rules of the United States Supreme Court, parties are typically referred to as petitioner and respondent under Rule 12 (when seeking discretionary review by writ of certiorari), but are occasionally referred to as plaintiff and defendant under Rule 17 (when invoking the court's original jurisdiction as provided for in the U.S. Constitution) or as appellant and appellee under Rule 18 (when direct review is provided for by federal statute).

- 410 is the volume number of the "reporter" in which the Court's written opinion in the Roe v. Wade is published.

- U.S. is the abbreviation of the reporter. In this sample, "U.S." stands for United States Reports.

- 113 is the page number (in volume 410 of United States Reports) where the opinion begins

- 1973 is the year in which the court rendered its decision

The abbreviated name of the court will be included inside the parenthesis before the year if the name of the court is not obvious from the reporter; this rule comes into play because certain reporters, such as the West National Reporter System, which publishes opinions originating from multiple courts. In this example, the name of the court (United States Supreme Court) is obvious (since only decisions of the U.S. Supreme Court are published in the U.S. Reports) and is thus omitted.

Here are two more examples:

- Brown v. Board of Education, 347 U.S. 483 (1954).

- Miranda v. Arizona, 384 U.S. 436 (1966).

When *lower federal court* opinions are cited, the citation includes the name of the court. This is placed in the parentheses immediately before the year. Examples:

- *Geary v. Visitation of the Blessed Virgin Mary Parish Sch.*, 7 F.3d 324 (3d Cir. 1993) - a case in the U.S. Court of Appeals for the Third Circuit

- *Glassroth v. Moore*, 229 F. Supp. 2d 1290 (M.D. Ala. 2002) - a case in the U.S. District Court for the Middle District of Alabama

Here are examples of how to cite West reporters:

- *Jackson v. Commonwealth*, 583 S.E.2d 780 (Va. Ct. App. 2003) - a case in the Virginia Court of Appeals (an intermediate appellate court) published in the South Eastern Reporter

- *Foxworth v. Maddox*, 137 So. 161 (Fla. 1931) - a case in the Florida Supreme Court published in the Southern Reporter

- *People v. Brown*, 282 N.Y.S.2d 497 (1967) - a case in the New York Court of Appeals (New York's highest court) published in the New York Supplement. The case also appears in West's regional reporter: People v. Brown, 229 N.E.2d 192 (N.Y. 1967).

Abbreviations for lower courts vary by state, as each state has its own system of trial courts and intermediate appellate courts.

Some states, notably California and New York, have citation systems that differ significantly from the various federal and national standards. Citations in California style put the year between the names of the parties and the reference to the case reporter. Citations in New York style wrap the year in brackets instead of parentheses. Both New York and California wrap an entire citation in parentheses when it is used as a stand-alone sentence. New York puts the terminating period outside the parentheses, but California puts it inside. New York wraps just the reporter and page references in parentheses when the citation is used as a clause. Either way, both state styles differ from the national/Bluebook style of simply dropping in the citation as a separate sentence without further adornment. Both systems use less punctuation and spacing in their reporter abbreviations.

The Brown case above would be cited (using the official reporter) to a New York court as:

(*People v Brown*, 20 NY2d 238 [1967]).

The famous Greenman product liability case would be cited to a California court as:

(*Greenman v. Yuba Power Products, Inc.* (1963) 59 Cal.2d 57.)[3]

FULL CITATION FORMAT:

Each specific source requires a slightly different component and is subject to special forms. Types of information typically include the author's name, the title or name of the source, the volume, if any, page, section, or other subdivision where the referenced material is located within the source, the publisher and the date

SHORT CITATION FORMATION:

The short form is used only after citing once in the full citation format. It typically omits some of the full citation elements but still provides enough information to identify and locate the original citation.

3. Citation Manuals

As has been explained, courts expect lawyers to follow specific formats in briefs and memoranda. Specific manuals for citations are prepared and published to provide authoritative guidelines and acceptable standards for locating and incorporating citations into cases for trial. In this way, the law as it is understood as to how it applies to a given situation with reference to statutes, regulations, and prior decisions is cited. Using legal citation, you check all references you find. Do not assume that what you find in another's work is in proper form or even accurate. Also remember, citations are not necessarily always current and are revised frequently. Legal documents published in prior years (though perhaps conforming to the citation references at the time of writing may need reformatting to comply with more recent standards. The most recent edition should be obtained when possible.

The first book we will discuss is: The Bluebook: A Uniform system of Citation, 18th, Edition. It has been around for 80 years and is used for citing cases.

Visit the website now: **www.legalbluebook.com/**

Read the home page in its entirety, noting the acknowledgements at the end of the page. They pretty well sum up their "authority."

Now visit www.alwd.org/ (Scroll to Publications on the drop down menu, and then click on ALWD Guide to Legal Citation)

The ALWD has published its own Citation Manual and notes on its website that it uses the simpler, yet long overdue changes from the Bluebook, in that the ALWD Citation Manual contains one system for all legal documents, making no distinction between law review articles and other types of writing. The Manual has been adopted by professors at more than ninety law schools, many paralegal programs, and a number of law reviews, moot court competitions, and courts.

You may want to review both of these manuals before you make a decision as to which you would like to use in your own practice. If you work in a legal office, they will already likely employ one or the other (or both).

4. Internet Citations

With the advent of the Internet and the explosion of the case information available online, the standards for citing were subjected to quite a bit of debate and ultimately to rule changes related to Civil Procedure. Here are samples of the rule changes:

Rule 18 of the Federal Rules of Civil Procedure has changed considerably, primarily to allow increased citation to Internet sources. Specific changes include:

> **Rule 18.2.1**(a) now provides guidance allowing citation to authenticated and official Internet sources as well as exact digital scans of print sources as if they were the original print source.

These changes in rule 18 allowing citation to official, authenticated, or exact Internet copies of cited materials are also reflected in rules 10, 12, 15, 16, and 17. Guidance for citation to webpage titles of main pages and subheadings has been expanded in rule 18.2.2(b).

> **Rule 18.2.2(a)** now states that when no author of an Internet source is clearly announced, the author information should be omitted from the citation, unless there is a clear institutional owner of the domain. Additionally, institutional authors of Internet sources should be abbreviated according to rule 15.1(d).

> **Rule 18.2.2(c)** states that citations to Internet sources should be dated as they appear on the Internet site, using only dates that refer clearly to the material cited. When material is undated, the date of the author's last visit to the website should be placed in a parenthetical after the URL.

> **Rule 18.2.2(c)** also states that for blogs and other frequently updated websites, citations should include timestamps whenever possible.

> **Rule 18.2.2(h)** still encourages the archiving of Internet sources, but does not require the citation to indicate the location of an archival copy.

> **Rules 18.6 and 18.7** allow for the use of timestamps in citations to audio and video recordings.

> **Rule 18.7.3** provides citation guidance for podcasts and online recordings.

QUESTIONS CHAPTER 8B (2-4)

TRUE/FALSE

1. The following citation element should be italicized: case names (including procedural phrases) T / F

2. "Ex parte" means the party is excused. T / F

3. Rule 18.2.2(b) allowed expanded use of the Internet and its web pages. T / F

4. You must never use a short form citation. T / F

5. The surname on individual suits are used in citation formats, e.g., Davis v Smith. T / F

6. When *lower federal court* opinions are cited, the citation includes the name of the court. This is placed in the parentheses immediately before the year. T / F

7. Rule 18.2.1(a) does not allow citation any Internet sources. T / F

8. Rule 18.2.2(c) states that for blogs and other frequently updated websites, citations should include timestamps. T / F

5. Shepardizing

Try to imagine the impact of the millions of cases decided in this country over the past 200 years. Because the principle of stare decisis (to adhere to or abide by past decisions) forms the basis for our legal system, every legal decision has potential precedential value. For example, some cases are followed as precedent; i.e., they are "good law, "while others can no longer be used to support future decisions and are considered "bad law." As a legal researcher, you must be aware of both types of decisions. Yet how could you possibly remember or even find out what happened to each and every case?

Thanks to Frank Shepard, that is not necessary. In the early 1870s, he realized the necessity for tracking the discussion of principles of law in court opinions, and also tracking the history of these opinions. He devised a method for extracting this information from published opinions and indexing it for the benefit of legal researchers. This information is compiled in <u>Shepard's Citations</u>.

Shepard's Citations is a citator, providing a list of all the authorities citing a particular case, statute, or other legal authority. The verb *Shepardizing* refers to the process of consulting Shepard's to see if a case has been overturned, reaffirmed, questioned, or cited by later cases.

In 1996, Shepard's was purchased by LexisNexis (a subsidiary of Reed Elsevier since 1994). After this acquisition, LexisNexis engaged in a "multi-million-dollar Citations Redesign (CR) project" to fully address and design a research system to manage the way we process case law and employ citations.

On-Line Version and Decline of Print Version

In March 1999, LexisNexis released an online version of the Shepard's Citation Service. While print versions of Shepard's remain in use, their use is declining. Although learning to Shepardize in print was once a rite of passage for all first-year law students, the Shepard's Citations booklets in hard copy format are extremely cryptic compared to the online version, because of the need to cram as much information about as many cases in as little space as possible.

Go to LexisNexis and search for Shepard's Citations.

There is information on Shepard's Citations on LexisNexis. To get to it, you'll have to sign up for a free trial, and it might be worth subscribing to this service for future reference. At the very least, you'll want to read up on Shepard's Citations.

Shepard's paper format consists of long tables of citations (with full case titles omitted) preceded by one or two-letter codes indicating their relationship to the case being Shepardized. Before Lexis became widely available, generations of lawyers (and law clerks and assistants) had to manually locate the Shepard's entry for a case, decipher all the cryptic abbreviations, and then manually retrieve all the cases which were marked by Shepard's as criticizing or overruling a particular case, to determine whether the more recent cases had been overruled on a specific issue. In many jurisdictions in the U.S., it is still possible to cite a case as good law even though it has been overruled, as long as it was overruled on another issue and not the specific issue for which it is being cited.

In 2004, market research by LexisNexis indicated that most attorneys and librarians conduct the majority of their research online, but "that there are a number of experienced attorneys, principally in smaller firms, who still prefer print and who are extremely unlikely to change their ways." A company representative noted given the ripe old ages at which many lawyers continue to practice their profession, "we don't see the market for Shepard's in print disappearing any time soon. " But, clearly, subscription lists for Shepard's products are declining as online usage grows. Attrition has been steepest in large law firms, where relatively junior associates conduct a great deal of citation research online. For many years, attrition in academic law libraries was relatively low. Many law school libraries continued to retain substantial collections of Shepard's in print. In recent years, attrition has increased—especially in law schools that no longer teach students how to Shepardize in print. But because many law school libraries are open to the public (or at least to graduates of the school), including practicing attorneys in the communities they serve, a typical law school library continues to retain at least a basic collection of Shepard's print products.

Today, LexisNexis users can Shepardize citations online; all cases displayed on LexisNexis bear a "Shepardize" link in their header and nearly always show an icon in the upper left corner of the Web page indicating the status of the case as citable authority. The icon itself, when clicked, brings up a full Shepard's report for the case.

The report indicates exactly how later cases cited the case being Shepardized with plain English phrases like "followed by" or "overruled" rather than by using the old abbreviations. In addition, the report shows the full case title (that is, the names of the plaintiff and defendant) and full citation for each of the later cases. This is important because law researchers can usually distinguish criminal from civil cases by looking at the title. Criminal cases (with the exception of habeas corpus cases) are always titled "People v. [defendant]" or "State v. [defendant]." Often, a criminal case may cite a civil case for a point of law which a civil litigator does not care about, and vice versa.

Finally, the online report has the convenience of allowing the user to simply click on the hyperlink for any listed case to retrieve it instantly (if it is within the user's access plan), whereas users of Shepard's print version had to dash through long law library aisles to retrieve heavy legal reporter volumes, one for each case.

Although the name *Shepard* is trademarked, it is also used informally by legal professionals to describe citators in general—for example, Westlaw's similar tool called *KeyCite*.

Westlaw (Key Cite) is another of the primary online legal research services for lawyers and legal professionals in the United States and is a part of West, a part of Thomson Reuters.

www.westlaw.com – you will immediately note it is a subscription website.

West's attorney-authored case law headnotes and the West Key Number System are used to determine and immediately alert legal professionals the case law they are reviewing has been either overturned, or may have history which deems the precedential value of the opinion invalid.

KeyCite was introduced to Westlaw in 1997 and was the first service to seriously challenge the Shepard's Citations, on which legal professionals had relied for generations. Shepard's had become such a necessary part of legal research, that citation checking is still informally referred to as "Shepardizing." In 2004, KeyCite was determined to be the most-used citation checking service in an annual survey of law firm technology use conducted by the American Bar Association.

West American Digest System is a system of identifying points of law from reported cases organized by topic and key number. The system was developed by West Publishing. This extensive taxonomy makes the process of doing case law legal research less time consuming as it directs the researcher to cases that are similar to the legal issue under consideration.

Westlaw's international content is available at www.westlawinternational.com. For instance, Westlaw Canada from Carswell includes the Canadian Abridgment and KeyCite Canada, and Westlaw UK provides information from Sweet & Maxwell and independent law reports, case analysis and case status icons. More recently, Westlaw China was introduced, with laws and regulations, cases, digests, and status icons (similar to KeyCite flags), for the law of the People's Republic of China. In total, Westlaw is used in over 68 countries.

Headnotes and Digests

Each case published in a West reporter is evaluated by an editor who identifies the points of law cited or explained in the case. The editor places the summaries of the points of law covered in the case at the beginning of the case. These summaries are usually a sentence long, and are called *headnotes*. Each headnote is then assigned a topic and key number. The headnotes are arranged according to their topic and key number in multi-volume sets of books called *Digests*. A digest serves as a subject index to the case law published in West reporters. Headnotes are merely editorial guides to the points of law discussed or used in the cases, and the headnotes themselves are not legal authority.

West introduced *WestlawNext* on February 8th 2014. The main advances in this version are that a user can start a search without first selecting a database, and the search screen allows one to click checkboxes to select the jurisdiction and nature of material wanted. A new search algorithm, referred to as **WestSearch,** claimed to be the world's most advanced legal research engine, executes a federated search across multiple content types. Users can either enter descriptive terms or *boolean* connectors and select a jurisdiction. Documents are ranked by relevance. WestlawNext also supports retrieval of documents by citation, party name or KeyCite reference. An overview page enables users to see the top results per content type or they can view all results for a particular content type. Filters can also be applied to refine the result list even further. On the results page, users can also see links to related secondary sources relevant to their research.

As you Shepardize cases, remember to make sure that the cases cited in your writing clearly and articulately support the arguments you have, then you have completed your task. Shepardizing can be reduced to a fairly easy process of simply locating the entries in Shepard's for your case, and looking to see if it has been reversed, modified, overruled, limited, criticized, or questioned.

How is Shepard's organized?

Shepard's Citation consists of at least three, sometimes four, parts:

> 1. hardbound main set of volumes (Case Edition or Statute Edition)
>
> 2. softbound Cumulative Supplement(s)
>
> 3. softbound Update(s)
>
> 4. Some Editions may also contain a hardbound Supplement Edition.

To get the full picture regarding your case you must consult all parts of Shepard's.

Shepard's Citations are available for U.S. laws and cases and each of the 50 states.

Case citations are arranged in the following order:

> 1. Parallel citations (in parentheses)
>
> 2. Federal and state cases that have a relationship to the case

3. Other federal cases arranged by federal circuit

4. Federal administrative decisions

5. Other state cases, arranged alpha by state

6. Selected secondary sources

Examples of changes for cases include:

a – affirmed

d – dismissed

r – reversed

v – vacated

cert gran - certioriari granted

Examples of changes for statutes include:

A – amended

C – constitutional

Re-en – reenacted

S – superseded

U – unconstitutional

- questionable

What do the symbols mean?

Within each volume of Shepard's, there is a detailed explanation of how to read the entries and how to decipher abbreviations and symbols.

On the front and on the title page of each volume there is a list of each reporter cited (for cases) or the name of each code cited (Labor Code, Revenue & Taxation Code, etc.).

There is also a list of materials where the citations originally appear (reporters, law reviews, statutes, etc.).

Following each citation are letters and numbers identifying "citations" of later documents that have cited the item you are Shepardizing.

For example, "685 FS 1220 Cir.9". indicates a later case from the U.S. Court of Appeals, 9th Circuit, published in volume 685, pp. 1220 et seq., of a series called Federal Supplement. (For abbreviations, check the Tables of Abbreviations, at the front of Shepard's bound volumes.)

The very small numbers and letters in front of, or after, each citation tell you how the later material treated your document in hand. For example, a small "f" indicates the later case "followed" the case being shepardized, an "o" that it was overruled. Sometimes, when Shepardizing a case, you will find very small numbers inserted within cites for later cases and printed somewhat above the line. These very small numbers (example: 3) and indicate the later case cited the document in hand specifically for the rule of law laid out in headnote number "X" of the case being Shepardized (headnote 3 in our example). Be sure to check all Shepard's volumes/pamphlets that cover time periods after the date of your document (pocket supplements).

How to Use Shepard's

Choose the *Shepard's* citator for the type of case you have. Include all the softcover supplements.

1. Find the volume and page of the case you are Shepardizing.

2. Use the volume numbers shown in the *sideheads* on each page to speed your search. On the appropriate page, use the *boldface* numbers to find the case you seek, as in the example below, volume 386 page 780.

3. Cited cases will be listed followed by case name, decision date, parallel citations in parentheses (legal citations to the same case in other reporters), and the citing references.

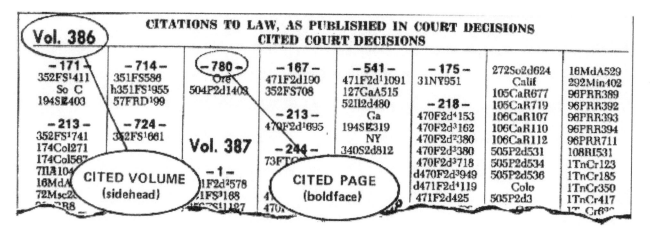

Shepard's Abbreviations

History of Case   Treatment of Case

a (affirmed)

m (modified)

r (reversed)

s (same case)

S (superseded)

v (vacated)

c (criticized)

d (distinguished)

e (explained)

j (dissenting opinion)

~ (consenting opinion)

L (limited)

o (overruled)

q (questioned)

The CITATION WORKBOOK, the final module of the training course will provide more exposure and practice on citating.

QUESTIONS CHAPTER 8B-5

TRUE/FALSE

1. "Good law" refers to cases that are followed as precedent. T/F

2. Shepardizing is checking to see if a case has had more action, been overturned, etc. T/F

3. LexisNexis owns Shepard's Citations. T/F

4. The on-line LexisNexis report indicates exactly how later cases cited the case being Shepardized with plain English phrases like "followed by" or "overruled" rather than by using the old abbreviations. T/F

5. The full case names of the plaintiff and defendant in a LexisNexis lookup or report is not available. T/F

6. Criminal versus civil cases cannot be differentiated using LexisNexis. T/F

7. Though Shepard is trademarked, there are other citators that work in a similar fashion, Westlaw's _____ for example.

8. Criminal cases are always titled "People" or _____" v. [defendant].

9. In the West reporter system, headnotes are _____ usually a sentence long.

10. Topics and key numbers are found in books called _____ .

11. Shepard's is organized as at least _____ part edition.

12. In Shepard's parallel citations appear in

    a. Line order

    b. Parentheses

    c. The headnote

13. In Shepard's cases, "r" stands for _____.

Answers to Chapter Questions

1. It is the law

2. Bar associations, state and US supreme courts, state legislatures and self-regulating

3. NFPA and NALA

4. Indirectly by using the same ethical codes attorneys do

5. Known as attorney client privilege – can't discuss client business with outsiders, can't be compelled to testify personally related to those communications

6. Unauthorized practice of law

7. Granting of permission

8. No specific answer – did you find it interesting?

9. Certainly, she instructed clients to lie, gave legal advice, both of which were unethical and could have been potentially detrimental to both cases

10. Research only, no answer required.

11. Research only

12. Research only

13. Research only

14. Research only

15.

ANSWERS CHAPTER 2 AND 3

1. A process wherein a court/judge reviews a decision (judgment) of another court/judge

2. (a) First Amendment, freedom of religion (b) Eighth Amendment, cruel and unusual punishment, (c) Fourth Amendment, unreasonable searches and seizures (d) First Amendment, freedom of speech (e) both the Sixth and Eighth – speedy trial and cruel and unusual punishment (f) Fifth Amendment, self-incrimination

3. (a) The case can be brought before either a state or federal court since both have jurisdiction, (b) Both state and federal laws prohibit gender discrimination

4. They can decide any type of case

5. Permits a state to obtain jurisdiction over nonresident individuals, companies

6. Yes, it limits jurisdiction based exactly on the subject matter, e.g., bankruptcy courts, probates, etc.

7. Yes, under the U.S. Constitution, it specifically states the jurisdiction of such courts is limited

8. A rule or a body of rules established by authority, society or custom

9. England

10. Law derived from custom and precedent

11. Rules of law which resulted from decisions rendered by judges

12. A term for a court decision which provides an example of authority

13. Yes, it is a flexible doctrine relating to prior decisions or precedents

14. <u>Brown v Board of Education of Topeka.</u>

15. Relate mostly to law and fairness and the various remedies

16. Maxims and Remedies (a) He who seeks equity must do equity (b) He who comes into equity must come with clean hands (c) Equity will presume that to be done which should have been done (d) Equity aids the vigilant, not those who slumber on their rights (e) Equity follows the law. (f) Equity regards substance rather than form

17. Specific performance, rescission, and injunction

18. What he bargained for – for instance, if a person bought a home and the documentation or deed were all screwed up, the court can reformulate to describe what the person thought he bought and reform the documents accordingly

19. Ordinances

20. Administrative

21. (a) no (b) supremacy clause

22. (a) state (b) federal (c) federal, though states have some jurisdiction over workers (d) state

23. FBI, Treasury, FDA, SSA, FTC, CIA, EPA, FCC, ICC, etc.

24. An administrative law judge (ALJ)

25. Yes – appeal to the next level for appellate review

26. Assignment only

27. Assignment only

ANSWERS- CHAPTER 4

1.   Plaintiff

2.   Defendant

3.   c

4.   d

5.   b

6.   c

7.   d

8.   d

9.   F

10.   (a) prepares some of it – (b) includes pleadings, interrogatories, depositions, summaries, motions, exhibits witnesses, citations

11.   Where the judge orders the parties to meet to see if they can work out their differences without the need for a trial.

12.   Voter registration, driver's license registration

13.   Asks questions to determine any biases, prejudices, may accept or reject juror

14.   Instructions by the judge to the jury setting forth the rules the jury must follow to reach a decision

15.   Getting all the facts – learning everything possible underpinning the case

16.   c

17.   c

18.   It is a process by which the verdict/ruling of the trial court is subjected to a reviewing process by a higher court with appropriate motions

19. The trial court is the initial trier of fact and the appellate is the court hearing the appeal from the verdict/judgment of the first court in which the case is heard

20. To obtain written answers to a list of questions (under oath)

21. Oral recording of a session with questions and answers tendered to a potential witness or participant in a lawsuit

22. The Defendant _____moves this court, pursuant to *Rule 50 (b) of the Federal Rules of Civil Procedure*, to set aside the verdict and judgment entered on _____, and to enter instead a judgment for the Defendant as a matter of law. In the alternative, and in the event the Defendant's motion for judgment as a matter of law is denied, the Defendant moves the Court to order a new trial.

23. (a) absolutely no – we have covered confidential information and ethics earlier (b) you should not answer it at all – ethics and legal ramifications of tampering with a witness

24. Subpoenas

25. Trial court is the first to hear the case and (b) the appellate court is the appeals court to which the trial court decisions are proffered for review and perhaps getting overturned.

26. They are the questions sent to either party requiring written answers and are a cheaper way to get them than depositions (oral testimony).

27. The documents which present the legal basis for a motion, citing any statutes and cases that support the claim.

ANSWERS CHAPTER 5

1. Sole, small, large, boutique, corporate, government, clinic
2. True
3. False
4. A Model Rule of Professional Conduct 5.4(a)
5. True
6. Percentage
7. False
8. Yes – a charge for a specific service
9. Partners, associates, paralegals, law clerks
10. False – free, no charge
11. True
12. Model Rule of Professional Conduct 7.1
13. False, believe it!!
14. Policies and procedures

ANSWERS CHAPTER 6

1. Plaintiff
2. Defendant
3. Demand letter
4. Yes – by rules established by courts or legislatures
5. Procedural and substantive
6. The amount of time governing when a person has to bring a lawsuit
7. Facts which tend to prove or disprove a theory of law
8. They state the client's position or goal
9. A. Client / B. client / C. client / D. client
10. The Bluebook
11. Rule 34
12. No, at least not generally, though in special cases, one could be compelled
13. Rule 1.6
14. True
15. Any of: Put the client at ease, calm organized workspace, nonjudgmental,   empathy, preliminary questions prepared,
16. Please describe as accurately as possible the weather and road conditions at the time of the accident.
17. Detail of a situation
18. Keep it Simple Stupid
19. False
20. (a) 1974, (b) Freedom of Information Act
21. False – require a written request authorized signature of the person to whom they relate, or if a minor (under 18 years) the signature of the parent or guardian
22. Determination of the direct and proximate cause of something
23. SOL stands for Statute of Limitations
24. False, each type of action or case has its own SOL and they are not the same for all types of cases.

ANSWERS TO CHAPTER 7

English grammar answers follow the question sets.

ANSWERS – CHAPTER 7-I-K

Answers you provided may vary some from the ones offered here. Edits are presented as alternatives and of course may not match up with those you wrote. The practice in the editing process is the point.

1. appraised
2. affected
3. principal
4. than
5. accept
6. memoranda (plural)

7. orally
8. liable
9. libel
10. proscribing
11. disinterested
12. hears
13. The plaintiff must state a cause of action, and seek actual damages
14. The court ruled there was jury misconduct
15. The court decided (or ruled) the contract had been rescinded
16. The judge held the lease had been terminated
17. The parties agreed to hold a pretrial settlement
18. The jurors reviewed the exhibits
19. The landlord terminated the lease
20. The court ruled the defendant's statements were actionable
21. The judge looked at the exhibits, and felt they were irrelevant
22. This letter explains the settlement proposed following the June 8 telephone conversation
23. The petitioner must meet the time limits required by the law to initiate a cause of action
24. The documents we discussed in previous correspondence are enclosed
25. All rent payments must be made by the first of each month in spite of anything else noted herein
26. The plaintiff, a vexatious litigant, refused and failed appear for his hearing
27. The defendant's actions, and conduct resulted in the injuries and damages to the plaintiff
28. The agreement was signed by the parties, but exhibits were not attached, making it necessary to resign, and redate it.
29. Defendant asserted the plaintiff had refused and failed to wear her seatbelt at the time the accident occurred
30. The jurors were unable to decide, though they had attempted to reconcile testimony, reviewed jury instructions, and examined exhibits

ANSWERS 7-L-N

1. False

2. False

3. True

4. False

5. False

6. False

7. False

8. False

9. True

ANSWERS CHAPTER 8A-1

1. True
2. False
3. False

4. True
5. True
6. True

7. False
8. False
9. True
10. False
11. True
12. False
13. True
14. True

15. True
16. d
17. c
18. b
19. d
20. b
21. d

ANSWERS – CHAPTER 8A-2

1. True
2. True
3. True
4. False
5. False
6. False – William Cranch was the compiler and seller
7. True
8. True

9. False – Illinois (Ill)
10. d
11. d
12. d
13. b
14. b
15. Official
16. Parallel
17. Lawyers' Edition

ANSWERS CHAPTER 8B 1

1. True
2. True
3. False
4. True
5. True
6. True
7. False

8. False (U.S.C.)
9. True
10. pinpoint
11. Westlaw
12. D
13. A
14. Page number

ANSWERS CHAPTER 8B (2-4)

1. True
2. False
3. True
4. False

5. True
6. True
7. False
8. True

ANSWERS CHAPTER 8B-5

1. True
2. True
3. True
4. True
5. False
6. False
7. KeyCite

8. State
9. Summaries
10. Digests
11. 3
12. B
13. Reversed

CONGRATULATIONS,
you have completed the first module of the training.
Be confident! You know a lot more than you think you do.

You will now move on to Volume 2.

References

Primary Authorities

I. Constitutions   Federal: Consult U.S.C.A., or U.S.C.S.

website: www.constitutioncenter.org

State: Consult your state's annotated code - www.findlaw.com/casecode/state.html

II. Statutes

Federal   - Consult U.S.C.A. or U.S.C.S.

State - Consult your state's annotated code

https://www.ncsc.org/consulting-and-research/areas-of-expertise/court-leadership/gavel-to-gavel

III. Cases

Federal   - Consult digests (American Digest System or Federal Practice Digest)

Website : www.findlaw.com -   Click on American Digest System or Federal Practice Digest

State -   Consult your state's digest - www.findlaw.com

Secondary Authorities

Encyclopedias

C.J.S.   All U.S. law

                American Jur. 2d   All U.S. law

                State-specific sets   Law of one state

A.L.R.

Annotations

                A.L.R. Fed   Federal issues

                A.L.R., A.L.R., 2nd, 3d, 4th, & 5th   State and common law topics

Texts and Treatises Law related to one topic

Legal Periodicals   Various topics

Restatements   Various topics

Attorney General

Opinions (attorney general)

U.S.A.G. Opinions   Federal topics
www.law.cornell.edu - www.justice.gov

State A.G. Opinions State topics (your state) - www.findlaw.com

Dictionaries   Black's Law Dictionary - www.westlaw.com

Martindale-Hubbell Law   International and state law

    Digest   www.martindale.com

    Uniform Laws   www.findlaw.com - "uniform laws, or codes."

    Jury Instruction   Federal or state -   www.morelaw.com,

        https://www.juryresearchinstitute.com/

The American Civil Liberties Union   www.aclu.org

Internet Resources

Management Information   https://mielegalaid.org/

Exchange

The Tenants Union   www.tenantsunion.org

Counsel Quest   https://www.ncsc.org/consulting-and-research/areas-of-expertise/court-leadership/gavel-to-gavel

Cornell University Legal   www.law.cornell.edu

Information Institute

Findlaw   www.findlaw.com

Hieros Gamos   www.hg.org/

Supreme Court Case   https://www.thecre.com/fedlaw/legal30/supcourt.htm

American Bar Association   www.abanet.org

The Internet Law Library   www.priweb.com/internetlawlib/1.htm

The Federal Judicial Center   www.fjc.gov

Tenant Net Home Page   www.tenant.net/

Equal Justice Network　　　www.equaljustice.org/

Government Websites

Department of Justice　　　www.jsutice.gov

Federal Regulations　　　www. gpo.gov

Federal Case Law　　　https://caselaw.findlaw.com/

Official State Government Sites　http://www.usa.gov

(you may start by clicking on the drop down menu for Government Agencies and Elected Officials, and then find the link for State, Local, and Tribal Governments)

State Government links　　　Use state name for government sites and related links

State Codes and Statutes　https://www.ncsc.org/consulting-and-research/areas-of-expertise/court-leadership/gavel-to-gavel

US Senate　　　www.senate.gov

The White House　　　www.whitehouse.gov

Corporate Business Information

Company Finders

　　　www.hoovers.com

Bloomberg　　　www.bloomberg.com

Criminal Law And Procedures

www.courttv.com/

Bankruptcy Law

– current bankruptcy issues can be found at the American Bankruptcy Institute; www.abiworld.org

Labor & Employment

post their newsletters on the Web. Arent Fox, one such law firm, can be accessed at: www.arentfox.com

Estate Planning & Probate

To locate wills of famous people (Jacqueline Kennedy Onassis, Elvis Presley and dozens of others are at: www.ca-probate.com/

Intellectual-Property Law

If you are interested in how cyberspace is affecting the laws governing intellectual property, a good general site covering current issues is offered by the Bureau of National Affairs at: www.bna.com

Legal Directories

Plan your career wisely—defining long-term goals, short-term goals, networking, locating sources that list paralegal job opportunities and identifying possible employers.

Search Yellow Pages, including Yahoo's Yellow Pages at www.yp.yahoo.com

There are numerous legal directories that provide lists of attorneys, their locations, and areas of practice. The Martindale-Hubbel Law Directory is located online at: www.martindale.com

Another valuable source of information is West's Legal Directory www.wld.com

In addition, you can find links to more than one hundred other directories listing

Attorneys and legal professionals at the following government website: www.house.gov.

Visit these job boards and search for paralegal positions: www.careerbuilder.com **and www.indeed.com**

Made in the USA
Middletown, DE
27 June 2025

77596472R00157